A

HISTORY OF THE

PROTESTANT REFORMATION.

B. BENTLEY, PRINTER, ANDOVER.

B. BENSLEY, PRINTER, ANDOVER.

A

HISTORY OF THE

PROTESTANT REFORMATION

IN

𝕰𝖓𝖌𝖑𝖆𝖓𝖉 𝖆𝖓𝖉 𝕴𝖗𝖊𝖑𝖆𝖓𝖉;

SHOWING HOW THAT EVENT HAS IMPOVERISHED THE MAIN BODY OF THE
PEOPLE IN THOSE COUNTRIES; AND CONTAINING A LIST OF THE ABBEYS,
PRIORIES, NUNNERIES, HOSPITALS, AND OTHER RELIGIOUS FOUNDATIONS
IN ENGLAND, AND WALES, AND IRELAND, CONFISCATED, SEIZED ON, OR
ALIENATED, BY THE PROTESTANT "REFORMATION" SOVEREIGNS AND
PARLIAMENTS.

BY WILLIAM COBBETT.

IN A SERIES OF LETTERS
ADDRESSED TO ALL SENSIBLE AND JUST ENGLISHMEN.

IN TWO VOLUMES.

VOL. II.

LONDON:

PUBLISHED BY THE AUTHOR, AT No. 183, FLEET STREET.

1829.

INTRODUCTION.

1. THE foregoing volume of this Work contains the History of the Protestant " Reformation," the object of which was to show, and, I trust, it has shown most clearly, that that event " has impoverished and degraded the main body of the people." In speaking of the motives to the producing of the event, I said, that a fair and honest inquiry would teach us, that the chief of those motives was PLUNDER. The inquiry was fair and honest, and it has taught to every reader, that plunder was the main object, and, indeed, the only object, with all the most active, and the most powerful, of the actors in that drama of devastation. The chief object of the present little volume, is, to show, as far as my means will enable me, the enormous extent and amount of that plunder.

2. To this end I here present to the reader the LIST, which is described in the title-page, but which stands in need of those short explanations which I am now about to give ; and, when I have given which, I shall add some observations, which, while they are suggested by bare justice to our well-fed and well-clad Catholic forefathers, are, as the reader will see, imperiously de-

Introduction to the Second Volume.

manded at my hands by mercy to ourselves, their unfortunate, half-famished, ragged, pauperized descendants.

3. The EXPLANATIONS, to which I have alluded in the last paragraph, relate chiefly to the *arrangement* of the several articles in the LIST. The order is Alphabetical throughout, except that WALES follows ENGLAND, leaving IRELAND to come last. The List, for England, begins, of course, with Bedfordshire, and ends with Yorkshire. Then, under the name of each county, the order is alphabetical again; the List for Bedfordshire, for instance, beginning with Bedford, and ending with Woburn.

Explanations of its contents.

4. In each article I have given, as far as my materials would enable me, 1. a description of the nature of the foundation ; 2. the name of the founder; 3. the date of the foundation; 4. the estimated yearly value at the time of the confiscation by Henry VIII.; 5. the present yearly value, according to the change in the value of money; 6. by what king, or queen, the property was granted away; 7. to whom it was granted. I will here give a specimen in the article just mentioned. " At WOBURN. A Cistercian Abbey, " founded near this place, in the year 1145, by " Hugh de Bolebec. Valued at 430*l*. 13*s*. 11½*d*., " now worth 8,613*l*. 19*s*. 2*d*. Granted, 1 Ed- " ward VI., to John Lord Russell."

Woburn Abbey.

5. Alas ! when the Russells were hunting the poor Catholics about, in the reign of Charles II., I wonder whether they ever thought of pious and generous Hugh de Bolebec ! Bishop TAN-

The Russells, and Hugh de Bolebec.

NER tells us, that this grant was made to Russell
in the first year of Edward VI.; Doctor HEYLIN
tells us that the people of Devonshire rose, in the
second year of Edward VI., and, amongst other
things, demanded that some of the monasteries
should be re-established; and HUME tells us,
that they were, at last, quelled, and punished by
martial law, by LORD RUSSELL, aided by German
troops! Alas! and poor Hugh de Bolebec
never thought of all the while, I would almost
be sworn!

6. The whole of the articles are not so perfect
in their information as is the one above cited. In
some the name of the grantee has not been to be
come at; in others the valuation is not recorded;
in others the name of the founder is wanting; and,
with regard to Ireland, the information is still
more scanty, and that, too, in every respect, and
in a very great degree. Nevertheless, the LIST,
taken altogether, is, I trust it will be thought, a
very interesting historical and statistical docu-
ment, and will be found very commodious as a
work of reference; for, if you see, or hear of,
any ancient foundation, in any part of the kingdom, and wish to know what it was, and when it
arose, how it was put down, and who got it;
knowing in what county it is, or finding this out by
the Index at the end of the Volume, you turn to the
county, which you will find in the order of the
alphabet. Then, knowing in or near what city,
town, or village it is, you turn, according to the
alphabet, to the city, town, or village; or, to
the usual name of the Abbey, Priory, or other

foundation. Thus you, with as little inconvenience as possible, get at the best information that I have been able to give.

Chief use of this volume. 7. But, it is in the mass, it is as the ground of a general conclusion, that the contents of this volume are of the greatest importance. Here are about three hundred pages of close print filled with a bare list of pieces of once public property, now worth from one hundred pounds to upwards of fifty thousand pounds a year each! Some few of the things in the List, as in the cases of several of the Colleges, Chapters, Hospitals, and other foundations, still continue to be public property; but, these form but a comparatively small part of the general mass; and there is, after all, wholly left out of the List, the numerous private estates, seized on and granted away by the "Reformation" sovereigns, in virtue of acts of attainder and other means, grounded on the adherence of the owners to the religion of their fathers. As, for instance, estates like that of which *Cowdry House.* COWDRY-HOUSE, in Sussex, was the chief seat, and which was seized on by Henry VIII., in virtue of the attainder of the Countess of Salisbury and her heirs, and granted by him to his physician, Sir ANTHONY BROWN, who obtained, from that execrable tyrant, manors and estates running over a considerable part of the north-west of Sussex and of the south-west of Surrey.

Tithes in the possession of lay persons. 8. Besides the public property described in this List, there were the tithes, which were thus seized on and granted away to lay persons by the Protestant "Reformation" sovereigns. Until that event took place, no man had an idea, that it could be possible for tithes to be claimed by any but those who administered religion. But, it was soon found, that a large part of those tithes, the sole objects of which were the promotion of religion, and the relief of the poor and the stranger, had, all at once, by a mere touch of the Protestant Wand, been converted into estates for the already nobles and rich men. Such they continue to this day; and, hence those monstrous things, called lay-impropriations, giving, in many cases, thousands of pounds a year to a layman, who never sees the parish, and a few pounds a year to a clergyman who does whatever clerical duty is done in that same parish. The whole affair was a real taking away from the middle and lower class, and a giving to the nobles and the rich. Yet are there men so blind, or so perverse, as to think, or to pretend to think, that the thing, called the " Reformation," ought to be looked upon as " a blessing " !

9. The whole of the rents of the estates of the Church, including those tithes which were confiscated and transferred to lay-parsons, amounted to, perhaps, a third part of the whole rental of the kingdom. There are no means of knowing what the amount really was; for the valuation was, in fact, no valuation at all. It was all plundering with one hand and squandering with the other, as may well be imagined, when the historians tell us, that OLD HARRY (the name which the English gave to the Devil for many

Enormous amount of the tithes of the whole kingdom.

years after Old Harry's death, and the name which the Americans give to the Devil to this day); when historians tell us that OLD HARRY gave a church-estate to a woman, who had made a pudding to please him, and that Sir MILES PARTRIDGE won a ring of church bells of him at dice! It is impossible to come at any thing like an exact account of the worth of the possessions of the Catholic Church. Protestant writers have endeavoured to make the Churches' rental as great as possible, in order to exhibit the clergy as monstrous devourers of the national income. According to the recorded valuations, the rental did not amount to more than a tenth part of the rental of the kingdom. But, then, these valuations were founded, apparently, solely upon the reserved rents, leaving out fines, renewals, heriots, deodands and various other sources of income ; and, therefore, I agree with those historians, who think that the Church income, including the impropriated tithes, amounted to a full third part of the income of all the landowners (clergy included) in the whole nation.

Gambling for church bells.

The charge of the laziness of monks and nuns.

10. Well, then, the good and thoughtless Protestant, who has been, as I was, duped from infancy to manhood; well, then, such good Protestant will ask: " Was not this a great deal too " much to be devoured by a parcel of lazy " monks and priests and nuns, who did no work " of any kind, who lived but to eat and drink " and sleep, and who kept the people in ig- " norance ? " Now, my good brother Protestant, be you who you may, you cannot be more zealous

or more loud upon this score than I was, for many years of my life; until I, at last, examined for myself, not the pages of lying, hired, place-hunting, pension-hunting, benefice-seeking, or romancing historians; but the pages of the sta-tute-book and of the books of the ancient laws of my country. This being the case, you are en-titled to a patient hearing and a kind answer from me, to this, your very natural question; a question such as I should, about ten years ago, have been very likely to put myself.

11. Now, then, if the monks and priests and nuns were such lazy people; if they worked neither by hand nor head; if they did nothing but eat, drink and sleep; if this were their real character, and this the habit of their lives, how can you possibly believe, that they had any in-fluence at all over the minds of the people? And, unless they had very great influence over their minds, how can you possibly believe, that they kept the people in ignorance? What, my friend! Were the people susceptible of know-ledge? Had they (just as we have) nature's works and laws to enlighten them? Had they a desire to become skilful and learned? And were they kept in a state of ignorance, were their capacities benumbed and their propensities thus completely thwarted by lazy creatures who lived only to eat, drink and sleep?

If true, how came they by such in-fluence?

12. By this time, you, I am sure, begin to be ashamed of these assertions; and, the further I go, the more fully will you be convinced, that you have been and are, as I formerly was, the

Find the falsehood of it in the present vo-lume.

dupe of those, who now live upon the spoils of the Church of our fathers. Now, then, is it a fact, is it true, that the Catholic clergy kept, or endeavoured to keep, the people in IGNORANCE? This is a charge that fat and luxurious fellows of the present day are incessantly preferring against them; but, is it not a false charge? That it is a false charge you will find proved in the most satisfactory manner, in the first Volume of this work, in paragraphs from 28 to 36, and in paragraphs from 129 to 134. But, my friend, look into the present volume. Turn over, zealous hater of " monkish ignorance "; turn over to the county of Oxford; then go on to Oxford city.

Colleges of Oxford. Aye! there it is, in that "learned University ", the colleges of which are all filled with rosy-gilled and most doctor-like Protestants, and the walls of which colleges incessantly ring with abuse poured forth on the Catholic religion, and especially on the clergy of that Church, who are here, above all the places in the world, accused of keeping the people in ignorance; there it is, surely, that you will, my good Protestant friend, find something in the way of *proof* to make good this accusation! Turn over the leaves, then, and come to the word " OXFORD."

What! all the halls and colleges founded by Catholics. 13. What! Aye, do! Rub your eyes bright, and then look again. What! nothing at all! Oh! everlasting shame on the name of Protestant! Not one single college, hall, or school, founded by Protestants, nor since the day that the word Protestant was pronounced in England! About twenty colleges in all, and all founded and endowed by Catholics; and, as if to put the calumniators of the Catholic clergy to shame eternal, as if to make them undergo a sort of hell in this world, out of the twenty, *eleven* were founded by CATHOLIC BISHOPS; *two* by MONKS; *one* by NUNS; and *five* by Catholic kings, nobles, gentlemen and ladies. Aye, and here is the record, that the University itself was founded by ALFRED, whose father took him to Rome, where he was anointed by the Pope himself! Nay, as if all this were not enough, here is the record, that the teaching at this University was begun by a monk, who came to England for the express purpose, and in gratitude for the services of whom Alfred founded and endowed a monastery for him at Winchester.

14. Thus, then, my good and true Protestant friend, we have, I think, settled the question about keeping the people in ignorance. We now come to the other assertion which is put forth by you, namely, that this full third part of the rents of the nation "was a great deal too "much to be devoured by the monks and priests "and nuns," and which you have, as I used to do, repeated out of the books of the really devouring vermin of the present day. Yes, it was "a great deal too much to be so devoured"; but, then, my friend, you are not yet aware, that your basis is an assumed fact; and that this assumed fact is a most monstrous lie! In the first place it was physically impossible that they should devour a fiftieth part of it. How, for instance, were the fourteen monks in the Abbey of

Leave the charge of ignorance.

Chertsey, in Surrey, to devour rents, which, in our money, amounted to 14,893*l.* a year ? BISHOP TANNER (a Protestant bishop, mind), says, that " all the monasteries were, in effect, great " schools and great hospitals (meaning, in those " days, places of hospitality) ; and were, many " of them, obliged to relieve many poor people " every day. They were likewise houses of " entertainment for almost all travellers. In " short, their hospitality was such, that, in the " Priory of Norwich, one thousand five hundred " quarters of malt, and above eight hundred " quarters of wheat, and all other things in pro- " portion, were generally spent every year."

Bishop Tanner's charac- ter of the monasteries.

15. There ! my good duped Protestant friend; that is the way in which monks and nuns " de- voured " their rents ! There were but twenty- two monks in this Priory ; so that, in fact, they were the mere agents for distributing amongst the needy and the strangers the rents of their estates. Ah! Good God! what has the thing called the " Reformation " produced at Norwich! Who is there at Norwich NOW to keep hospi- tality ? " St. ANDREW'S HALL," as it is now called, which was the church of this Priory, is the Corn-market, and now hears, instead of the chantings of its benevolent monks, the chaffer- ings and the cheapenings, the lying and roguish cant, of sly Quaker corn-monopolizers. The questions here now are, not how and when malt and wheat shall be distributed to the poor and the stranger; but, how they shall be hoarded up, made dear, and kept from the thirsty and the

Former hos- pitality at the Priory at Norwich.

St. Andrew's Hall.

hungry. It was from the platform, on which once stood the high-altar of this Priory, that I tendered to the people of Norfolk, that Petition, which they did me the honour to pass, which was afterwards presented to the Parliament, which now lies on the table of the House of Commons, and which is, I trust, destined finally to be the ground-work of measures, calculated, not, certainly, to restore to us the happiness enjoyed by our Catholic fathers, but to take away by law, and to give back to the poor, a part, at least, of those Church-revenues, which, in Catholic times, were deemed to be, and actually were, the inheritance of the poor and the stranger; for, this is the grand thing for which that Petition prays; and, certainly, if the spot from which it sprang could be supposed capable of giving it any degree of effect, one more appropriate than the altar-base of this munificent Priory could not have been chosen.

Norfolk Petition.

Revenues of Catholic church disposed of to the benefit of the poor;

16. Yes, my good and duped Protestant friend, "a great deal too much to be devoured "by monks and priests and nuns"; and, accordingly, the monks and nuns did not, as you have seen, devour it, nor hardly any part of it. And now, as to the priests, including the bishops. They could not marry; they could have no wives; they had, in fact, no families to provide for; while, as to the monks and nuns, they could possess no private property, could leave nothing by will, and, therefore, were completely trustees for the poor and the stranger. Of the manner, in which the bishops spent their incomes, we

and not devoured by monks and nuns.

have a specimen in the eleven colleges, out of twenty, founded and endowed by them at Oxford. But the main thing of all is, that the Catholic priesthood, taken all together, wholly maintained the poor and the stranger, and suffered not the name of pauper to be known in England; and, it never was known in England, until the thing, called the "Reformation," came.

17. This is a matter, which is, at this time (July, 1827), of infinite importance. In the *Prayer of the Norfolk Petition.* Norfolk Petition, before mentioned, we prayed that "a part of the public property, commonly called Church property," might be taken away by law, and applied to other public purposes. My anxious wish, and my hope, is, that the prayer of this Petition may finally be granted by the Parliament; whether before the Parliament be reformed, I cannot say; but, granted it will be, in the end, I have no doubt; and, with this in my mind, it is, that I put forth this little volume, the utility of which, in the case thus hoped for, we shall presently see. But, first, we ought to consider a little the origin of this "Church property," as it is now called, and as it never was called, and as no one ever presumed to call it, until it had the name given it by Protestant priests and bishops, when they once got it into their hands. It was, in fact, the portion of the poor, the infirm, the aged, the widow, the orphan, the stranger, and of all the necessitous, which portion was lodged in the hands of the clergy for just and wise distribution.

18. In the first Volume of this Work, in para-

graphs from 49 to 59 inclusive, this matter is
fully and clearly stated. To those paragraphs
I beg to refer the reader. There it is clearly
shown, that tithes, and every other species of income of the clergy, were looked upon, and were,
in fact and in practice, more the property of the
poor than of the monks, nuns, priests, and
bishops. Thus it was that there were, in this
then happy country, neither paupers nor common
beggars. But, when a part of the tithes and
estates had been seized and taken away from the
clergy altogether, and when the remainder had
been given to bishops and priests, who were
allowed to marry, and who, of course, had
families of their own to feed and clothe and to get
fortunes for, the beggars, as we have seen in
paragraphs 471 and 472, began to appear, and
they soon " covered the land," as the lice did the
land of Egypt. Attempts were, as we have
there seen, made to keep down their numbers by
punishments the most horrible ; so that England,
which had never before known what poverty
was, now saw it in all its most hideous forms.

*Tithes for-
merly looked
upon as the
property of
the poor.*

19. At last, when the butchering and racking
Elizabeth had tried whipping, scourging, and
even martial law, in vain, and when she and the
principal plunderers began to fear, that raging
hunger would, if not, by some means or other,
assuaged, deal them deadly blows ; then, and
not till then, the POOR-LAWS were passed; and
this fruit of the famous " Reformation " sticks to
the landowners, clings fast to them, unto the
present day. The real history of the poor-

*Poor-laws
tried after
whipping and
martial law
failed to sup-
press beg-
ging.*

rates and of English pauperism is given Vol. I., paragraphs from 227 to 237; and in paragraphs from 457 to 478. And, we are always to bear in mind, that the money, or food, or clothing, proceeding from the poor-rates, is the poor's property. It is not alms; it is what they have a right to by the law of nature, by the law of God, and by the common law of the land; aye, that same law, which, and which alone, gives a man a right to the enjoyment of his field or garden, also gives the poor and necessitous a right to be relieved out of the fruits of the earth.

Private property.

20. Civil society it was that caused that which is called private property. In a state of nature, when man was and the lands were as God made them and left them, the lands were for the common use of all the people. When the people of any country agreed to give up their common right, and to permit private ownership to exist, they must have done it with a view to make their lives safer and happier; and, therefore, it is impossible; it is absolutely impossible, that they could have contemplated, as a consequence of their social compact, that the lives of the millions would ever be placed at the mere mercy of the thousands, or, perhaps, of the hundreds. MAL-

Malthus' denial of the right of the poor to relief.

THUS denies the right of the poor to relief; he denies that they have any right to claim relief from those who hold the lands and houses as their private property; and he actually recommends to the Parliament to be so foolish as well as so unjust and cruel as to pass a law to refuse relief to all who shall be born after a certain day, and also to all the parents of such persons. In the way of justification of this horrid proposal, he says, that the man wanting relief after this, " should be left to the punishment of nature."; that he should be told, that the " laws of " nature had doomed him and his family to " starve"; and that, whatever might be their state of distress, they " had no claim on so- " ciety for the smallest portion of food "! I need hardly say, that this came from the pen of a Church of England Parson! Arro- gant, insolent, stupid, and cruel as it is, its source will be a question of doubt with few men.

21. To the "punishment of nature" this stupid and cruel projector would leave the necessitous. Well, Parson, the poor would, I dare say, take you at your word, and jump for joy to be thus referred to the laws of nature. Those laws, Parson, bid them, when they want food, to take it where they can find it, and to care nothing about the place or the person that they take it from. The laws of nature know nothing about theft or robbery or bur- glary. When, indeed, in no shop, house, barn, mill, or other place, the hungry man can discover food sufficient to satisfy his hunger; or, when finding it, he has not, whether by force of arms or otherwise, the ability to get at it and eat it; then, indeed, I allow, that, "the laws " of nature have doomed him to starve"; but, Parson, it is only when he cannot discover the existence of the food, or when, knowing where

The "punish-ment of na-ture."

The laws of nature far different to what Mal-thus thinks them.

it is, he has not force to seize it, that the "laws of nature doom him to starve."

22. We very well know, that all men are subject, and ought to be subject, as I have, on more than one occasion, before stated, to be called forth, to be compelled to come forth, and, at the risk of their lives, defend their country against a foreign enemy, and also to defend the lands or houses, which are the private property of the possessors, in case of any illegal attempt to take away, or to injure, those lands or houses. Now, suppose the country invaded, or suppose a band of rebels to be gutting, or pulling down, the house of a Lord. Suppose PARSON MALTHUS to go to a poor man, to whom he has before been preaching his doctrine; and suppose him to call upon this man to come forth, as a militia-man, to repel the invaders, or to quell the rebels.

PARSON.—Here, CHOPSTICK! Come away, and bring your arms to defend your country.

CHOPSTICK.—My country, Parson: how is it mine, if I have not in it even a security against being starved to death while the land abounds in food?

PARSON.—But, here is the law, and forth you must come, or be punished severely.

CHOPSTICK.—Law! Why, the law of nature bids me, first, not to risk my life; next, it bids me stay at home in these times of peril, to quiet the alarms of, and to protect, my wife and children.

PARSON.—But, here are a parcel of rebels,

gutting and pulling down the good Lord
Rottenborough's house.

CHOPSTICK.—Well! let him drive them away.

PARSON.—But, he cannot; he is not able;
one man cannot fight with a thousand; and
the law commands us to come forth to the
protection of each other.

[*Enter* OVERSEER.]

CHOPSTICK.—Law! Oh, no! Parson, the law *Chopstick,*
of nature bids the strong to do what they please *and*
with that which the weak have got; that law
bids these strong poor men to go and take the
goods and to pull down and divide amongst
them the big house of this rich weak man; and,
if I be to be referred to that law, when I and
my wife and children are starving for want of
relief; if the Overseer be to answer my application by telling me, "that the law of nature has
doomed us to starve," surely I may refer my
Lord to the sentences of the same law.

OVERSEER.—Why, John, who has been filling *the Overseer.*
thy head with this nonsense? When did I talk
to you about the law of nature? Are there not
the poor laws to provide for you, in case of distress; and do you not, in this way, partake in
the yearly rents, and, in fact, in the ownership,
of my Lord's estate?

[*Exit* PARSON, *slipping off.*]

CHOPSTICK.— Aye! That's another man's
matter, Master Pinchum! Then, indeed, if I be
a sort of a part-owner with my Lord, it is just
that I should [*taking a club down from the
rack*] go and fight for the protection of his

goods and his house; and here I go to do my best against these rebels.

23. This is the true, the common-sense, view of the matter. Agreeably to these principles there are, and always have been, in all countries except in ill-fated Ireland, since the " Reformation," a legal provision, of some sort or other, for the necessitous; a law of some sort, that effectually provided that they should not die for want of food and raiment; and, though in England, many attempts have been made, by STURGES and others, to alter the law in such a way as to make it more and more difficult for the indigent to obtain relief; though attempts of this sort are continually making; they never can, upon the whole, be attended with success; for, before they could obtain that success, the kingdom would be convulsed to its centre; and, indeed, it is clear to every man of sense and reflection, that it is the poor-rates, and the poor-rates alone, which, at this very moment, cause the peace of the country to be preserved.

Attempts to alter the poor-laws.

24. But, though these rates are just and necessary, we are never to forget, that they were not at all necessary, that they never existed, and that the hateful name of pauper never was known in England, until that " Reformation," as it is called, which caused the enormous confiscations, the particulars of which are stated in this second Volume of my History. Before that time, the indigent were relieved out of the produce of the tithes, out of the revenues of the monasteries, and out of those of the manors and other estates

of the bishops. We have seen, in the first volume of this work, how a large part of the tithes and almost all the revenues of the monasteries were alienated from the poor and from the public, and in what manner they became private property. As to the poor, they, after about fifty years of whipping, branding, iron-collaring, shooting, and hanging, got a provision, such as it was, in the poor-rates; but, observe, the public got no compensation for what the aristocracy had taken from it; and every man had now, if not a pauper himself, to pay poor-rates, to make up for what the aristocracy had got divided amongst them!

25. A pretty large part of the tithes and of the manors and the other estates belonging to the Bishops, the Cathedrals, and the Colleges, remained unconfiscated, and were turned over to the Protestant Parsons, Bishops, Deans, Prebendaries, Fellows of Colleges, and other " spiritual persons" (as the law calls them) of the present "Protestant Church of England, as by law established." Now, it is a clear case, that the Parliament, which could take this property from the clergy of one religion, and give it to those of another religion; the Parliament that could, in spite of Magna Charta and in spite of the law of the land of a thousand years' standing, do this, though, in doing this the Parliament set at nought the wills, or grants, of all the founders of the numerous religious houses and establishments; it is a clear case, that all those who contend, that the Parliament had a right to do these things, must allow, that the Parliament has

A large part of the tithes turned over to the Protestant clergy

by Act of Parliament.

a right to dispose as it pleases of all that part
of the Church property, which still continues to
belong to the nation, or, in other words, which
is not private property. The divers religious
foundations were made agreeably to the law. If
the religion was to be changed, and a new one
was to be established, the property in the foundations ought, in justice, in bare justice, to have
reverted to the founders, or to their heirs, who,
in most cases, were to be found, and were ready
to put forward their claim to it. If the religion
were found to be bad, the property, the lands,
the trees and the buildings, had committed no
offence. Nevertheless, the property was all
seized on by the King and Parliament. The
Parliament gave it all to the King; and the
King, and his successors, gave the greater part
of it, in return, amongst the members of the two
houses of Parliament, or their relations ! Now,
if the King and Parliament had a right to deal
thus with property, the heirs of the founders of
which were ready to claim it, surely no one can
deny, that the present King and Parliament
have a right to apply to public purposes
that part of this great mass of property, which,
as stated above, continues to be the property of
the public. There is, I venture to assert, no man
that will deny this, and especially no man, who
possesses, by descent or otherwise, any part of
the Catholic Church estates; for, what title has
such man to his estate? What plea has he
against an ejectment? He has no title, he has
no answer, except those which are furnished

by those Acts of Parliament of Henry VIII., which seized, and granted to the King, the estates of the Church. This sauce for the goose, so delicious as it long has been acknowledged to be, must, when the time for another repast shall arrive, be allowed to be sauce for the gander; and, of this sauce, Norfolk Petition would, if acted upon, give the nation a taste.

26. PLUNKETT, who has now been made a lord, and about whom the bleaters in Ireland are, just now, making such a fuss, asserted, in the debate on Mr. HUME's motion for applying part of the clerical incomes in Ireland to other public purposes; this PLUNKETT asserted, in the most unqualified terms, that all tithes, glebes, and all sorts of property, called Church property, were as sacred from the touch of the Parliament, that the Parliament had not more right to sell them, or to apply them in any way, than it had to sell, or otherwise dispose of, any parcel of any man's private property! Indeed, Plunkett! What, then, are any of those titles good for, by which men now hold the immense masses of property described in this volume? If this King and Parliament have no right to touch that which belongs to the nation, could Harry VIII. and his Parliament have a right to seize and to alienate all these masses of property, great part of which were really private property, and had claimants, legal claimants, to demand them? If this King and Parliament have no right to take public property, and to apply it to public purposes, can those titles be worth one single

Lord Plunkett's assertion as to the inviolability of Church property.

straw, which rest on Acts of Parliament, which Acts seized on private property and applied it to private purposes? I might, by comparing the tenure of what the Church parsons hold with the tenure of private property, show the gross absurdity of the doctrine of this Plunkett, who, I recollect, was anxious to check the circulation of small pamphlets, because the mass of the people were now become so much more enlightened than formerly; I might, by the comparison just mentioned, show the monstrous absurdity of the doctrine of this Plunkett: but, I say, No: I say, Let his doctrine stand, if the parsons like; and, then, all the tithes of all the holders of Abbey-lands, aye, and of the greater part of the Cathedral and College-lands, are not worth one single pinch even of Scotch snuff.

Very few who agree with him.

27. However, as there certainly is not a man in the kingdom (except some parson, perhaps), besides PLUNKETT, to hold a doctrine like this, we will leave PLUNKETT to have his hearing faculties tickled by the bleaters of Ireland, and will now go on to see a little how, if applied to this mass of "public property, commonly called Church property," Norfolk Petition would work.

Property now remaining to the nation.

28. The property which remains to the nation is, I. THE PAROCHIAL TITHES AND GLEBES. II. THE BISHOPRIC REVENUES. III. THE DEAN AND CHAPTER REVENUES. IV. THE COLLEGE REVENUES. Here is still an immense mass of property, and all of it, or nearly all of it, diverted from the uses to which it was formerly applied, and to which it was intended that it should always be applied.

PROTESTANT REFORMATION.

But, the questions for us here are, whether it be now well applied; and whether it could not be much better applied than it now is. As to the real amount of it, that will never be got at by the public, as long as it shall remain in the hands in which it now is. No man has ever been able to get an account laid before Parliament, of the amount of this property! Accounts of every thing else can be got; but, of this no account can ever be come at. Some years ago, a return was made to Parliament, stating, the name of each living, the population of the parish, the size of the church, the state of the parsonage-house, and the annual worth of the living, IF UNDER ONE HUNDRED AND FIFTY POUNDS! Here was a crafty trick! Why not state the annual worth, if ABOVE one hundred and fifty pounds! Why this close disguise if ABOVE that mark? Is not the answer ready?

Return made to Parliament of the number and value of Livings.

To have stated the annual worth of the whole of the livings would have shown to this beggared people what an immense sum is swallowed annually by these comparatively few men and their families, whose Catholic predecessors kept all the poor, and also kept the churches in repair out of these same tithes. The tithes of England, Wales and Ireland have been estimated, by several writers, at eight millions a-year. The parsons affect to say that this is an over statement. But, when any public functionary hears his gains over stated, and knows that he is thereby placed before the public in a disadvantageous light, what is his remedy? Why, to publish an exact account of what he really does receive.

Estimate of the total value in England and Wales.

INTRODUCTION.

Aye, and this is what the parsons would do, to be sure, if they had it in their power to prove that their gains had been over-rated. For my part, I am convinced, that, if we include the rent of the parsonage-houses and glebes, the compulsory offerings and fees, and all the estates of the Bishops, Chapters, Colleges and other foundations, which, though not legally, nor necessarily, engrossed by the Church-parsons, are so in fact ;

if we include the whole, I am convinced, that this Church-Establishment costs this "enlightened Protestant nation," more than TWELVE MILLIONS OF POUNDS STERLING A YEAR; and this, too, observe, without including further millions that are required to maintain the POLICE-Establishment and the TROOPS, which the public papers so frequently exhibit to us as employed in collecting, or in aiding and defending those who are employed in the collecting of tithes! This "Church property," as it is called, must, like the Debt, not be estimated by the bare amount of itself, but, there must be added to this amount, the cost of the army, which is required on account of it. If we leave this out of our estimate, we shall be as far short of the true mark, as we should be if we were to leave out of the estimate of the custom and excise taxes the amount of the salaries of the custom-house and excise officers ; or as if we were, in our account of the cost of post-chaise hire, to leave out the amount of the sums paid to the post-boy and the ostler. The cost, then, of this establishment is perfectly enormous : and, what is the establishment worth to the nation? Is the "service" rendered by this body of persons, called the clergy, worth twelve or fifteen millions a year? Is it worth one million? Is it worth one pound? Is not the name of "service" wrongly applied in this case? Has not this establishment now been proved, by ample experience, to be injurious, rather than beneficial, to the country? Ought the incomes to be applied to other public purposes? The stating, and shortly remarking on, a few well-known facts, relating to each of the above four classes of "spiritual persons," taking the classes in the order in which they there stand, will enable us to answer these questions; and, if we find the last of these questions to be answered in the affirmative; that is to say, if we find, that these several parcels of public property ought to be applied to other public purposes, there will remain for us to determine only on the manner and degree, in which it is our duty to petition the King and Parliament to cause the taking away, or alienation, to be made.

29. To begin with the first class, the TITHES and GLEBES, or property now possessed by the common parsons, or parish clergy, it must always be borne in mind, that this property was only so much put into the hands of the priests for the purposes of relieving their indigent parishioners, of showing hospitality to the stranger, of keeping the church in repair and keeping up its ornaments, and of furnishing a decent maintenance for the parish priests themselves. This was not only the intention of the founders and

Purposes for which tithes were originally granted.

endowers of parish-livings; but, it was the law of the land as well as the law of the church. In the first volume, paragraph 51, I have shown by a reference to the canon-law, that the poor were to have relief out of the tithes. And, to prove beyond all doubt, that this was the practice as well as the law, I need only mention an Act of the 15th year of Richard II., which provides that, if the living of the parish be in the hands of any convent, the convent shall always leave in the hands of their vicar, a part of the income sufficient for the relief of the poor. Another Act, enforcing this Act, was passed in the 4th year of Henry IV. So that it is quite clear, that the tithes, glebe, and all the income of every church living, were to be employed, as far as necessary, in relieving and in otherwise doing good to the poor and the stranger.

Wholly diverted from those purposes.

30. It is not necessary to say, that the income arising from this class of public property has been wholly diverted from the purposes to which it was, at first, destined, and to which it was, until the " Reformation," as we Protestants call that sad event, fairly applied. Why, therefore, should these parcels of property remain any longer, at any rate, in the hands of the present possessors? If they would, even now, do as the Catholic priests did; if they would maintain the poor of their parishes, and would entertain and help all strangers in distress; if they would repair the churches, keep up the ornaments (there are none left, by the bye); if, in short, they would put an end to

poor-rates and church-rates, and keep the poor and repair the church, they might still keep the tithes and the glebes and parsonage-houses and gardens. But, if they will do neither of these, what reason is there for their having the property? "They have law for it." Oh, aye! And the Catholic clergy, and more especially the monks and nuns, had " law for it " too, and law a little older, at any rate, than the law that our parsons have for it. They have law for it till another law come to take this their law away ; and what reason is there, I again ask, for leaving the property in their possession? What REASON is there that another law should not come to take this their law away !

31. Most monstrously have they always been afraid of questions like this. Most anxious have they always been to keep out of sight the origin of the poor-rates. A Hampshire farmer, who had read the "PROTESTANT REFORMATION," told me a few weeks ago, that, at a meeting, relative to the poor, lately held at the poor-house, in his parish, and at which meeting the parson presided, there was a great deal said about the frightful increase of, and great hardship inflicted by, the poor-rates, of which the parson complained more vehemently than any body else. He (the farmer) took this occasion to ask, in all simplicity, of his Reverence, "How there came to " be such a thing as poor-rates in England, and " who it was that used to maintain the poor in " old times?" " Well," said I, " and what did " he say to you in answer?" " Zay," replied he,

The Hampshire Farmer's question to his Parson.

" ha did n't zay much; but ha screwed down
" 's brows, and, looking as black as the very
" devil; ha zed, that tw'oud be a good deal better
" if every man wou'd mind 's woan business."
This was a pincher indeed! Our parsons know
all about the Catholic claims to tithes; they
know all about the collection of tithes; all about
moduses and endowments and the like; they
have at their fingers' ends all the history of the
" superstitions and idolatries" of the Catholic
Church; but ignorant as horses they appear
with regard to the way in which the poor were
kept in Catholic times; and, I can tell you another thing; namely, that whoever dares to make
any thing public on that subject, is, if they can
reach him, sure to feel, in some way or other,
the effects of their implacable vengeance; of the
truth of which we have the most complete proof
in the curious affair of Mr. RUGGLES, to the circumstances of which I have once before merely
alluded, but which, in justice to myself as well
as my subject, and, which is of still more importance, in justice to the middle and working
classes of my countrymen, I must here fully relate.

*Ruggles's
History of
the Poor.*

32. In the year 1793, DEIGHTON, bookseller,
Holborn, published a book in two vols. octavo,
with the following title: " The History of the
" Poor: their rights, duties, and the laws
" respecting them: in a Series of Letters. By
" THOMAS RUGGLES, F. A. S. One of His Ma-
" jesty's Justices of the Peace for the Counties
" of Essex and Suffolk." In this work, Mr. Ruggles explained the foundation of the right of

the poor to a maintenance from the land; he explained the principle on which the Catholic Church took charge of the poor; he traced the Church-estates, including tithes, glebes, personal tithes and all, back to one and the same source; namely, CHARITY; he insisted, that gifts, out of which the Church-property arose, were gifts not to bishops and priests, or to any religious order, for their own use, but that they were gifts IN TRUST to them for certain purposes, one of which purposes was, the maintenance of the poor; and this his doctrine he founded and upheld on the canons of the Church, on the writings of the fathers, on the common-law of England, and on the statute-law of England.

33. Having established his doctrine of gifts in trust, he proceeded to inquire, whether this doctrine ought not now to be acted upon; and, he came to the conclusion, that it ought to be acted upon; that, not only the holders of what is still called Church-property, but the holders of abbey-lands also, ought, EVEN NOW, to be made to pay annually, towards the maintenance of the poor, a full fourth, at least, of the net yearly profits of such property, and this, observe, over and above the proportion that might be called for from those who held no such property! For, he contended, and, indeed, he proved, that the grants of the Parliament to Henry VIII. did not set aside, nor at all enfeeble, the claim of the poor to their share of the benefit of the gifts in trust; and that, though

The author contends for reviving the claim of the Poor.

the claim had lain DORMANT for a long while, it WAS BY NO MEANS BECOME EXTINCT. In short, he proposed to revive the claim, to act upon it, and to call upon all the holders of Church-property, whether coming from the Catholic seculars or regulars, whether now held by clerical or lay persons, to give up, if it should be wanted by the poor, a fourth part of the net profits of their estates, be they of what nature they might, for, or towards, the maintenance of the poor, and this, too, over and above the rates paid by other people. He proposed, in short, that the poor should be maintained out of the Church-property, if a fourth of its income would do it, and, if it would not, he proposed first to take that fourth, and then to raise in the present manner, and by general assessment, whatever might be wanted further.

Mr. Ruggles no Jacobin, but a magistrate.

34. Observe, now, that it was no jacobin, no radical, no republican, who proposed this ; but, in the first place, a land-owner ; in the next place, a Justice of the Peace in two counties; in the next place, a most loyal gentleman; in the next place, one of the adorers of the " Heaven-born" Pitt ; and, lastly, a most zealous Protestant, asserting that the Catholic Church had " rested on fear and superstition," and that the " Reformation," springing up at the " magic " touch of Henry VIII.," gave rise to a system " more consonant to the principles of sober " piety and good sense"! A sort of " piety " and " good sense" that had, it seems, Mr. Ruggles, little to do with charity, or with an honest execu-

tion of "trusts"! However, such was the author of this book; such was the maintainer of
these doctrines. "And," the reader will exclaim, "why were the doctrines not acted
"upon?" Aye! that is the pith of the story: that
is the very thing we are going to see. "See!"
the reader will exclaim; "but, what answer
"was given to Mr. Ruggles?" Alas! reader, no
answer was given to poor Mr. Ruggles; but
he soon found himself under the necessity of an-
swering himself. In short HE PUBLISHED A SECOND
EDITION OF HIS BOOK, LEFT OUT ALL HIS ABOVE-
MENTIONED DOCTRINES AND PROPOSALS, AND ALMOST
BEGGED PARDON FOR HAVING PUT FORTH THOSE
DOCTRINES AND PROPOSALS!

Obliged to eat his words.

35. "What!" exclaims the honest reader,
"an Englishman do this! an English Gentle-
"man do such a thing as this!" O, yes! And
your "Gentlemen of England," as that former
demagogue and now creeping courtier, Sir
Francis Burdett, calls them, have proved to the
world, by a long series of acts, that they are,
generally speaking, the meanest and most cow-
ardly of all mankind. But, what was it, then,
that this poor Thomas Ruggles, Esq. this unfortunate Justice of the Peace for the counties of Essex and Suffolk; what was it that the
poor man left out of his second edition?
We will now see what it was that he left out,
what words he ate, in order to appease the
wrath of the parsons; for he expressly says,
in the preface to his second edition, that "HIS
"PRINCIPLES AS A FRIEND TO THE HIERARCHY, HAD

BEEN SOMEWHAT CALLED IN QUESTION," in consequence of his attempt "to revive the claim" of the poor on the revenues of the clergy. Poor fellow! That was enough for him! He was marked out for vengeance : he evidently saw it ; and published his "second edition" in order to save himself, if possible. And, now let us see what it was that the poor, terrified "Esquire" left out.

36. In the Preface to his first edition, he is speaking of the monstrous burdens on the land, especially of the poor-rates ; and, here he says, that, in his book, he has made an inquiry into the matter. "More especially," says he ; and then he goes on in the following words ; and, mind, these words that I am now going to copy here, are left out in the second edition. The poor "'Squire" re-publishes, in the second edition, the Preface to the first edition ; and, at the end of the thirteenth paragraph of that preface he leaves out, he sinks, he eats the words, and every word, of the following passage :

Preface to his book.

" More especially as to that part of the case, " which relates to the productiveness and appli- " cation of those estates which were originally " given to the clergy, in trust for eleemosy- " nary purposes ; but if the laity were to claim " from the legislature that equity which the " Court of Chancery would decree on a bill " filed in common cases, on complaint of a " cestui. que trust ; that the trustees should ful- " fil those trusts, for the purposes for which the " estate was granted ; a cry of, 'The church

" is in danger,' much more serious and dis-
" tressing would arise throughout the land, than
" any attempts of the sectaries have occasioned.
" This also requires the attention of the Minis-
" ter ; but the pen of no individual can ever be
" expected to rouse him to action on this point ;
" nothing but the public voice is equal to that
" effect ; such an equitable decree of the egisla-
" ture, clashing with the interests of so reverend
" a portion of our fellow subjects." Poor
'Squire ! He was compelled to eat these words
even in his Preface ! But we are now to see
what a dreadful meal, or, rather, counter-vomit,
he had to undergo, in the work itself.

37. In his 27th Letter, first edition, after
describing the origin of tithes, he speaks of the
practice as to the distribution of them. The following are his words, which words he leaves
out in the second edition.—" That such was
" their origin, is not only the true theory ;
" but, that, in former days, the practice
" flowed in conformity with the principle,
" has been already proved in the instance
" of an application from St. Augustine to
" Pope Gregory, with respect to the distribution
" of tithes ; from ancient canons of the church,
" and from other instances, where the three-
" fold or four-fold division of the tithes was di-
" rected, as the sees of the Bishop were, or
" were not, endowed. The writings of the
" fathers also corroborate the proof of this
" theory, as well as of the practice ; and the
" evidence of those who first held these fiduci-

His explanation of the origin of tithes.

INTRODUCTION.

" ary estates for the benefit of the poor and the
" church, is evidence of the highest authority,
" and establishes the most convincing proof.
" The statute law also proceeded on this idea;
" or else the legislature looked on the possessions
" of the ecclesiastics as the property of the
" kingdom, in the reigns of Richard II. and
" Henry IV."—Yes! the parsons of Essex and
Suffolk did not like to hear of any " divisions
" of the tithes, or any distribution of them." They
did not like to hear of " fiduciary estates"; that
is to say, trust-held estates. And so the poor
'Squire found that his safest way was to swallow
all this down again.

38. The next is a still bigger mass for poor
'Squire Ruggles to get back down his throat.
He has been, in the sentences immediately preceding what I am now about to quote, speaking
of the turbulent times (from Henry V. to Henry
VIII., and the still more turbulent in and after
this last reign) which caused the above-mentioned
claim of the poor to lie dormant. Then he goes on
in the words which I am just about to quote, and
which words the poor 'Squire has wholly sunk in
his second edition :—" No wonder, that " [during
The claim of the turbulent times, and after the Reformation,]
the poor, " these claims should have remained dormant,
though long " but it by no means follows, as a consequence,
dormant, not " that because such rights of charity as these,
extinct. " owing to the rough and unsettled circumstances
" of the times, were dormant, they should BE-
" COME EXTINCT, especially when so large a
" portion of the revenue still remained to the
" Church; the possessors of which, however cha-

" ritable in their DOCTRINES, by DEGREES WITH-
" DREW THE RIGHTFUL AND ACCUSTOMED PROPOR-
" TION OF THEIR ESTATES FROM THE REPAIR OF
" CHURCHES AND THE MAINTENANCE OF THE POOR ;
" and although they still presided in our high
" court of conscience, and through the ensuing
" century gave us chancellors, were, notwith-
" standing, very careful how they permitted
" such a claim to be established over the es-
" tates of the dissolved monasteries : knowing
" that their own possessions were held by the
" same tenure, given, at first, for the same
" purposes, and liable to similar trusts."—No
wonder that the 'Squire's "principles" as a
friend to the hierarchy, were somewhat " called
in question." No wonder that he was compelled
to swallow these words.

39. Having told us, that the claims, though
they had been dormant, were not extinguished,
he proceeded to prove, that the right still existed in 1793, as good as it was, as complete as it
was, in the 12th or 14th century, never having
been weakened by any positive law. The following is the passage ; most excellent it is ; and
it is unnecessary for me to add, that it was left
out of the second edition.—"We all know, that a *His law of*
" claim to the third or fourth part of the eccle- *the case.*
" siastic revenue for the benefit of the poor, is
" nearly vanished in the oblivion of past times ;
" but a right may remain, although the use of it
" has been long neglected. A maxim of law
" prevails in ecclesiastical rights, nullum tempus
" occurrit ecclesiæ ; the poor are a part of the

INTRODUCTION.

" Church; the possessions of the Church are the
" possessions of the poor; the revenues have
" been so styled by the fathers of the Church;
" they were obtained in the name of the poor,
" for the love of God : are not the poor, there-
" fore, permitted to claim the benefit of the
" same maxim? Is not that the law of the part,
" which is the law of the whole? At least there
" is as much justice in the maxim for the one, as
" for the other; therefore, nullum tempus occur-
" rit pauperibus. If positive ordinances of the
" state have not destroyed this right, no length
" of time should be allowed to weaken it. Let
" those who doubt the truth of these assertions,
" find, if they can, an affirmative injunction, that
" the Church should hold its revenues free and
" clear of those trusts, for the benefit of the
" poor, which were created by the donors,
" when they gave their lands and tithes for ele-
" emosynary purposes; no such discharge is to
" be seen in the Acts of Parliament in the 27 and
" 31 Henry VIII., which empowered the crown
" to alienate the possessions of the monasteries :
" those, therefore, who are possessed of estates,
" which were formerly monastic, held them
" QUOD HOC, subject to the same equitable
" claim."—Alas! for poor Justice Ruggles! No
wonder, good God! that his " principles, as a
" friend to the hierarchy, were somewhat called
" in question." However, here we have law, not
only equity, but law also, for going with a demand, if we chose it, on the holders of Abbey-
lands for a part, at least, of their revenues !

40. One more extract shall finish; and a pretty complete finish it is : for, it contains nothing short of a proposition, to take away from all holders of what is, or what ever was, ecclesiastical property, a full fourth part of the net annual profits of such property ! Not, a word, not a breath of this, in the 'Squire's second edition ! " MUM !" says the Squire; but I have found out the first edition ; and in that the 'Squire shall now be heard.—" In any future revisal of the *His proposal.*
" laws, respecting the poor, their maintenance,
" employment, and relief, it may be worth the
" attention of the legislature to call to mind for
" what purposes the ecclesiastical revenues of
" the kingdom were originally granted, to in-
" quire whether they are employed in those pur-
" poses ; to investigate the fact, on what trusts
" and on account of what duties, the clergy
" originally received the clerical estates ; and to
" ask whether those duties and those trusts are
" now fulfilled ? and when they are convinced of
" the purposes for which those estates were
" originally granted, and can find no positive law
" to abrogate those purposes, and perceive that
" the poor stand as much in need of the per-
" formance of those duties, as they did when
" the estates were first granted to the Church ;
" the principle on which the legislature should
" proceed is manifest. I am aware of the nature
" of such investigations, and fully sensible that
" no man can expect, in those whose performances
" of the duties, for which they have received
" their estates, is challenged and brought to the

INTRODUCTION.

" test, a favourable audience, nor expect from
" them a candid interpretation of the motives
" which instigate to the enquiry ; but be that as
" it may ; the present situation of the poor ; their
" wretched state ; their increasing misery ; the
" increasing burthen upon the people for their
" maintenance ; these warrant the enquiry ; the
" inquiry brings to light the evidence ; the de-
" ductions are the consequence of a free and
" candid use of the reasoning faculties ; if any
" error lie either in fact or argument, candour
" requires an explanation from those who con-
" ceive that there is the least intention in the
" writer to mislead the judgment of the public ;
" which explanation will be thankfully received ;
" as it will, nevertheless, tend to establish one
" great object of this investigation, that is truth.
" Assuming, therefore, the foregoing state of
" the matter as fact, would it be a hard compro-
" mise with the possessors of ecclesiastical estates,
" that those in the possession of lay patrons,
" on whom no parochial duty is incumbent,
" should, after a medium of the poor rates has
" been taken throughout the kingdom for the last
" three years, bear the increased expense of the
" maintenance of the poor alone, until the rate
" upon their ecclesiastical estates amount to one-
" fourth of the net annual receipt of their pro-
" fits, before the lay estates be further encum-
" bered ; and that the clergy should be rated
" in the same proportion ?"—Not one word of
all this in the second edition !

PROTESTANT REFORMATION.

Circum-stances under which Mr. Ruggles published his work.

41. These opinions, doctrines, and, especially, this last PROPOSITION, to take away a fourth part of the revenues even of the lay impropriators and from the abbey-land holders, as well as from the parsons and bishops, must have obtained for, and secured to, poor 'Squire Ruggles a comfortable time of it! This book came out just before high Anti-Jacobin times, when it was pretty nearly as much as a man's life was worth to express a doubt of the excellence of the Church establishment. The Church property and all private estates in general had been confiscated, or nearly so, together, in France; plunder, guillotining, burning of nobles' houses, putting royal persons in prison, and, finally, to death: all these had, in France, come along with, in company with, a taking away of tithes. "Look you there!" said "our parsons: "see the dreadful consequences "of touching tithes! If you touch tithes, you "see, plunder, murder, house-burning and king-"killing, and atheism must follow! They must "all follow, if you touch tithes." This was the cry of the parsons, throughout the whole of this then deluded country. Every one was called an enemy of GOD as well as of the King, if he but hinted a doubt of the wisdom of suffering this Church clergy to swallow up so many millions a year. In this state of things, the arrogance of the parsons was beyond description. They were as active as they were arrogant. And, at a time when a man dared hardly speak his mind in private conversation, if his sentiments were at all hostile to the parsons, judge, reader, of the life that poor Justice Ruggles must have

led, until he publicly, in a second edition, published his recantation, and in the face of the nation, did as good as do penance for his sins against Tom Cranmer's and Old Betsey's Church "as by law established." Judge of the life that he must have led, at a time, when not to bow to the earth before a Church parson, was to run a risk of being deemed an atheist and a jacobin, and when such deeming had its practical effects always at hand, ready for the victim. As to tradesmen and farmers, they dared not open their mouths to speak of a parson in any terms but those of positive praise. It was during this "reign of terror," real reign of terror, much more real than it ever was in France, that poor 'Squire Ruggles recanted! It is very curious to observe the effect of the reign of terror in this case. The 'Squire wrote the matter of his book in 1792, and published it in a periodical work, called the " ANNALS OF AGRICULTURE." He published the first edition, in the book-shape, very early in 1793. Now, observe, the war against France was not begun when this edition must have been in the press. So that the reign of terror had not commenced, and could not have been anticipated, when this first edition, with all the above-quoted passages in it, went to the press from the hands of Mr. Ruggles. But when the second edition went to the press, the reign of terror was in full swing; the Act of Habeas Corpus was suspended; and there was an Act to empower the Ministers to imprison, just where and when they pleased, any body ('Squires not excepted) THAT THEY MIGHT SUSPECT of treasonable practices!

No wonder, therefore, that Mr. RUGGLES changed his tone, recanted, and expunged the passages which were offensive to the parsons, who now saw plenty of barracks and German troops in the country, and who, to use their own phraseology, made the " enemies of social order " and our holy religion" shake in their shoes.

42. Without stopping here to congratulate my readers (which, had I room, I would, in the strongest and fullest terms that our language admits of) on the change which thirty years of war and borrowing money have produced relative to the parsons: without stopping to congratulate my readers on the amazing change in the minds of the people, relative to these same Church parsons, I now proceed again to ask, what reason is there that this great mass of property, now used solely by the clergy, should not be applied to some other public purpose ; and, again I come (after my long but most useful digression relating to Mr. Ruggles) ; again I come, to that class of property, which is in the hands of the common parsons, or parish clergy. This class of property consists of several sorts, tithes, great and small, land, glebes, tithes in money, parsonage-houses and gardens, compulsory offerings, compulsory fees. These, like all other religious property, whether secular or regular, were made, granted, or established, in trust. The objects, that they were intended to effect, were, to make a sure provision for the poor, to build, repair, and ornament churches, to keep hospitality for the stranger, and to support unmarried priests, to be the personal friends, comforters, advisers,

admonishers of all their parishioners ; and, particularly, to teach all the CHILDREN of the parish their moral and religious duties : and that, too, not by merely the reading of prayers to them and the reading of what are called sermons to them from the desk, or pulpit; but by personal, individual teaching, the church being, at certain appointed times of very frequent occurrence, a real religious and moral school. Are these objects now effected by the means of these several sorts of parish-church property? Will any man say, that any one of these objects is now effected by the parish clergy? Will any man say, that any one of these objects is now effected, or attempted to be effected, by means for instance, of the 2s. 9d. in the pound, which the citizens of London pay, for tithe, on the rack-rent of their houses? When that tithe was settled, there were no poor-rates, no church rates ; and the poor and church were, of course, to be maintained out of this 2s. 9d. in the pound ; and, as Mr. Ruggles most justly observes, there never has been any law passed to release the city-clergy of this claim on the tithes.

Inefficiency of the Established Church.

43. Besides, as to the public utility of the thing, it is perfectly notorious, that there are now about forty different religions, all professing to be founded on the Bible ; it is equally notorious, that a very small proportion of the people, even in England and Wales, go to the Established Church, and that, in Ireland, there is not above one person out of seven that goes to that Church. In the Hampshire list of persons taking out game

certificates for 1825, there was one parson out of every thirteen persons; so that, if this were the case generally, a thirteenth part of all the sportsmen in England consisted of parsons alone. It is notorious, that there is a very large part of the parishes, even in the finest counties in England, in which the parsonage-houses have been suffered to fall down and totally disappear; and it is equally notorious, that, in more than one half of the parishes, there are no houses that the parsons deem fit for them to live in, while, at the very same time, large, even enormous, sums of money have been voted out of the taxes for the " relief of the poor clergy of the Church of England." It is notorious, that, in numerous parishes, the churches have been suffered to tumble down, and to leave scarcely a trace behind, while the tithes do, nevertheless, continue to be most rigidly exacted by the parsons. It is notorious that many of the parsons have several livings ; and that many receive the tithes for years together, without ever setting their eyes on the parish. It is notorious, that a considerable part of the parish-parsons are, at the same time, colonels, captains, or subalterns, in the army, or navy, and that they continue to receive half-pay as such officers, though the half-pay is held, by the Government, to be a retaining fee for future service, and though the law forbids these men ever to be military or naval officers again. Lastly (for the enumeration would never end), it is notorious that a large part of these parsons are Justices of the Peace, and are, at the same time, rectors or vicars of several parishes each.

44. It being manifest, then, that the revenues received by these persons are not applied as they formerly were, and that they are not applied to any beneficial public purpose, we must determine, that they ought to be otherwise applied; that they ought to be applied to some really useful public purpose. To what public purpose I will speak of by-and by, and also of the manner and degree of the alienation, or subtraction.

Enormous revenues of the Bishops.

45. Next come the ENORMOUS REVENUES OF THE BISHOPS, several of whom have died, of late years, each leaving personal property to an amount exceeding two hundred thousand pounds, after having lived in the style of princes. Will any man say, that this ought to be, and that, at the same time that these men's gains and accumulations are thus going on, the people at large ought to see one million six hundred thousand pounds of the money raised on them, taken from them, in taxes, or out of public loans, voted away for the " relief of the poor clergy of this same church?" Will any man say, that this ought to be? Will any man say it, let him be who or what he may?

Deans and chapters.

46. As to the Deans and Chapters, of what use are they to the nation? As far as I have ever heard, it is not even pretended that they perform any duty, any services at all to the public, to either king or people : and, besides, the persons who receive the revenues of the Cathedral

churches, have generally, if not always, a parish-living besides, at many miles' distance, and, sometimes, two or three such livings! Yet, as this SECOND VOLUME of my work will show, the Chapters have immense estates. And is there a man on earth, except he be one who gains by the thing, who will say, that the nation's estates ought thus to be used? Will even Sir James Graham say, that the fundholder, who has lent his money to those, who, in fact, enjoy the greater part of these and all such like estates; will even Sir James Graham say, that a farthing of interest ought to be deducted from the fund-holder, while there is any part of this public pro-perty unapplied to the liquidation of the debt due to him!

47. The Colleges present us with another im- *The Colleges.*
mense mass of public property, from which the parsons and the aristocracy alone derive, or can, under the present regulations, derive any pos-sible advantage. The estates of these Colleges are very great in worth, and, of course, in yearly amount. This amount is divided amongst par-sons, who are the schoolmasters to the aristo-cracy! As to the nation at large, it can have no share in the benefit produced by these estates, seeing, that the scholars are admitted only on such terms as must effectually shut out all the middle and working classes. And, are we, then, going to back the men, who would strip our neighbours, the fundholders, while these estates remain to be used for the exclusive benefit of the aristocracy and their schoolmasters? These

estates, like all those which are held by the rest
of the clergy, are public property; as such they
may be dealt with by the King and Parliament.
It would be hypocrisy, calling for the punishment
of the cat o'nine tails, to pretend that this great
mass of public property, or, that the whole of
the Church Establishment, all taken together,
is of any use to the public, as it is now em-
All in the hands of the aristocracy. ployed. It is a large part of the property of the
whole country, divided amongst, and enjoyed ex-
clusively by, the aristocracy. That is the real
fact. The Bishopricks, the Parish-livings, the
Deanships, the Stalls, the Fellowships, are, in
fact, all in their gift. The property is, in short,
the public's in right and in name, and the aristocracy's in possession and enjoyment. And, as
to its being necessary for the religious instruction
of the people, that is the very thing that I have
showed to be false, in the very first Paragraph
of the first volume of this work; to which I beg
the reader to turn, if he have it not in his recol-
How it might be applied to public uses. lection. In short, this is a great and enormous
mass of public property, now enjoyed by the
few; and the time is apparently not far distant,
when all men will be convinced of the necessity
of applying it to purposes of a really public nature, or, in one word, to the liquidation of part
of the Debt.

Manner of doing this. 48. With regard to the manner of withdraw-
ing this public property from the control that it
is at present under, the means would be an Act
of Parliament, and, provided the provisions of
the Act were effectual, the manner might be as

mild as the parsons themselves could have demanded, even in " Anti-Jacobin " times, when the workings of our avenging friend, the DEBT, were not perceived. The degree would be a matter of more difficulty; or, I should say, it would require a little more thought. There are two opinions with respect to new regulations; the one is, that there ought to remain no Church-establishment at all, but that each sect, or sort, ought to be left to provide for its own religious instructors. The other is, that there ought to be an establishment upon an almost apostolical allowance. I am for the former; because, as long as there is an establishment, making a part of the state, there must always be a contest going on amongst the divers sects for a preference of some kind or other. Before, however, we can say, what the degree of alienation or subtraction ought to be, we must know which of these two changes would be adopted. But, one thing I am fixed on, and that is, that I, for my own part, would never join in any petition to king or parliament, for any new modelling or any alienation, or subtraction, of these public revenues, if such petition stopped short of taking, and applying to public purposes, nine-tenths of these revenues, taken as a whole.

49. If any one should be disposed to characterize such a deduction as harsh, I here, beforehand, beg leave to observe to him, that I have no desire to see any deduction at all, if the nation can continue to pay the interest of the Debt in full and in gold of standard weight and fineness.

Justice of the measure.

I look upon this immense mass of public property as enjoyed almost exclusively by the aristocracy and its immediate dependants. I do not like this; but, for me, let it still be thus, if the fundholders can continue to be paid as I have just stated. But, is there a man in the world, who will not say, that every shilling's worth of public property ought to be applied to the payment of the Debt, before a thought be entertained of taking from those who have lent their money, any portion of their right to a demand of payment? We have seen, that Mr. Ruggles insists on the right, the legal right, of the nation, to demand, that the Abbey-lands, that is, that all property seized and granted away by the "Reformation" sovereigns and Parliaments, whether it consist of lay impropriations, Abbey-lands, or what not, though now in the hands of lay persons, and deemed private property; we have seen, that he, who was a land-owner, a Justice, and, I believe, a lawyer, insists, that a part of even this property could be legally, and might be justly, applied to the public purpose of relieving the poor. Now, as for me, I never wish to see proposed any measure that shall touch this description of property, which may now fairly be called private property. But, is not a man's stock-certificate; is not that private property also? Has he not, to a certainty, given his money for it? Therefore, though God forbid the necessity should arise, I have no hesitation in saying, that I would rather see even the lay-impropriations and the abbey-lands resumed by Act of Par-

PROTESTANT REFORMATION.

liament, than see an Act of Parliament making
a great deduction from the property of the fund-
holder; and most assuredly, I would much rather
see a resumption of grants by the Crown of the
lands and houses and mines and other property,
which the Crown has granted away since the
reign of Henry VIII., out of the ancient crown
estate; and, as we always ought to bear in mind,
which granting away has been the cause of that
continual and copious drain, the Civil List. But
of all the horrible things in this world, would not
the most horrible be, to borrow 1,600,000l. to
make a present of to the parsons of the Church;
and, to reduce the interest of the Debt; that is
to say, to take away a part of the property of the
fundholder, who lent the money thus made a
present of; to take, I say, part of his property
away while the clergy were suffered to keep the
1,600,000l.! Observe, that, during the years,
during all the years, that the Parliament was
making the Church clergy a present of 100,000l.
a year, the making of loans was going on: so
that, this 100,000l. a year came out of the loans:
it was borrowed money; the lender is to be paid
his interest: and, will any man say, that it is not
most horrible to think of deducting from this
interest; to think of doing this on account of the
poverty of the state, while the state suffers the
clergy to keep this money?

50. The thing called QUEEN ANNE'S BOUNTY, *Queen Anne's Bounty.*
an annual sum, taken from the people, to be
given to the Church parsons, in addition to all
their monstrous revenues. What pretty names

they give to these things! The Crown had, for part of its income, the tenths and first fruits of the clergy. QUEEN ANNE was the sovereign when this branch of income was granted away from the Crown, in order to augment the value of small livings; but, one good turn deserves another; such "generosity" in the Queen merited a return; but, alas! the people had to make the return; and, accordingly, they have had to pay more to the Civil List ever since, on account of this "Bounty" than the "Bounty" itself amounts to. However, here is another great annual sum (in addition to the tithes and all the other things that we have before seen) going from the pockets of the people into those of the clergy.

Civil List.   51. Here, again, we have another effect of the Protestant "Reformation." Before that even there was no Civil List. Poor-rates, Civil List Queen Anne's Bounty, Septennial Bill, NATIONAL DEBT; all, yea all, are the fruit of the event, called "the Reformation"; and, though the rest might, or may be overcome, THE DEBT CANNOT, without making a change in that Protestant Church, to establish which on the ruins of the Catholic Church, the debt was made! All history, though full of instances of retribution does not, I verily believe, throughout its thousands of volumes, furnish us with one so complete so striking, and reading to mankind so tremendous a lesson as this. Here, at this moment, in England, famed, during fifty ages, for her liberties and her laws; but, still more famed for the happiness of her people, and the plenty in which they lived : here she is, and here she has been for years, avowedly in deep distress, engaged in contrivances for getting rid of her people, who are petitioning to be transported from their native land, in the hope of mending their miserable lot! Here she is, covered with the disgrace of ten times the gaol-room that was formerly necessary, and with that of a regulation, which allots to the convicted felon in her gaols more and better food and raiment than to the honest labouring man in her woods and fields ! And, what is the cause of this? The Debt is the sole cause ; for that renders monstrous taxes necessary; they render a great standing army necessary; so that it is the Debt, and that alone, which has made England the most degraded and miserable of countries, Ireland always excepted. And what caused the Debt? An Act of Parliament for the making of loans and paper-money. And for what were loans and paper-money made ? Why, the very act itself declares, that they were made for the purposes of waging war, in order " to keep out Popery, and to preserve the Protestant Church as by law established;" so that the Debt is an invention and institution as purely Protestant as half-pay parsons are, or as is the tread-mill itself. And, at last, that Debt, that Protestant Debt, which was created for the declared, nay, the boasted, purpose of preserving this Church, now threatens this very Church with destruction ; now fixes its eyes on the property of that Church as the first

thing to fly to in case of necessity; and that such
necessity will and must arise, and is even now a
hand, where is the man of sense who does no
believe? And, where is the just man who wil
not say, that those who have lent their money
for the waging of wars to "keep out Popery,"
ought not to be bilked of one farthing of their
demand, while there is left to the Protestan
clergy a single ear of wheat, or a single blade o
grass?

Conclusion.   52. Here I conclude. I have (in the first V
lume), given a history of the manner in whic
Church property had been dealt with heretofore
In this second Volume I give an account of th
property, show the worth of it, and who has i
In this INTRODUCTION, I have endeavoured to shov
that it is just and reasonable, that the immens
mass which still continues to be public property
ought to be dealt with again, and legally applie
to purposes really public; and, as a reward fo
all the labour I have bestowed, I am quite sati
fied with the firm belief, that the day is not fi
off, when the knowledge that I have commu
cated, and when the principles that I hav
taught, relative to this great subject, will I
adopted by persons in authority, and acted up
to their full extent. . . . .
Here I had signed my name, and was about
put the date. It was on its way from my mi
to my hand, when I stopped my hand all
once and exclaimed: "Good God! the ninth
" July! the anniversary of my sentence of t
" years' imprisonment in a felon's gaol, with

" fine of a thousand pounds to the King, and, at
" the end of the two years, with seven years'
" bail, myself in three thousand pounds and two
" sureties in a thousand pounds each; and all
" this monstrous punishment for having expressed
" my indignation at Englishmen having been
" flogged, in the heart of England, under a
" guard of German troops! Good God!" exclaimed I again; " What! am I, on the anni-
" versary of that day, which called forth the
" exultation of the Hampshire parsons, who
" (though I had never committed any offence, in
" private life, against any one of them) crowed
" out aloud, in the fulness of their joy, ' Ha!
" he's gone for ever! He will never trouble us
" any more!' and who, in a spirit truly charac-
" teristic of their corps, actually had, as a stand-
" ing toast, ' Disgrace to the MEMORY of Cob-
" bett.'—What!" exclaimed I again, " and am
" I, on the anniversary of that very day, putting
" the finishing hand; yea, sending from under
" my fingers to the press, the last, the very last
" words, the completing words, the closing
" point, of a work, which does the JOB for them
" and for all their tribe; of the former part of
" which work, I, myself, have sold forty thousand
" copies, containing six hundred and forty thou-
" sand Numbers; and which work is now sold in
" English, in two Stereotyped Editions in the
" United States of America; which work has
" been published at Madrid and at New York
" in *Spanish,* at Paris, Geneva and Alost in
" *French,* at Cologne in *German,* and at Rome

PROTESTANT REFORMATION.

" in *Italian;* and all this took place just about
" sixteen years after these Hampshire parsons
" had taken for a standing toast: ' Disgrace to
" the MEMORY of Cobbett!'" And, then, feeling health and vigour in every vein and in every
nerve; seeing, lying before me, manuscript
(equal to twenty pages of print) written by me
this very day; knowing the effects, which, in the
end, that manuscript must have on these parsons, and the great good that it must do to the
nation; reflecting, feeling, seeing, knowing,
thus, it is, that I, in justice to our pious, sincere,
brave, and wise forefathers, and in compassion
to my suffering countrymen, and to the children
of us all, send this little volume forth to the
world.

WM. COBBETT.

Kensington, 9th July, 1827.

LIST

OF

ABBEYS, PRIORIES, &c.

BEDFORD (County).

At BEDFORD. An Hospital of St. Leonard's Hospitalers, founded in the reign of Edward IV., by a townsman, the yearly revenue of which was 16l. 6s. 8d. in 26 Henry VIII.; now worth 326l. 13s. 4d.

A Franciscan Friary, founded by Mabilea de Plateshull, in the reign Edward II., valued yearly at 5l., now worth 100l.; granted, 31 Hen. VIII., to John Gostwyke.

At BIGGLESWADE. A Chantry; revenue 7l., now worth 140l.

At BISSEMEDE. A Priory of Augustine Canons, founded by Hugh Beauchamp, in the reign of Henry II.; annual revenue, 81l. 13s. 5½d., now worth 1,623l. 9s.2d.; granted, 29 Hen.VIII., to Sir William Gascoigne.

At CALDWELL. An Augustine Priory, founded in the reign of John, by Robert of Houghton. Revenue 148l. 15s. 10d., now worth 2,975l. 16s. 8d.; granted, 5 Elizabeth, to Thomas Leigh.

BEDFORDSHIRE.

At CHICKSAND. A Priory of Nuns of St. Gilbert, founded, in the year 1150, by Pain de Beauchamp and his wife. Yearly value, 230*l.* 3*s.* 4½*d.*, now worth 4,603*l.* 7*s.* 6*d.* Granted, 31 Hen. VIII., to R. Snow.

At DUNSTABLE. A Priory of Augustine Canons, founded by Henry I. Yearly value 402*l.* 14*s.* 7½*d.*; now worth 8,054*l.* 12*s.* 6*d.* Granted to Sir Leonard Chamberlayne.

At EATON. A College, or Guild. Yearly value 7*l.* 16*s.* now worth 156*l.*

At ELSTOW. An Abbey of Benedictine Nuns, founded by Judith, niece to the Conqueror, and wife to Waltheof, Earl of Huntington. Yearly value 325*l.* 2*s.* 1½*d.*, now worth 6,502*l.* 2*s.* 6*d.* Granted, 7 Edward VI., to Sir Humphrey Radcliff.

At FARLE. An Hospital, founded by Hen: II. Granted, 26 Hen. VIII., to the Provost and Fellows of Cambridge College.

At GROVESBURY. Priory of Aliens, whose possessions still remain. Revenue uncertain.

At HARWOOD. A Priory of Augustine Nuns, founded, in the reign of Stephen, by Sampson le Forte. Yearly value 47*l.* 3*s.* 2*d.*, now worth 943*l.* 3*s.* 4*d.* Granted to William Lord Parr, 35 Henry VIII.

BEDFORDSHIRE.

At MELCHBURN, or MECHELBURN. A Preceptory of Knights Hospitalers, with a Manor and a Church, settled by Lady Alice, or Adelize, de Claremonte, Countess of Pembroke, in the reign of Henry I. The Lands belonging to this Preceptory were valued at 241*l.* 9*s.* 10*d.*, now worth 4,829*l.* 16*s.* 8*d.*; granted, 3 Edward VI., to John Earl of Bedford.

At MERGATE, or MARKET-STREET. A Nunnery of Benedictine Nuns, founded in a wood, near this place, in the parish of Caddington, by Ralph, the Dean and Chapter of St. Paul's, London, in the year 1145. Valued, 26 Henry VIII., at 143*l.* 18*s.* 3*d*; now worth 2,878*l.* 5*s.* Granted, 2 Edward VI., to George Ferrers.

At NEWENHAM, near BEDFORD. A Monastery of Augustine Canons, founded in the reign of Henry II., by Simon Beauchamp. Yearly revenue 343*l.* 15*s.* 5*d.*, now worth 6,875*l.* 8*s.* 4*d.*; granted, 32 Henry VIII., to Urian Brereton.

At NORTHWELL, NORTHILL, or NORRELL. A Collegiate Church, founded, 6 Henry IV., by Sir Gerard Braybroke, Knt., Thos. Pevre, John Harvey, John Ward, Edm. Hampden, and John Hertshorne, for the souls of Sir John Traylly and son. Yearly value at the dissolution, 61*l.* 5*s.* 5*d.*, now worth 1,225*l.* 8*s.* 4*d.*; granted, 2 Edward VI., to William Fitzwilliam.

At WARDEN. An Abbey of Cistercian Monks, founded, in the year 1135, by Walter Espec.

Yearly value 442*l.* 11*s.* 11*d.*, now worth 8,851*l.* 18*s.* 4*d.*; surrendered, by the Abbot and fourteen Monks, December 4, 1538.

At WOBURN. A Cistercian Abbey, founded near this place, in the year 1145, by Hugh de Bolebec. Valued at 430*l.* 13*s.* 11½*d.*, now worth 8,613*l.* 19*s.* 2*d.*; granted, 1 Edward VI., to John Lord Russell.

BERKS (COUNTY).

At ABINGDON. Here was an Abbey of Benedictine Monks, 500 in number, in the time of the Ancient Britons, where Constantine the Great is said to have been educated; it was destroyed by the Danes, A.D. 955; but afterwards rebuilt by the Abbot Ethelwold, through the bounty of King Edred and King Edgar. Valued, at the dissolution, at 2,042*l.* 2*s.* 8½*d.* yearly, now worth 40,842*l.* 14*s.* 2*d.*; granted, 1 Edw. VI. to Sir Thomas Seymour; and 5 Edward VI., to Sir Thomas Wroth.

At BUSTLESHAM. A Priory of Augustine Canons, founded by Hugh de Spencer, Jun., originally for the Knights of St. John of Jerusalem. Valued, at the dissolution, at 661*l.* 14*s.* 9*d.* yearly, now worth 13,234*l.* 15*s.*; granted, 7 Edward VI., to Sir Edward Hoby.

At CHOLSEY, near WALLINGFORD. Monastery destroyed; founded by King Ethelred, in the year 986. The revenue, at the general dissolution, granted to Sir Francis Englefield.

At DONINGTON, near NEWBURY. A Friary, of the Order of the Blessed Trinity, founded 16 Richard II. Valued at 20*l.* 16*s.* 6*d.*, now worth 416*l.* 10*s.*

At FARENDON. A Cistercian Cell was settled here, by some Monks, in the year 1203. The possessions were granted to Sir Francis Englefield.

At HURLEY. A Priory, or Cell of Benedictine Monks, founded in the reign of William the Conqueror, by Godfrey de Magna Villa. Valued, 26 Henry VIII., at 134*l.* 10*s.* 8*d.*, now worth 2,690*l.* 13*s.* 4*d.*; granted to Leonard Chamberlayne, 36 Henry VIII.

At POUGHELY, in the Parish of Chaddleworth, A Priory of Augustine Canons, founded in the year 1160, by Ralph de Chaddleworth. Valued at 71*l.* 10*s.* 7*d.*, now worth 1,430*l.* 11*s.* 8*d.*

At READING. In the year 1121, Henry I. founded here an Abbey for 200 Benedictine Monks; income, at the dissolution, 2,116*l.* 3*s.* 9½*d.*, now worth 42,323*l.* 15*s.* 10*d.*; granted, 4 Edward VI., to Edward Duke of Somerset.

A Friary, in the north side of Castle-street, founded in the year 1400. Granted to the Mayor and Burgesses, as a site for a bridewell!

BERKS.

At SANDLEFORD. A Priory of Augustine Canons, founded in the year 1205, by Jeffrey, Earl of Perch and Maud his wife : value 10*l.* yearly, now worth 200*l.*

At SHOTTESBROOKE. A Chantry or College ; founded in the year 1337, by Sir William Trussel, Knt. ; valued 33*l.* 18*s.* 8*d.*, now worth 678*l.* 13*s.* 4*d.* ; granted, 2 Edward VI., to Thomas and Edward Weldon.

At STEVENTON, or STENNINGTON, near Abingdon. An Alien Priory of Monks, founded by the Abbey of Bec, in Normandy, prior to the reign of Henry I.

At STRATFIELD-SAY. A Priory of Alien Benedictine Monks, founded in the year 1170, by Nicholas de Stotevile.

At WALLINGFORD, or WARING. A Benedictine Cell, founded in the reign of William the Conqueror, by Gilfrid, Abbot of St. Alban ; granted, 38 Henry VIII., to John Norres.

A College, endowed before or during the reign of King John, by Edmond, Earl of Cornwall ; yearly revenue 147*l.* 8*s.* 0½*d.*, now worth 2,848*l.* 0*s.* 10*d.* ; granted, 2 Edward VI., to Michael Stanhope and John Bellew.

BUCKINGHAM (County).

At ANKERWYKE. A Benedictine Nunnery, founded in the reign of Henry, by Sir Gilbert de Montficet, Knt. and his son; yearly value 45*l.* 14*s.* 4*d.*, now worth 914*l.* 7*s.* 8*d.* Granted to Lord Windsor, 31 Hen. VIII. and to Sir Thomas Smith, 4 Edward VI.

At BITTLESDEN. A Cistercian Abbey, founded here through the bounty of Ernald de Bosco, in the year 1147; yearly value 142*l.* 1*s.* 3*d.*, now worth 2,842*l.* 5*s.*; granted, 32 Hen. VIII., to Thomas Wriothesley.

At BRADEWELL. A Benedictine Priory, founded in the reign of Stephen, by the Baron of Wolverton; valued at 53*l.* 11*s.* 2*d.* yearly, now worth 1,071*l.* 3*s.* 4*d.*; granted 34 Henry VIII. to Arthur Longfield.

At BURNHAM. An Augustine Nunnery, founded in the year 1265, by Richard, King of the Romans; yearly value 91*l.* 5*s.* 11½*d.*, now worth 1825*l.* 19*s.* 2*d.*, granted, 36 Hen. VIII. to William Tyldesly.

At ESSERUG, OR ASKERIDGE, in the Parish of Pitston. A College of Bonhommes, founded by Edmond, Earl of Cornwall, in the year 1283; valued yearly at 447*l.* 18*s.* 0½*d.*, now worth 8,958*l.* 10*d.*; granted, 17 Elizabeth, to John

Dudley and John Ayscaugh; it is now the seat of the Duke of Bridgewater.

At GARE, or GORE, in the Parish of Hanslap. A Nunnery, destroyed.

At HOGSHAW. An Hospital of the Knights of St. John of Jerusalem, founded about 1180; granted, 35 Henry VIII., to Matilda Lane.

At LAVINDEN. An Abbey of Premonstratensians, founded and endowed in the reign of Henry II., by John de Bidun. Yearly revenue 91l. 8s. 3$\frac{1}{2}d$., now worth 1,828l. 5s. 10d.; granted, 35 Henry VIII., to Sir Edmond Peckham.

At LUDGARSHALL, or LITTERSHALL. An Alien Hospital, founded through the bounty of Henry II.

At MEDMENHAM, or MENDHAM. A Cistercian Abbey, founded in the year 1204, by Hugh de Bolebec. Revenue, at the dissolution, 23l. 17s. 2d.; now worth 477l. 3s. 4d.; granted, 38 Hen. VIII., to Robert Mone, and others.

At LITTLE MERLOW, or MINCHIN MARLO. A Benedictine Nunnery, founded by Jeffrey, Lord Spensar, about the year 1244. Yearly revenue, 37l. 6s. 11d., now worth 746l. 18s. 4d.; granted, 32 Henry VIII., to John Titley and E. Restwold.

BUCKINGHAM.

At MEURSLEY, or ST. MARGARET'S. A Benedictine Nunnery, founded by Henry de Blois, Bishop of Winchester, in the year 1160. Here nine Nuns were turned out, and their yearly property, 22*l.* 6*s.* 7*d.*, now worth 446*l.* 11*s.* 8*d.*, granted, 29 Hen. VIII., to Sir John Dance.

At MISSENDEN. An Abbey of Augustine Canons, founded by Sir William de Missenden, in the year 1133; yearly value, at the dissolution, 285*l.* 15*s.* 9*d.*, now worth 5,715*l.* 15*s.* : granted, 7 Edward VI., to the Duke of Northumberland; and, 16 Elizabeth, to Robert Earl of Leicester.

At NEWINTON-LONGAVILLE. A Priory of Foreign Monks, founded in the reign of Hen. I. granted to the College of Oxford.

At NOCTELE, or NUTTLEY. An Abbey of Augustine Canons, founded in the year 1162, by Walter Giffard, Earl of Buckingham, and Ermangard his Lady; yearly revenue 495*l.* 18*s.* 5½*d.* ; now worth 9,918*l.* 9*s.* 2*d.* ; granted, 1 Edward VI., to Sir William Paget.

At RAVINSTON. An Augustine Monastery, founded in the reign of Henry III., by the bounty of Peter de Chaseport, Pastor of Ivingho; value yearly 66*l.* 13*s.* 4*d.*, now worth 1,333*l.* 6*s.* 8*d.*; granted, 2 Edward VI., to Sir Francis Bryan.

At SNELLSHALL. A Benedictine Priory,

founded, 10 Henry III., by Ralph Mortel; yearly revenue 24*l.*, now worth 480*l.*; granted, 30 Henry VIII., to Francis Piggot.

At STONY STRATFORD. An Hospital, founded prior to 1240.

At TYKEFORD, or TICKFORD, near Newport St. Mary. A Priory of Aliens, founded before 1475; yearly value 126*l.* 17*s.*, now worth 2,537*l.*; sold by James I. to Henry Atkins, M.D.

At WENGE. A Priory of Aliens, bestowed, by Maud the Empress, to the Monastery of St. Nicholas; but granted, by Henry VIII., to Sir Robert Dormer.

CAMBRIDGE (COUNTY).

At ANGLESEY. A Priory of Augustine Canons, founded by Henry I.; yearly value 149*l.* 18*s.* 6*d.*, now worth 2,998*l.* 10*s.*; granted to John Hynde, 30 Henry VIII.

At BAREHAM, or BERCHAM, in the Parish of Lynton. A Priory, founded before the reign of Edward I.; granted, 31 Henry VIII., to Philip Paris, and afterwards to John Millecent, Esq.

At BARNWELL. A Priory, founded in the

year 1092, by Picot, a Norman Lord, and his Lady; yearly value 351*l.* 15*s.* 4*d.*, now worth 7,035*l.* 6*s.* 8*d.*; granted, 38 Henry VIII., to Antony Brown; and, 6 Edward VI., to Edward Lord Clinton.

At Cambridge. A Benedictine Cell, founded by John de Cranden, Prior of Ely, in the reign of Richard III.; granted to William Bateman, Bishop of Norwich.

A Gilbertine Priory, founded prior to the year 1291, by the bounty, or gift, of B. fil. Walteri; yearly revenue, 16*l.* 16*s.*, now worth 336*l.*; granted, 35 Henry VIII., to Edward Ebrington and Humphrey Metcalf.

Catherine Hall, founded aud endowed about the year 1474, by Robert Wood-lark, D.D.; yearly revenue at the suppression 39*l.* 2*s.* 7*d.*, now worth 782*l.* 11*s.* 8*d.*

Christ's College, for twenty-four Scholars in Grammar, founded by William Bingham, in the year 1442, Pastor of St. Zachary, London; being afterwards augmented by the bounty of others. Yearly revenues at the dissolution, 26 Henry VIII., made 190*l.* 10*s.* 10½*d.*, now worth 3,810*l.* 17*s.* 6*d.*

King's College, built and endowed in the year 1443, by Henry VI.; revenues valued at 751*l.* 8*s.* 1*d.*, now worth 15,028*l.* 1*s.* 8*d.*

Queen's College, founded by Margaret of Anjou, Queen of Henry VI., about the

VOL. II.   F

year 1448; yearly income 230*l.* 15*s.* 2½*d.*, now worth 4,615*l.* 4*s.* 2*d.*

An Augustine Friary, founded by Sir Jeffrey Picheford, Knight, before the year 1290; granted, 36 Henry VIII., to William Keynsham.

A Dominican Priory, founded by some pious persons before the year 1275; granted to Edward Elrington and Humphrey Metcalf, 35 Henry VIII.

A Friary of Mendicant Franciscans, founded by the bounty of Edward I. Sold, 38 Henry VIII., to the Executors of Lady Frances Sidney.

A Friary of Carmelites, founded by Edward I. and by some noblemen; granted, 36 Henry VIII., to John Eyer.

At CHATERIS. A Benedictine Nunnery, founded by Alfwen, Wife of Ethelstan, Earl of the East Angles, with the advice and assistance of her brother Ednod, Bishop of Ramsey, in the year 980; yearly revenue 112*l.* 3*s.* 6*d.*, now worth 2,243*l.* 10*s.*; granted, 5 Edward VI., to Edward Lord Clinton.

At CHIPPENHAM. An Asylum of Knights Hospitalers, founded, in the year 1184, most bountifully, by William de Mandevill; valued at 33*l.* 6*s.* 8*d.* yearly, now worth 666*l.* 13*s.* 4*d.*; granted, 32 Henry VIII., to Sir Edward North.

At Denny. An Abbey of Minor Nuns, founded, 15 Edward III., by Mary de St. Paulo, Widow of Adomarc Earl of Pembroke; revenues yearly 218*l.* 0*s.* 1½*d.*, now worth 4,360*l.* 2*s.* 6*d.*; granted, 31 Henry VIII., to Edward Elrington.

At Ely. A great Benedictine Priory and Cathedral, that had been often destroyed and rebuilt again during the various invasions of the Danes, and other convulsions of the country, were finally rebuilt and richly endowed, in the year 970, by Ethelwold, Bishop of Winchester, through the bounty of King Edgar and others. Revenues of the Cathedral at the dissolution 2,134*l.* 18*s.* 6½*d.*, and of the Monastery 1,084*l.* 6*s.* 9½*d.* yearly; now worth 42,698*l.* 10*s.* 10*d.*, and 21,686*l.* 15*s.* 10*d.*; granted in the year 1541.

An Hospital of Hospitalers, founded here early by a Bishop; yearly revenue 25*l.* 5*s.* 3½*d.*, now worth 505*l.* 5*s.* 10*d.*; granted, 4 Elizabeth, to the Master and Fellows of Clare Hall, in Cambridge.

At Fordham. A Convent of Gilbertine Canons, founded near this town by the Dean of Fordham, in the reign of Henry III.; yearly value 46*l.* 3*s.* 8*d.*, now worth 928*l.* 13*s.* 4*d.*; granted, 32 Henry VIII., to Philip Parry.

At Ikelington. A Benedictine Nunnery, founded in the reign of Henry II., by Aubery

de Vere, Earl of Oxford; yearly value 80*l.* 1*s.*
10½*d.*, now worth 1,601*l.* 17*s.* 6*d.*; granted,
30 Henry VIII., to the Bishop of Ely.

At ISELHAM. An Alien Priory, founded here
at an early period; valued yearly 10*l.* 13*s.* 4*d.*,
now worth 213*l.* 6*s.* 8*d.*

At LYNTON. An Alien Priory.

At MIRMAUD, MARMONDE, or WELLE. A
Gilbertine Priory, founded in the reign of
Richard I., by Ralph de Hauvill; valued, 26
Henry VIII., at 13*l.* 6*s.* 1½*d.* yearly, now worth
266*l.* 2*s.* 6*d.*; granted, 10 Elizabeth, to Per-
cival Bowes and John Mosyer.

At SHENGAY, near Wendy. A Preceptory of
Knights Hospitalers, endowed, in the year
1140, by Sibylla de Raynes, Daughter of the
Earl of Montgomery; valued at 175*l.* 4*s.* 6*d.*
yearly, now worth 3,504*l.* 10*s.*; granted, 32
Henry VIII., to Richard Longe.

At SPINNEY, in the Parish of Wykes, or
Wicken. An Augustine Priory, founded by Sir
Hugh de Malebisse and Beatrix his Wife, in the
reign of Henry III.; granted, 36 Henry VIII.,
to Sir Edward North.

At STERESBERGH, or STURBRIDGE, near
Cambridge. An Hospital of Lepers, founded
prior to the year 1245, under the patronage of

the Bishop of Ely; but granted, 36 Henry VIII., to the Mayor and Bailiffs of Cambridge; and, 4 James I., to John Shelbury, and Philip Chewte, Gentleman.

At SWAFAM. A Benedictine Nunnery, founded by one of the Bolebec family, before the reign of King John; yearly value 46*l*. 10*s*. 8*d*., now worth 930*l*. 13*s*. 4*d*.; granted, 30 Henry VIII., to the Protestant Bishop of Ely.

At THORNEY. A Benedictine Abbey, founded by the first Abbot of Peterburgh, as early as the time of St. Etheldreda; yearly value 508*l*. 12*s*. 5*d*., now worth 10,172*l*. 8*s*. 4*d*.; granted, 3 Edward VI., to John Earl of Bedford.

CHESTER (COUNTY).

At BARAW. An Hospital of the Knights of St. John of Jerusalem, founded in the reign of Edward I., by Robert de Bachepuz; yearly value at the dissolution 107*l*. 3*s*. 8*d*., now worth 2,140*l*. 13*s*. 4*d*.

At BERKINHEAD. A Benedictine Priory, founded in the reign of Henry II., by Hamon Massy, Baron of Dunham Massy; valued at 102*l*. 16*s*. 10*d*. yearly, now worth 2,056*l*. 16*s*. 8*d*.; granted, 36 Henry VIII., to Ralph Worseley.

At DUNBURY. A College, founded in the year 1386, by Sir Hugh Calvely, Knight; value 42*l.* 2*s.* 8*d.*, now worth 842*l.* 13*s.* 4*d.* yearly; sold by Queen Elizabeth to Thomas Aldersey, London, Merchant Taylor.

At CHESTER. A Benedictine Abbey, or Nunnery, founded in the time of the Saxons, but afterwards enlarged by Elfleda, Countess of Mercia, and by other benefactors; yearly revenue 1,073*l.* 17*s.* 7½*d.*, now worth 21,477*l.* 12*s.* 6*d.*; granted 26 Henry VIII.

A Benedictine Nunnery, founded in the reign of William the Conqueror, by Randal, Earl of Chester; valued at 99*l.* 16*s.* 2*d.*, now worth 1,996*l.* 3*s.* 4*d.*; granted, 33 Henry VIII., to Urian Brereton and Son.

St. John's College, founded by King Ethelred, in the year 689; yearly income at the dissolution 88*l.* 16*s.* 8*d.*, now worth 1,776*l.* 13*s.* 4*d.*; granted, 4 Elizabeth, to John Fortescue.

St. John's Hospital, outside the north gate, possessing anciently great privileges, and containing at the dissolution, 26 Henry VIII., a Chaplain and six poor Brethren; yearly income 28*l.* 10*s.* 4*d.*, now worth 570*l.* 6*s.* 8*d.*

A Friary, founded southward of the city, by a Bishop of Chester; granted, 36 Henry VIII., to John Coke.

A Franciscan Friary, founded in the reign of Henry III.; granted to John Coke.

A Carmelite Friary, founded in the year 1279, by Thomas Stadham, Gentleman; granted by Henry VIII. to John Coke.

At COMBERMERE. A Cistercian Abbey, founded in the year 1133, by Hugh de Malbane, Lord of Nantwich; yearly value 255l., now worth 5,100l.; granted, 32 Henry VIII., to William Cotton, Esq., and now it belongs to Sir Robert Salusbury Cotton.

At NANTWICH. An Hospital anciently founded here held the tythes, which were granted, 6 Elizabeth, to William Grys.

At NORTON. A Priory of Augustine Canons, founded by a Mr. Williams of Chester; yearly value at the dissolution 258l. 11s. 8d., now worth 5,171l. 13s. 4d.; granted, 37 Henry VIII., to Richard Brook.

At PULTON. A Cistercian Abbey, founded by Robert, butler to the Earl of Chester, in the year 1153; granted, 36 Henry VIII., to William Cotton, Esq.

At STANLAW. A Cistercian Abbey, founded by John Constable and Baron Holton of Chester, in the year 1172; granted, 7 Edward VI., to Sir Robert Cotton, Knight.

At VALEROYAL. King Edward, in the year

1277, expended on building a Monastery here 32,000*l.*; yearly value at the dissolution 540*l.* 6*s.* 2*d.*, now worth 10,806*l.* 3*s.* 4*d.*; granted, 35 Henry VIII., to Thomas Holcroft.

CORNWALL (County).

At St. Antony. A Benedictine Cell, founded here as early as Richard's time; granted, 6 Elizabeth, to William and John Killigrew.

At Bodmin. A Priory of Augustine Canons, founded, in honour of the bones of St. Petroc, that are deposited there, in the year 905; yearly income at the dissolution 289*l.* 11*s.* 11*d.*, now worth 5,791*l.* 18*s.* 4*d.*; granted, 36 Henry VIII., to Thomas Sternhold.

At St. Burien. A College, founded by King Athelstan near the Land's End, in honour of St. Buriena, a holy woman from Ireland, who had an oratory and was buried here. Yearly income 55*l.* 7*s.* 1*d.*, now worth 1,107*l.* 1*s.* 8*d.*; granted to the Duke of Cornwall.

At German's. A Collegiate Church, founded in honour of St. German, one of the famous French Bishops who came into Britain to oppose the Pelagian heresy, in the year 936; yearly revenue 243*l.* 8*s.*, now worth 4,868*l.*; granted, 33 Henry VIII., to Catharine Champernoun, John Ridgway, &c.

At HELSTON. A Hospital, founded by a Mr. Kyllegrew, at an early period; yearly value 14*l*. 7*s*. 4*d*., now worth 287*l*. 6*s*. 8*d*.

At ST. KARENTOC. A College, founded in the reign of Edward the Confessor, in honour of St. Carantocus, disciple of St. Patrick; yearly value 89*l*. 15*s*. 8*d*., now worth 1,795*l*. 13*s*. 4*d*.; now in the patronage of John Buller, Esq.

At LANACHEBRAN. A Cistercian Cell, founded about the Conquest, under the tutelage of St. Achebran; granted, 2 Elizabeth, to Francis Earl of Bedford.

At LAUNCESTON. A College of Augustine Canons, founded before the Conquest, about half a mile from this town; yearly revenue 392*l*. 11*s*. 2*d*., now worth 7,851*l*. 3*s*. 4*d*.; granted 26 Henry VIII.

At ST. MICHAEL'S MOUNT. A Priory of Alien Monks, founded in the year 1085, by Edward the Confessor; yearly value 110*l*. 12*s*. 0½*d*., now worth 2,212*l*. 10*d*.

At PENRYN, or GLASENEY, in the Parish of Gluvias. A College, built by the good Bishop of Exeter, Walter Bronescomb, in the year 1270; valued at 205*l*. 10*s*. 6*d*., now worth 4,110*l*. 10*s*.

At ST. PROBUS. A College, founded before

the Conquest; yearly income 22*l.* 10*s.*, now worth 450*l.*; granted 26 Henry VIII.

At St. Syriac. A Cluniac Cell, founded as early as the time of Richard I.; granted, 37 Henry VIII., to Laurence Courtney.

At Treleigh, or Turleigh. A Preceptory of Knights Hospitalers, founded by the bounty of Henry de Pomerai and Reginald Marsh; yearly value 81*l.* 8*s.* 5*d.*, now worth 1,628*l.* 8*s.* 4*d.* This, among other undisposed possessions, belonged to the Hospitalers, 5 Philip and Mary; but was granted at their dissolution, 16 Elizabeth, to Henry Wilby and George Blythe.

At Truro. A Dominican Convent, founded by the Reskiner family, in the reign of Hen. III.; granted, 7 Edward VI., to Edward Anglianby.

At Truwardraith, in the Deanery of Pawder. An Alien Priory of Benedictine Monks, founded in the year 1169, by some Noblemen; yearly value 151*l.* 16*s.* 1*d.*, now worth 3,036*l.* 1*s.* 8*d.*; granted, 34 Henry VIII., to Edward Earl of Hertford.

CUMBERLAND (County.)

At Armethwait. A Benedictine Nunnery, endowed by William Rufus; yearly value

18*l.* 8*s.* 8*d.*, now worth 368*l.* 13*s.* 4*d.*; granted, 6 Edward VI., to William Gryme, or Carleil.

At ST. BEE'S. A Benedictine Cell, or Monastery, founded in the year 650, by Bega, a holy Woman from Ireland. There were a Prioress and six Nuns at the dissolution. Yearly income 149*l.* 19*s.* 6*d.*, now worth 2,999*l.* 10*s.*; granted, 7 Edward VI., to Sir Thomas Challoner.

At CALDRE, in Copeland, near Egremond. A Cistercian Abbey of Monks, founded in the year 1134, by Ranulph, Earl of Chester; income at the dissolution 64*l.* 3*s.* 9*d.*, now worth 1,283*l.* 15*s.*; granted, 30 Henry VIII., to Thos. Leigh.

At CARLISLE. An Augustine Priory of Monks, and a Nunnery, founded in the year 686; were destroyed in the Danish wars, but rebuilt by William Rufus, and Walter, a Norman Priest. Income 531*l.* 4*s.* 11*d.*, now worth 10,624*l.* 18*s.* 4*d.*

St. Nicholas' Hospital, founded by the Ancestors of Richard I. for thirteen Lepers; granted, 33 Henry VIII.

At GRAYSTOKE. A Collegiate Church, founded before the year 1359, by William Lord Graystock; yearly income 82*l.* 14*s.*, now worth 1,654*l.*; granted, 6 Elizabeth, to William Grice, and Antony Foster.

At HOLM CULTRAM. A Cistercian Abbey,

founded by Henry, Son to David King of Scotland, in the year 1150 ; income 535*l.* 3*s.* 7*d.*, now worth 10,703*l.* 12*s.* 6*d.*

At KIRK OSWALD. A College of twelve secular Priests, founded, 20 Henry VIII., by Robert Threlkeld; valued at 78*l.* 17*s.*, now worth 1,577*l.*; granted, 30 Elizabeth, to Edward Downinge, and Miles Doddinge, Esqrs.

At LANERCOST. An Augustine Monastery, founded in the year 1169, by Robert de Villibus, Lord of Gilleisland; yearly value 79*l.* 19*s.*, now worth 1,599*l.*; granted to Thomas Lord Dacre.

At SETON, alias LEKELY. A Benedictine Nunnery, founded by Henry Kirby; yearly income 13*l.* 17*s.* 4*d.*, now worth 277*l.* 6*s.* 8*d.*; granted, 33 Henry VIII., to Hugh Askue.

At WETHERALL. A Benedictine Cell, founded in the reign of William Rufus, by Ranulph Meschin, Earl of Cumberland; income 128*l.* 5*s.* 3½*d.*, now worth 2,565*l.* 5*s.* 10*d.*; granted, 33 Henry VIII.

DERBY (COUNTY).

At DE BELLO CAPITE, near Norton. An Abbey of White Canons, founded in the year 1183, by Robert Lord Alfreton, one of the executioners of the Archbishop of Canterbury, Thomas à Becket; income 157*l.* 10*s.* 2*d.*, now worth 3,150*l.* 3*s.* 4*d.* ; granted, 28 Henry VIII., to Sir Nicholas Strelly.

At BRISOLL. An Augustine Friary, founded in the reign of Henry III.; income 10*l.* 17*s.* 9*d.*, now worth 217*l.* 15s.; granted, 6 Edward VI., to Henry Duke of Suffolk.

At CALKE. An Augustine Cell, founded in the year 1161, by Maud, widow of the Earl of Chester; granted, 1 Edward VI., to John Earl of Warwick.

At CHESTERFIELD. An Hospital of Lepers, founded as early as the reign of Richard I.; suppressed by Henry VIII.

At LE DALE, in the Deanery of Derby. A Premonstratensian Abbey, founded in the reign of Henry II., by Sterlo de Grendon; yearly income 144*l.* 12*s.*, now worth 2,892*l.* ; granted, 36 Henry VIII., to Francis Poole.

At DERBY. A Cell of Cluniac Monks, founded in the year 1140, by Waltheof; yearly income 10*l.*, now worth 200*l.* ; dissolved in the reign of Henry VIII.

All Saints College ; income 38*l.* 14*s.* now worth 774*l.*

A Monastery of Friars (Dominicans); granted, 35 Henry VIII., to John Hynde.

At LITTLE DIRBY, or DARLEY. An Augustine Friary, founded in the reign of Henry I., by Robert de Ferraris, Earl of Derby; yearly income 285*l.* 9*s.* 6½*d.*, now worth 5,709*l.* 10*s.* 10*d.*; granted, 32 Henry VIII., to Sir William West.

At GREISLEY, in the Deanery of Repingdon. A Priory of Augustine Canons, founded in the reign of Henry I., by William de Greisley; income 39*l.* 13*s.* 8*d.*, now worth 793*l.* 13*s.* 4*d.*; granted, 35 Henry VIII., to Henry Crutch.

At KING'S MEAD, near Derby. A Benedictine Nunnery, founded in the year 1160, by the Abbess of Derby; value 21*l.* 18*s.* 8*d.*, now worth 438*l.* 13*s.* 4*d.*; granted, 35 Henry VIII., to Francis Earl of Shrewsbury.

At REPINGDON. A Monastery of Augustine Monks stood here in the year 660; destroyed in the Danish Wars, but rebuilt in the year 1172, by Maud, widow of Ranulph, Earl of Chester; yearly income 167*l.* 18*s.* 2*d.*, now worth 3,358*l.* 3*s.* 4*d.*

At SPITTEL, on the Peak, between the villages of Hope and Castleton, an Hospital, founded 12 Edward III.; valued 26 Henry VIII., at 2*l.* yearly, now worth 40*l.*

At YEVELEY, or STEDE. A Preceptory of Knights Hospitalers, founded in the reign of

Richard I., by Ralph le Fun and Sir William Meynill, in the year 1268; valued at 107*l*. 3*s*. 8½*d*. yearly, now worth 2,143*l*. 14*s*. 2*d*.; granted 35 Henry VIII., to Charles Lord Montjoy.

DEVON (County).

At AXMINSTER. A College, founded by King Elhelstan, for seven Priests, to pray for the souls of those who were slain in a battle which he fought against the Danes, at Bremaldown, near this place.

At AXMOUTH. An Alien Priory, founded by Richard de Rivers, Earl of Devonshire, in the reign of Henry II.; granted, 6 Edward VI., to Walter Earl.

At BARNSTAPLE, in the Deanery of Barnstaple. A Cluniac Priory, founded in the reign of William the Conqueror, by Johel, of Totness; yearly value 129*l*. 15*s*. 3½*d*., now worth 2,595*l*. 5*s*. 10*d*.; granted, 29 Henry VIII., to William Lord Howard.

At BUCKLAND, in the Deanery of Tamerton. A Cistercian Abbey, founded in the year 1278, by Amicia, Countess of Devonshire; yearly income 341*l*., now worth 6,820*l*.; granted, 33 Henry VIII., to Richard Greynfeld.

At BUCKFASTRE. A Cistercian Abbey, founded in the year 1137, by Ethelwerd, son of William Pomerei; income 466*l.* 11*s.* 2½*d.*; now worth 9,331*l.* 4*s.* 2*d.*: granted, 31 Henry VIII., to Sir Thomas Dennys.

At CARESWELL. A Cluniac Cell, founded at some early period; granted, 38 Henry VIII., to John Etherege or Athrege.

At CHULMELEIGH. A College, said to have been founded, before the time of Edward I., by the Lady of the Manor, for seven children, whom she saved from being drowned by their own father, who looked upon himself as unable to maintain them; yearly income 24*l.* 8*s.* 4*d.*, now worth 488*l.* 6*s.* 8*d.*

At CORNWORTHY, in the Deanery of Totness. An Augustine Nunnery, founded by the Edgecomb family; income 63*l.* 3*s.* 10*d.*, now worth 1,263*l.* 16*s.* 8*d.*; granted, 2 Elizabeth, to Edward Harris and John Williams.

At CREDITON, or KIRTON, in the Deanery of Kenne. A College, founded in the Saxon times, but underwent afterwards many alterations; yearly income, at the dissolution, 332*l.* 17*s.* 5½*d.*, now worth 6,657*l.* 9*s.* 2*d.* yearly; granted, 37 Henry VIII., to Elizabeth Countess of Bath and to Sir Thomas Darcy.

At DUNKESWELL. A Cistercian Abbey,

founded in the year 1201, by William Briwere; yearly income 298*l.* 11*s.* 10*d.*, now worth 5,971*l.* 16*s.* 8*d.*; granted, 26 Henry VIII., to John Lord Russell.

At EXETER. The number of religious houses here suppressed is not known; though, from the celebrity of this city, in the Roman, British and Saxon times, there is not the least doubt that vast numbers of religious, of all orders, flocked hither. There is particular mention of three religious houses, within the precincts of the city: first, a Nunnery, which is now the Dean's house; second, a Monastery, founded by Ethelred, in the year 868; and the third, a Monastery, founded in the year 932, by Ethelstan, and endowed with twenty-six villages for its support. The monks repeatedly fled, for fear of the Danes, but were finally recalled, and settled in more lands and privileges than ever, by King Canute, in the year 1019.

A Benedictine Priory, founded by William the Conqueror; yearly income 145*l.* 12*s.*, now worth 2,912*l.*; granted, 32 Henry VIII., to Sir Thomas Dennys.

Boneville's Hospital, founded in the year 1407, by Sir William Boneville, in Rockslane, for twelve poor people, with the income of fifty marks per annum. This Almshouse was demolished, and the site converted into a garden, and granted to ——Newton, Esq.

DEVON.

St. Mary Magdalene Hospital, founded prior to the year 1163, without the south gate, to which Bishop Bartholomew Iscanus was a benefactor; granted, 26 Henry VIII.

A Dominican Friary, founded on the north side of the Cathedral Church; granted, by Edward I., to John Lord Russell, now called Bedford house.

A Franciscan Friary, founded without the south gate, in the reign of Edward I., by Bishop Button; dissolved and granted to Humphrey Rolles.

At FORD, in the parish of Thorncomb. A Cistercian Abbey, founded in the year 1136, by Richard Fitz Baldwin, Sheriff of Devonshire, and by Andelicia, his sister and heiress; yearly income 381*l.* 10*s.* 6$\frac{1}{2}$*d.*, now worth 7,620*l.* 10*s.* 10*d.*; granted, 32 Henry VIII., to Richard Pollard.

At FRETHELSTOKE, or FRISTOKE. An Augustine Friary, founded, 8 Henry III., by Sir Robert Beauchamp, Knt.; yearly income 127*l.* 2*s.* 4$\frac{1}{2}$*d.*, now worth 2,542*l.* 7*s.* 6*d.*; granted, 29 Hen. VIII., to Arthur Viscount Lisle.

At HERTLAND. An Augustine Monastery, founded, in the reign of Henry II., by Githa, wife to the Earl Godwin; yearly income 306*l.*

13s. 2½d., now worth 6,133l. 4s. 2d.; granted, 37 Hen. VIII., to William Abbot.

At LEGH, or LEYE, in the parish of Burlescomb. An Augustine Nunnery, founded, in the reign of Henry II., by Walter Clavell; yearly income 202l. 15s. 3d., now worth 4,055l. 5s.; granted, 35 Henry VIII. to Sir John St. Leger.

At MODBURY, in the Deanery of Plymton. An Alien Priory, founded, in the reign of Stephen, by Sir Peter sur Dive, in Normandy.

At NEWENHAM, or NEUHAM, in the parish of Axminster. A Cistercian Abbey, founded, in the year 1246, by Reginald de Mohun, Earl of Somerset: income 231l. 14s. 4d. yearly, now worth 4,634l. 6s. 8d.; granted, 5 Elizabeth, to Thomas Duke of Norfolk.

At OTTERY. A College, founded in the year 1337, by John Gradison, of Exeter; income 303l. 2s. 9d. yearly, now worth 6,062l. 15s.; granted, 37 Henry VIII., to Edward Earl of Hertford.

At OTTERINGTON. An Alien Priory, founded in the reign of William the Conqueror, by the Monks of St. Michael, in Normandy, income 87l. 10s. 4d. yearly, now worth 1,750l. 6s. 8d.; granted 31 Henry VIII., as parcel of Sion, to Richard Duke.

DEVON.

At PILTON, near Barnstaple. A Benedictine Cell, founded, by King Ethelstan; valuation 56*l*. 12*s*. 8½*d*., now worth 1,132*l*. 14*s*. 2*d*.

At PLYMOUTH. A Friary, in the east part of the town; granted, 38 Henry VIII., to Giles Iselham.

At PLYMTON. A Free Chapel of Augustines, founded, in the year 1121, by William Warlewast, Bishop of Exeter; value 912*l*. 12*s*. 8½*d*., now worth 18,252*l*. 14*s*. 2*d*.; granted, 2 Elizabeth, to Arthur Champernoun.

At POLLESHOO. A Benedictine Nunnery, erected in the reign of Richard I., by William Briwere, Bishop of Exeter; value 170*l*. 2*s*. 3½*d*. yearly, now worth 3,402*l*. 5*s*. 10*d*.; granted, in the reign of Edward VI., to John Earl of Warwick.

At SLAPTON. A College, founded, in the year 1373, by Sir Guy de Brien; granted, 37 Henry VIII., to Thomas Arundel.

At TAVESTOCK. A Benedictine Abbey, founded, in the year 961, by Ordgar, Earl of Devonshire, and his son; valued at 902*l*. 5*s*. 7½*d*. yearly, now worth 18,045*l*. 12*s*. 6*d*.; granted, 31 Henry VIII., to John Lord Russell.

At TORR, in the Deanery of Iplepen. A Premonstratensian Abbey, founded, in the year

1196, by William Briwere; yearly value 396*l*
0*s*. 11*d*., now worth 7,920*l*. 18*s*. 4*d*.; granted,
35 Henry VIII., to Sir John St. Leger.

At TOTNESS. An Alien Priory, founded, in
the reign of William the Conqueror, by John
Aluredi; value 124*l*. 10*s*. 2½*d*. yearly, now
worth 2,490*l*. 2*s*. 6*d*.; granted, 35 Henry VIII.,
to Catherine Champernoun and others.

DORSET (COUNTY).

At ABBOTSBURY. A Benedictine Abbey,
founded by Orcius, steward to King Canute, in
the year 1026; income 485*l*. 3*s*. 5½*d*. yearly,
now worth 9,703*l*. 9*s*. 2*d*.; granted, 35 Henry
VIII., to Sir Giles Strangwaies.

At ATHELINGTON. An Hospital, founded at
an early time, by Mr. Chidiock; income 7*l*. 8*s*.
4*d*. yearly, now worth 148*l*. 6*s*. 8*d*.; granted, 3
Edward VI., to Sir Michael Stanhope.

At BINDON. A Cistercian Abbey, founded, in
the year 1172, by Robert de Burgo and his
wife Maud; income 229*l*. 2*s*. 1½*d*. yearly, now
worth 4,582*l*. 2*s*. 6*d*.; granted, 32 Henry VIII.,
to Sir Richard Poynings.

At BRIDPORT. A Priory, at the end of the

town, income 6*l.* yearly, now worth 120*l.* ; converted into a dwelling-house, called St. Jones.

An Hospital over the bridge to the west of the town ; income 8*l.* 6*s.* 1*d.* yearly, now worth 166*l.* 1*s.* 8*d.*

At CERN, or CERNELL. A Benedictine Abbey, founded in the Saxon times, by a Mr. Egelward ; underwent several changes in after times ; valued, at the dissolution, at 623*l.* 13*s.* $2\frac{1}{2}d.$, now worth 12,473*l.* 4*s.* 2*d.* ; granted, 17 Elizabeth, to John Dudley and others.

At CRANBURN, in the Deanery of Pimpern. A Benedictine Cell, founded in the year 980, by Elwardus Snew ; granted, 2 Elizabeth, to Thomas Francis.

At DORCHESTER. St John's Hospital.

A Franciscan Abbey, founded, 4 Edward II., by the ancestors of Sir John Chidiock ; granted, 35 Henry VIII., to Sir Edmund Peckham.

At FRAMPTON. An Alien Priory, founded by William the Conqueror ; granted, 14 Elizabeth, to Sir Christopher Hatton, who sold it to John Brown, Esq.

At HOLME. A Cluniac Cell, founded before the reign of Edward I. ; granted, 1 Edward VI., to John Hannon.

At HORTON. A benedictine Cell, founded in the year 970, by Ordgar, Earl of Devonshire; granted, 1 Edward VI., to Edward Duke of Somerset, and after his attainder, to William Earl of Pembroke, 7 Edward VI.

At LODRESS. An Alien Priory, founded in the reign of Henry I., by Richard de Redveriis.

At LYME. An Hospital; valued at 38*l*. 11*s*.; now worth 771*l*.

At MAYNE. A preceptory of Knights Hospitalers; granted, 6 Elizabeth, to William Pole and Edward Downing.

At MELCOMB, or MILTON. A Dominican Friary, founded by Rogers, of Brianston; granted, 35 Henry VIII., to Sir John Rogers, of the same family.

At MIDDLETON. A Benedictine Abbey, founded, by King Ethelstan, in the year 933, to expiate the murder of his brother Edwin; income 720*l*. 4*s*. 1*d*., yearly, now worth 14,408*l*. 1*s*. 8*d*. granted, 31 Henry VIII., to Sir John Tregonwall.

At SHAFTESBURY. A Benedictine Nunnery, founded, in the year 888, by King Alfred; value 1,329*l*. 1*s*. 3*d*. yearly, now worth 26,581*l*. 5*s*.; granted, 1 Edward VI., to William Earl of Southampton.

DORSET.

St. John's Hospital, super montem de Shaftesbury, founded; granted, 2 Edward VI., to Randle Burgh and others.

An Almshouse, in St. James's parish, in the west side of St. Mary's lane; granted, 28 Elizabeth, to Edward Read.

At SHIREBURN. A Benedictine Abbey, founded, about the year 1200, by King John; value, at the Dissolution, 692l. 14s. 7½d. yearly, now worth 13,654l. 12s. 6d.; granted, 31 Henry VIII., to Sir John Horsey.

At SPECTESBURY. An Alien Priory, founded, in the reign of Henry I., by Robert Earl of Mallent and Leicester; granted, 35 Henry VIII., to Charles Blount, Lord Mountjoy, as parcel of the possessions of Witham.

At TARENT. A Cistercian Nunnery, founded, in the year 1230, by Richard Power, Bishop of Chichester; valued, at the dissolution, at 239l. 11s. 10d., now worth 4,691l. 16s. 8d.; granted, 33 Henry VIII., to Sir Thomas Wyat.

At WARHAM. Alien Priory, bestowed in the reign of Henry I., to the Convent of Lira, in Normandy, by Robert Earl of Leicester; granted to Thomas Reve and George Cotton.

At WILCHESWOOD. A Priory, founded here, at a very early period; value 12l. 16s. 4d. yearly, now worth 256*l*. 6*s*. 8*d*. ; suppressed, with the minor Monasteries, in the reign of Henry VIII.

At WINBURN, or TWINBORN. A Nunnery, founded, in the year 705, by St. Cuthburga, daughter of Kenred, King of the West Saxons, where several of the Saxon Kings were buried ; valuation, at the dissolution, 131*l*. 14*s*. now worth 2,634*l*. ; granted, 1 Edward VI., to Edward Duke of Somerset, then to Giles Keylway and William Leonard, but finally to Edward Lord Clinton.

DURHAM (COUNTY).

At BISHOP's AUCKLAND. A College, founded, and well endowed by Anthony Beck, Bishop of Durham ; yearly value 180*l*. 3*s*. 2*d*., now worth 3,603*l*. 3*s*. 4*d*.

At CHESTER ON THE STREET. A College, founded in the year 883, by Bishop Eardulfus, who had been forced to flee hither with the body of St. Cuthbert from Lindisfarne. The seven Prebends here were valued, 26 Henry VIII., at 77*l*. 12*s*. 8*d*., now worth 1, 552*l*. 13*s*. 4*d*.

At DERLINGTON. A College, founded early, by Hugh Pusar, Bishop of Durham, in the reign of Henry II.; valued at 51*l.* 8*s.* 4*d.*, now worth 1,028*l.* 6*s.* 8*d.*

At DURHAM. A Cathedral, and Benedictine Priory, founded about the year 995. The body of the tutelar Saint, Cuthbert, was magnificently enshrined behind the high altar; yearly income 4,436*l.* 16*s.* 3*d.*, now worth 88,736*l.* 5*s.*

At FINCHALE. A Benedictine Cell, founded, in the year 1128, by Randal, Bishop of Durham, for the Monks of Durham; yearly value 146*l.* 19*s.* 2*d.*, now worth 2,939*l.* 3*s.* 4*d.*; granted, 26 Henry VIII., to the Dean and Chapter of Durham.

St. Edmond's Hospital, founded, by Nicholas de Farneham, Bishop of Durham, in the year 1247; yearly value 109*l.* 4*s.* 4*d.*, now worth 2,184*l.* 6*s.* 8*d.*; granted, 7 Edward VI., to the Mayor and Burgesses of Newcastle.

At GRETHAM. An Hospital, founded, in the year 1262, by Robert de Stichill, Bishop of Durham; yearly value 97*l.* 6*s.* 3½*d.*, now worth 1,946*l.* 5*s.* 10*d.*; granted, 26 Henry VIII., to the Bishop of Durham.

At JARROW. A Benedictine Cell, or Monastery, founded in the year 684, by King Egfrid. The learned and venerable Bede had his education here. Yearly income 40*l.* 7*s.* 8*d.*, now worth 807*l*. 13*s*. 4*d*.; granted, 36 Henry VIII., to William Lord Eure.

At KEYPIER, near Durham. An Hospital, founded, in the year 1112, by Randal Bishop of Durham, and Hugh, Bishop of the said place; yearly income 167*l*. 2*s*. 11*d*., now worth 3,340*l*. 18*s*. 4*d*.; granted, 36 Henry VIII., to Sir William Paget.

At LANGCESTER. A College, founded, in the year 1283, by Anthony Beck, Bishop of Durham; yearly income 49*l*. 3*s*. 4*d*., now worth 983*l*. 6*s*. 8*d*.; granted, 7 Edward VI., to Simon Weldbury, and Christopher Moreland.

At NORTON. A College, anciently founded, in the patronage of the Bishop of Durham; valued yearly at 34*l*. 13*s*. 4*d*., now worth 693*l*. 6*s*. 8*d*.

At SHIREBURN. An Hospital, founded by the above mentioned Hugh Pusar, Bishop of Durham, in the reign of Henry II.: yearly revenue 135*l*. 7*s*., now worth 2,707*l*. Here were maintained sixty-five Lepers, a Master, and some Priests. Granted, in the reign of Henry VIII., to the Bishop of Durham.

At STAINDROP. A College, founded, in the reign of Henry IV., by Ralph Nevill, Earl of Westmoreland, for six decayed Gentlemen, six poor Officers, and other poor Men; yearly revenue 126*l*. 5*s*. 10*d*., now worth 2,525*l*. 8*s*. 4*d*.

At WERMOUTH. A Benedictine Cell, built by the famous Abbot, Benedict Biscopius, in the year 674, who received this town from King Egfrid. Yearly value 26*l.*, now worth 520*l.*; granted, 37 Henry VIII., to Thomas White-head.

ESSEX (COUNTY).

At BERDEN. An Augustine Friary, founded, in the reign of Henry III.; yearly income 31*l.* 5*s.* 1½*d.*; now worth 625*l.* 2*s.* 6*d.*; granted, 30 Henry VIII., to Henry Parker.

At BERKING, or Bedenham. A Benedictine Nunnery, founded, in the year 675, by Erkinwald, son of Anna, King of the East Angles, and afterwards Bishop of London; yearly income 1,084*l.* 6*s.* 2½*d.*, now worth 21, 686*l.* 4*s.* 2*d.*; granted, 5 Edward VI., to Edward Lord Clinton.

At BILEIGH, near Maldon. Premonstraten-sian Abbey, founded, in the year 1180, by Robert Mantel; income 196*l.* 6*s.* 5*d.* yearly, now worth 3,926*l.* 8*s.* 4*d.*; granted, 32 Henry VIII., to Sir John Gate.

At BLACKMORE. An Augustine Monastery, founded, in the reign of King John, by Adam and Jordan de Samford; income 85*l.* 9*s.* 7*d.* yearly, now worth 1,709*l.* 11*s.* 8*d.*; granted, 32 Henry VIII., to John Smith.

At CHELMESFORD. A Dominican Friary, founded, at an early date here, or in the adjoining hamlet Fulsham; income 9*l.* 6*s.* 5*d.* yearly, now worth 186*l.* 8*s.* 4*d.*; granted, 34 Henry VIII., to Antony Bonvixi.

At CHICH. An Augustine Priory, founded, by Richard de Belmeis, Bishop of London and St. Osith, before the year 1118; income 758*l.* 5*s.* 8*d.* now worth 15,165*l.* 8*s.* 4*d.*; granted, 31 Henry VIII., to Thomas Lord Cromwel, and after his attainder, to Sir Thomas Darcy, 5 Edward VI.

At COGGESHALE, or COXHALL. A Cistercian Abbey, founded, in the year 1142, by King Stephen; yearly income 298*l.* 8*s.*, now worth 5,968*l.*; granted, 29 Henry VIII., to Sir Thomas Seymour.

At COLCHESTER. A Benedictine Abbey, founded, in the year 1096, by Eudo, courtier of William the Conqueror; income 523*l.* 17*s.* 0½*d.*; yearly, now worth 10,477*l.* 0*s.* 10*d.*; granted, 1 Edward VI., to John Earl of Warwick.

An Augustine Friary, founded, in the reign of Henry I., in the south part of the town, by Ernulphus, who became afterwards prior of it, income 113*l.* 12*s.* 8*d.* yearly, now worth 2,272*l.* 13*s.* 4*d.*; granted, 28 Henry VIII., to Sir Thomas Audley.

A Friary, without the walls of the town, on the southward, founded, in the year 1244, for the crouched Friars ; value 7*l.* 7*s.* 8*d.* yearly, now worth 147*l.* 13*s.* 4*d.*; granted, 35 Henry VIII., to Thomas Lord Audley.

Monastery of Grey Friars, founded, in the year 1309, by Robert Lord Fitzwalter, near the east gate, who became a Friar before his death, in 1325 ; granted, 36 Henry VIII., to Francis Jobson and Andrew Audley, and by King Edward VI., to John Earl of Warwick.

At COLUM, or COLUN. A Benedictine Priory, founded, in the reign of Henry I., by Albericus de Vere, who became a Monk there ; yearly value 175*l.* 14*s.* 8½*d.*, now worth 3,514*l.* 14*s.* 2*d.*; granted, 28 Henry VIII., to John Earl of Oxford.

At CRESSING TEMPLE. A Preceptory of Knights Templars, founded, by King Stephen, in the year 1150 ; granted, 35 Henry VIII., to Sir W. Hughes, Knight.

At DUNMOWE PARVA. An Augustine Monastery, founded, in the year 1104, by Lady

Juga; revenues 173*l*. 2*s*. 4*d*., now worth 3,462*l*. 6*s*. 8*d*.; granted, 28 Henry VIII., to Robert Earl of Sussex.

At HALSTEDE. A Benedictine Cell, founded, in the reign of William the Conqueror, by Ingelrica, wife of Ranulf Peverell; income 83*l*. 19*s*. 7*d*. yearly, now worth 1,679*l*. 11*s*. 8*d*.; granted, 29 Henry VIII., to Giles Leigh.

At HALFIELD REGIS. A Benedictine Priory, founded, in the year 1140, by Aubrey de Vere, father of the Earl of Oxford; revenues 157*l*. 3*s*. 2½*d*., now worth 3,143*l*. 4*s*. 2*d*.; granted, 32 Henry VIII., to Thomas Noke.

At CASTLEHEDINGHAM, or HENINGHAM. A Benedictine Nunnery, founded, in the year 1190, by Aubrey de Vere, first Earl of Oxford, or rather by his Countess Lucia, who became the first Prioress; revenues, at the suppression, 29*l*. 12*s*. 10*d*. now worth 392*l*. 16*s* 8*d*.; granted, 28 Henry VIII., to John Earl of Oxford.

At HORKESLEY PARVA. A Cluniac Priory, founded, in the reign of Henry I., by Robert Fitz Godebold; revenues 38*l*. 14*s*. 7*d*., now worth 774*l*. 11*s*. 8*d*.

At LATTON. An Augustine Priory, founded, before 20 Edward I., by some person, whose name is not known; granted, 28 Henry VIII., to Sir Henry Parker.

ESSEX.

At LAYER MORNEY. A College, founded, in the year 1330, by William de Morney, Lord of the Manor.

An Hospital, or Almshouse, erected in the year 1523, in pursuance of the will of Henry Lord Morney; granted, by Queen Elizabeth, to William Tipper and Robert Dawe.

At LIGHES. An Augustine Priory, founded, in the reign of Henry III., by Sir Ralph Gernoun; yearly revenue 141*l.* 14*s.* 8*d.*, now worth 2,834*l.* 13*s.* 4*d.*; granted, 27 Henry VIII., to Sir Richard Rich.

At MALDON. A Carmelite Friary, founded, in the reign of Edward II., by some persons unknown; value 26*l.* 0*s.* 8*d.* yearly, now worth 520*l.* 13*s.* 4*d.*; granted, 36 Henry VIII., to George Duke and John Sterr.

At MALDON JUXTA. An Hospital for the leprous townsmen, founded, by some one of the ancient Kings of England; granted, 30 Hen.VIII. to Thomas Dyer; and, 25 Elizabeth, to Theophilus and Robert Adams.

At LITTLE MAPLESTEAD. A Preceptory of Knights Hospitalers, founded, in the reign of Henry I., by Juliana, daughter and heiress of Robert Dorsnell; granted, at the dissolution, to George Harper.

ESSEX.

At MERCY, or WEST MERESEY. An Alien Priory, founded by King Edward the Confessor; granted, 34 Hen. VIII., to Robert Dacres, Esq.

At NEWPORTPOND. An Hospital, founded, in the reign of King John, by Richard Serlo; valuation 23*l*. 10*s*. 8*d*., now worth 470*l*. 13*s*. 4*d*.; granted, by Henry VIII., to Sir Martin Bowes.

At PAUNSFIELD. An Alien Priory, founded, 4 William the Conqueror, by Walteran Fitz Ranulph; granted, 30 Henry VIII., to Sir Giles Caple.

At PLECY. A College, founded, 17 Rich. II., by Thomas Duke of Gloucester; valuation 139*l*. 3*s*. 10*d*. yearly, now worth 2,783*l*. 18*s*. 4*d*.; granted, 38 Henry VIII., to John Gales.

At PRITTLEWELL. A Cluniac Priory, founded, in the reign of Henry II., by Robert Fitz Swain; yearly value, 194*l*. 14*s*. 3*d*., now worth 3,894*l*. 5*s*. 10*d*.; granted, 29 Henry VIII., to Thomas Audley; and, 5 Edward VI., to Sir Richard Rich.

At SEDEBURBROOK. A Free Chapel, founded, in the reign of Edward I.; granted, 7 Edward VI., to Sir Anthony Brown and Richard Weston.

At STANESGATE, in the Parish of Steeple. A Cluniac Priory, founded, by the predecessors of the Prior of Lewes, antecedently to the year 1176; value 43*l*. 8*s*. 6*d*. yearly, now worth 868*l*. 10*s*.; granted, 35 Henry VIII., to Edmund Mordaunt.

At STRATFORD, in the parish of West Ham. A Cistercian Abbey, built, in the year 1134, by William de Montfichet; income 573*l*. 15*s*. 6½*d*. yearly, now worth 11,475*l*. 10*s*. 10*d*.; granted, 30 Henry VIII., to Peter Meawtis, Esq.

At THOBEY, near INGATESTONE. An Augustine Priory, founded early, by Michael Capra and wife and son; value 75*l*. 10*s*. 6*d*. yearly, now worth 1,510*l*. 10*s*.; granted, 22 Henry VIII., to Sir Richard Page, Knt.

At THREMHALL. An Augustine Priory, founded, in the reign of William the Conqueror, by Gilbert de Montefixo; valuation 70*l*. 19*s*. 3¼*d*., now worth 1,419*l*. 5*s*. 10*d*.; granted, 28 Henry VIII., to John Carey.

At TILTEY. A Cistercian Abbey, founded, about the year 1152, by Robert Ferrers, Earl of Derby, and Maurice Fitz Jeffrey; valuation 177*l*. 9*s*. 4*d*., now worth 3,549*l*. 6*s*. 8*d*.; granted, 35 Henry VIII., to Thomas Lord Audley.

At TIPTREE. An Augustine Monastery, founded, in the reign of Edward I., by Ralph de Munchensi; value 22*l*. 16*s*. 4*d*. yearly, now worth 456*l*. 6*s*. 8*d*.

At LITTLE WALDEN. A Benedictine Abbey of Monks, founded, in the year 1136, by Jeffrey Mandevil, Earl of Essex; income 406*l*. 15*s*. 11*d*. yearly, now worth 8,135*l*. 18*s*. 4*d*.; granted, 29 Henry VIII., to Sir Thomas Audley.

At WALTHAM. An Augustine Monastery, founded, in the year 1062, by Earl Harold; value 1,079*l*. 12*s*. 1*d*. yearly, now worth 21,592*l*. 1*s*. 8*d*.; granted, 1 Edward VI., to Sir Anthony Denny.

At WIKES. A Benedictine Nunnery, founded, in the reign of Henry I., by Walter and Alexander Mascherell, brothers; value 92*l*. 12*s*. 3*d*., now worth 1,852*l*. 5*s*.; granted by Hen. VIII.

At WUDEHAM. An Augustine Monastery, founded, in the reign of Henry II., by Maurice Fitz Jeffrey and Tiretai, Sheriff of Essex; granted, 31 Henry VIII., to Henry Polstead.

GLOUCESTER (COUNTY).

At BECCANFORD. An Alien Priory, given, in the reign of Henry I., to the Abbey of St. Martin, in Normandy; value 53*l*. 6*s*. 8*d*. yearly, now worth 1,066*l*. 13*s*. 4*d*.; granted, 1 Edward VI., to Sir Richard Lee.

At CIRENCESTER. An Augustine Monastery, magnificently built, in the year 1117, by Hen. I. ; yearly value 1,051*l*. 7*s*. 1½*d*., now worth 21,027*l*. 2*s*. 6*d*. ; granted, 1 Edward VI., to Sir Thomas Seymour ; 6 Elizabeth, to Richard Masters.

At DAEGLESFORD. A Monastery, founded, in the year 718, by one Begia, on a site, granted him for that purpose, by King Ethelbald ; dissolved.

At DEREHURST. An Alien Priory, founded, about the year 980, by Doddo Duke of Mercia ; granted, 34 Henry VIII., to William Throckmorton.

At FLEXELEY, or DENE. A Cistercian Abbey, founded, in the time of Stephen, by Roger Earl of Hereford ; value 112*l*. 13*s*. 1*d*. yearly, now worth 2,253*l*. 1*s*. 8*d*. ; granted, 36 Henry VIII., to Sir Anthony Kingston.

At GLOUCESTER. A Benedictine Abbey, founded, in the year 680, by Wulphere, the first Christian King of Mercia, and Ethelred, his brother and successor, who was afterwards Monk and Abbot of Bardney. There were, according to the Saxon custom, religious of both sexes : this house was honoured by having, for ninety years, three Queens successively the presiding Abbesses ; valuation, at the dissolution, 1,550*l*. 4*s*. 5½*d*. now worth 31,004*l*. 9*s*. 2*d*. ;

granted, by Henry VIII., to the Bishop and his officers.

An Augustine Monastery, founded, as some writers say, in the year 660, by Mer-wald, Viceroy of West Mercia; or, as others, with more appearance of certainty, say, by Ethelred, Earl of Mercia, in the year 909; income 90*l*. 10*s*. 2½*d*. yearly, now worth 1,810*l*. 4*s* 2*d*.; granted, 31 Henry VIII., to John Jennings.

A Friary, not far from the south gate, founded, before the year 1268, by Lord Berkley; granted, 35 Henry VIII., to John Jennings.

A Monastery of Dominicans, founded, near the Castleyard, by Henry III., in the year 1239; granted, 31 Henry VIII., to Thomas Bell, who made it a drapering house.

A Carmelite Friary, founded in the suburbs without the north gate, by Queen Elenor, Sir Thomas Gifford and Sir Thomas Berkley, in the time of Henry III.; granted, 35 Henry VIII., to Richard Andrews and Nicholas Temple.

At MINCHIN HAMPTON. An Alien Priory, according to some authors, was founded here very early, but others say, that this idea took rise from the fact that the manor was given to the Nuns or Minchins of the Holy Trinity, in

Normandy, by William the Conqueror; revenues valued at 117*l.* 16*s.* 11*d.*, now worth 2,356*l.* 18*s.* 4*d.*; granted, 34 Henry VIII., to Andrews Lord Windsor.

At HAYLES, or TRAY. A Cistercian Monastery, founded, in the year 1251, by Richard Earl of Cornwall, afterwards King of the Romans and Emperor of Germany; valuation 357*l.* 7*s.* 8½*d.*, now worth 7,147*l.* 14*s.* 2*d.*; granted, 1 Edward VI., to Sir Thomas Seymour, and after his attainder, to William Marquis of Northampton, 4 Edward VI.

At HORKSLEGH, or HORSLEY. An Alien Priory, endowed, in the time of William the Conqueror, by Roger Earl of Shrewsbury; granted, 7 Edward VI., to Sir Walter Dennys.

At LANTONY, near Gloucester. An Augustine Monastery, founded, in the year 1136, by Milo Earl of Hereford, on the south side of the city; income 748*l.* 19*s.* 11½*d.*, now worth 14,979*l.* 19*s.* 2*d.*; granted, 32 Henry VIII., to Sir Arthur Porter.

At LECHELADE. An Hospital, founded, 30 Henry III., by Lady Isabel Ferrers; granted, 14 Elizabeth, to Denis Tappes.

At NOENT, or NEWENTON. An Alien Priory, founded, on the manor given by William the Conqueror to the Convent of Cormeili in Normandy; granted, 1 Edward VI., to Sir Richard Lee.

At QUEININGTON. A Preceptory of Knights Hospitalers, founded, through the bounty of Agnes de Lacy and her daughter before the reign of John ; valued at 137*l*. 7*s*. 1½*d*. yearly, now worth 2,747*l*. 2*s*. 6*d*.; granted, 37 Henry VIII., to Sir Richard Morisine and to Sir Anthony Kingston.

At STANLEY. A Benedictine Cell, founded, in the year 1136, by Roger Berkley; yearly income 126*l*. 0*s*. 8*d*., now worth 2,520*l*. 13*s*. 4*d*.; granted to Sir Anthony Kingston.

At STOW-ON-THE-WOLD. An Hospital, founded, about the year 1010, by Ailmar, Earl of Cornwall and Devonshire; valued at 25*l*. 4*s*. 4*d*. yearly, now worth 504*l*. 6*s*. 8*d*.

At THEOKESBURY, or TEWKESBURY. A Benedictine Monastery, built and endowed by two brothers, Oddo and Doddo, in the year 715, but enlarged in the year 1102, by Robert Fitz Haimon, a noble Norman ; valued at 1,598*l*. 1*s*. 3*d*. yearly, now worth 31,961*l*. 5*s*.; granted, 36 Hen. VIII., to Thomas Strowde, Walter Erle, and James Paget.

At WESTBURY ON TRIN, or TRYMME. A Benedictine Cell and College, founded, in the year 824, and endowed with several lands by

Ethelric, son of Ethelmund. Having suffered by wars and other convulsions it was rebuilt, in the year 1288, by Godfrey Giffard, Bishop of Worcester; valued at 232*l.* 14*s.* 0½*d.* yearly, now worth 4,654*l.* 0*s.* 10*d.*; granted, 35 Henry VIII., to Sir Ralph Sadler.

At WINCHELCOMBE. A Benedictine Monastery, or Nunnery, founded, 787, by King Offa; and, in 798, King Ranulph laid there the foundation of a stately Monastery; valued at 759*l.* 11*s.* 9*d.* yearly, now worth 15,191*l.* 15*s.*; granted, 1 Edward VI., to Sir Thomas Seymour.

HANTS. (COUNTY).

At SOUTH BADEISLEY. A Preceptory of Knights Templars; valued at 118*l.* 16*s.* 7*d.* yearly, now worth 2,376*l.* 11*s.* 8*d.*; granted, 31 Henry VIII., to Sir Nicolas Throckmorton.

At DE BELLO LOCO REGIS, or BEAULIEU, in the New Forest. A Cistercian Abbey, founded, by King John, in the year 1204, for thirty monks; income 428*l.* 16*s.* 8½*d.* yearly, now worth 8,576*l.* 4*s.* 2*d.*; granted, 30 Henry VIII., to Thomas Wriothesley, Esq.

At BROMERE. An Augustine Monastery, founded, by Baldwin de Redveriis, and his uncle,

Hugh, in the reign of Henry I.; valued at 200*l*. 5*s*. 1½*d*. yearly, now worth 4,005*l*. 2s. 6*d*.; granted, 28 Henry VIII., to Henry, Marquis of Exeter.

At BURTON, in the Isle of Wight. A College, founded, 1282, by John de Insula, rector of Shalfleet, and Thomas de Winton, rector of Godshill; granted, 18 Henry VIII., to Winchester College.

At HAILING. An Alien Priory, founded, by King William, and afterwards by King Hen. I.; granted, 33 Henry VIII., to the College of Arundel.

At MEREWELLE. An Augustine Priory, founded, in the reign of John, by Henry of Blois, Bishop of Winchester; granted, 5 Edward VI., to Sir Henry Seymour.

At MOTISFONT. An Augustine Priory, founded, by William Brimere, in the reign of John; valued at 167*l*. 15*s*. 8½*d*. yearly, now worth 3,355*l*. 14*s*. 2*d*.; granted, 28 Henry VIII., to William, Lord Sandys.

At NETTELY, near Southampton. A Cistercian Abbey, founded, 1239, by King Henry III.; valued at 160*l*. 2*s*. 9½*d*. yearly, now worth 3,202*l*. 15*s*. 10*d*.; granted, 28 Henry VIII., to Sir William Paulet.

At PORCHESTER. An Augustine Monastery, founded, 1133, by King Henry I.; valued at 314*l*. 17*s*. 10½*d*. yearly, now worth 6,297*l*. 17*s*. 6*d*.; granted, 30 Henry VIII., to John White.

At PORTESMOUTH. An Hospital, founded, in the time of John, by Peter de Rupibus, Bishop of Winchester; valued at 33*l*. 19*s*. 5½*d*. yearly, now worth 679*l*. 9*s*. 2*d*.

At QUARRER, in the Isle of Wight. A Cistercian Monastery, founded, 1132, by Baldwin de Redveriis, afterwards Earl of Devonshire; valued at 184*l*. 1*s*. 10*d*. yearly, now worth 3,681*l*. 18*s*. 4*d*.; granted, 36 Henry VIII., to John and George Mills.

At RUMESEY. A Benedictine Nunnery, founded, 967, by Edward, or Ethelwold, a Saxon nobleman; valued at 528*l*. 8*s*. 10½*d*. yearly, now worth 10,568*l*. 19*s*. 2*d*.; granted, 38 Henry VIII., to John Bellew and R. Pigot.

At SOUTHAMPTON. An Augustine Priory, built, by Henry I., upon the river, two miles above the town; valued at 91*l*. 9*s*. yearly, now worth 1,829*l*.; granted, 30 Henry VIII., to Francis Dawtrey.

An Hospital, called God's House, founded, in the time of Henry III., by two brothers, Gervase and Protase, of Hampton, for the poor.

HANTS.

St. Mary Magdelan Hospital, founded, 1179, for lepers.

A Franciscan Friary, founded, 1240, near the wall, in the south part of the town; granted, 36 Henry VIII., to John Pollard, and, 5 Edward VI., to Arthur Darcy.

At TWINHAM. An Augustine Priory, founded in the time of Edward the Confessor; valued at 541l. 16s. yearly, now worth 10,896l.; granted, 37 Henry VIII., to Joseph Kirton.

At TYCHFIELD. A Premonstratensian Abbey, founded, in the time of Henry III., by Peter de Rupibus, Bishop of Winchester; valued at 280l. 19s. 10½d. yearly, now worth 5,619l. 19s. 2d.; granted, 29 Henry VIII., to Sir Thomas Wriothesley, who built a stately house here.

At WHERWELL. A Benedictine Nunnery, founded, by Elfrida, Queen Dowager of King Edgar, in the year 986, to expiate the crime of her being concerned in the murders both of her first husband, Ethelwolf, that she might be queen, and of her son-in-law, King Edward, that her own son might be king; here she spent the latter part of her life in doing penance, like David, for her sins, and for regaining, like the prodigal child, the good graces of her heavenly Father; valued at 403l. 12s. 10d. yearly, now worth 8,072l. 18s. 4d.; granted, 31 Hen. VIII., to Sir Thomas West, lord de la Ware.

At WINCHESTER. A Benedictine Priory, founded, as they say, by King Lucius, but destroyed in Diocletian's persecution, in the year 266; rebuilt, by Deodatus, the Abbot, in the year 300; the monks were massacred, and the house perverted into a temple for the idolatrous worship of Dagon, by Cerdic, King of the West Saxons, but finally restored by the Saxon Christian Kings; value, at the suppression, 1,507*l.* 17*s.* 2*d.* yearly, now worth 30,157*l.* 3*s.*4*d.*

A Nunnery, founded, in the east part of the city, by King Alfred; here St. Edburg was Abbess; valued at 179*l.* 7*s.* 2*d.* yearly, now worth 3,587*l.*3*s.* 4*d.*; granted, 38 Hen. VIII., to John Bellew and John Broxholme.

A Monastery, founded, by King Alfred, for the learned Monk Grimbald, whom he had brought from Flanders. It was removed, 1110, to Hyde, without the city; valued at 865*l.* 1*s.* 6*d.* yearly, now worth 17,301*l.* 0*s.* 10*d.*; granted, 37 Henry VIII., to Richard Bethel.

St. Elizabeth College, founded, by John de Pontoys, Bishop of Winchester, 1300; valued at 112*l.* 17*s.* 4*d.* yearly, now worth 2,257*l.* 6*s.* 8*d.*; granted, 35 Henry VIII., to Thomas, Lord Wriothesley.

Wykeham College, founded, by the munificent prelate, William of Wykeham, Bishop of Winchester, 1387, outside the city to the southward; valued at 639*l.* 8*s.* 7*d.* yearly, now worth 12,788*l.*

St. Cross Hospital, founded, south-west of the town, by Henry le Blois, Bishop of Winchester, in the year 1132, for the whole maintenance of 13 poor brethren in lodging, clothing, and diet, and for dining 100 poor persons every day. In the year 1185, Richard, Bishop of Winchester, made provision for dining another 100 poor persons every day; and, in the time of Henry VI., Cardinal Beaufort made additional provisions for a rector, two chaplains, 35 poor men, and three poor women; value, at the dissolution, 184*l.* 4*s.* 2*d.* yearly, now worth 3,684*l.* 3*s.* 4*d.*

An Hospital, for the poor folk, stood outside the King's Gate, maintained by the Monks of St. Swithin, now suppressed.

An Augustine Friary, stood a little without the south gate, on the way to Hampton; the site of this as well as of three other Friaries, granted.

Grey Friary, founded, by King Hen. III., close by the east gate, on the inside; granted, 35 Henry VIII.

At WINTENEY. A Cistercian Nunnery, founded, in the time of William the Conqueror, by the son of Peter Jeffrey; valued at 59*l.* 1*s.* yearly, now worth 1,181*l.*; granted, 30 Henry VIII., to Richard Hill, Esq., Serjeant of the King's Cellar.

HEREFORD (County).

At Acley. An Alien Priory, founded, in the year 1160, by the ancestors of Robert Chandos; granted, 33 Henry VIII., to Sir Philip Hobby.

At Acornbury. An Augustine Nunnery, founded, by Margery, wife of Walter de Lacy, three miles south of Hereford, in the reign of King John; valued at 75*l*. 7*s*. 5½*d*. yearly, now worth 1,507*l*. 9*s*. 2*d*.; granted, 33 Hen. VIII., to Hugh de Harry.

At Bromyard. A College, founded, prior to the reign of Henry III.; granted, 14 Elizabeth, to one Henry James.

At Clifford. A Cluniac Priory, founded, in the time of Henry I., by Simon Fitz Richard; valued at 65*l*. 11*s*. 11*d*. yearly, now worth 1,311*l*. 18*s*. 4*d*.; granted, 7 Edward VI., to William Herbert, Earl of Pembroke.

At Dore. A Cistercian Abbey, founded, in the time of King Stephen, by Robert Ewyas; valued at 118*l*. 2*s*. yearly, now worth 2,362*l*.; granted, 31 Henry VIII., to John Scudamore.

At Dynmore. An Hospital of Knights Hospitalers, founded, by Sir Thomas ——, a brother of the order, in the time of Henry II.; granted, 2 Edward VI., to Sir Thomas Palmer.

At FLANESFORD. An Augustine Monastery, founded, 1347, by Richard, Lord Talbot; valued at 15*l*. 8*s*. 9*d*. yearly, now worth 308*l*. 15*s*.; granted, 30 Henry VIII., to George, Earl of Shrewsbury.

At HEREFORD. A Cathedral, founded here, in the year 680; again destroyed by the wars, and rebuilt by William the Conqueror; valued, at the general suppression, 831*l*. 4*s*. 1*d*. yearly, now worth 16,624*l*. 1*s*. 8*d*.

A Benedictine Cell, founded here very early, but enlarged in after times by several benefactors; valued at 121*l*. 3*s*. 3½*d*. yearly, now worth 2,423*l*. 5*s*. 10*d*.; granted, 34 Henry VIII., to John ap Rice.

St. John's Hospital of Templars, stood in the suburbs, without the north gate; granted, 6 Elizabeth, to Robert Freke and John Walker.

A Friary, founded, in the time of Edward III., in the north suburbs, by Sir John Daniel; granted, 5 Elizabeth, to Elizabeth Wynne.

A Friary, founded, without the Freregate, by Sir William Pembrugge, in the time of Edward I.; granted, 36 Hen. VIII., to James Boyle.

At KILPECKE. A Benedictine Cell, founded, about 1134, by Hugh, the son of William the

Norman; granted, 13 Henry VIII., to the Bishop of Gloucester.

At LEOMINSTER. A Benedictine Cell, founded, about 660, by Merwald, King of West Mercia, but destroyed and rebuilt in after times; valued at 660*l.* 16*s.* 8*d.* yearly, now worth 13,216*l.* 13*s.* 4*d.*; granted to the Bailiffs and Burgesses of the town.

At LYMBROKE. An Augustine Nunnery, founded, about a quarter of a mile from the left bank of the river Lugg; valued at 23*l.* 17*s.* 8*d.* yearly, now worth 477*l.* 13*s.* 4*d.*; granted, 7 Edw. VI., to John West and Robert Gratwick.

At WIGMORE. An Augustine Monastery, founded, in the year 1100, by Ralph de Mortimer; but, for want of water and convenience, shifted up and down, and finally settled into a stately monastery, a mile beyond the town; valued at 302*l.* 12*s.* 3½*d.* yearly, now worth 6,025*l.* 5*s.* 10*d.*; granted, 2 Edward VI., to Sir Thomas Palmer.

At WORMELEY. An Augustine Abbey, founded, in the time of King John, by Gilbert Talbot; valued at 83*l.* 10*s.* 2*d.* yearly, now worth 1,670*l.* 3*s.* 4*d.*; granted, 37 Henry VIII., to Edward, Lord Clinton.

HERTS. (County).

At St. Alban's. A Benedictine Abbey, founded, in the year 793, by King Offa, for 100 monks, in honour of St. Alban, the first Briton who suffered martyrdom; valued at 2,510*l.* 6*s.* 1½*d.* yearly, now worth 50,206*l.* 2*s.* 6*d.* ; granted, 7 Edward VI., to the Mayor and Burgesses.

St. Julian's Hospital, founded, in the time of Henry I., by Jeffrey, the Abbot, near this town, on the London road, for leprous persons; granted, 36 Henry VIII., to Richard Lee.

At Berkhamsted. Two Hospitals stood here in the reign of King John, for poor lepers; revenues granted, 36 Henry VIII., to Robert Hordem.

At Cestrehunt, or Chesthunt. A Benedictine Nunnery, founded, in the year 1183; valued at 27*l.* 6*s.* 8*d.* yearly, now worth 546*l.* 13*s.* 4*d.* ; granted, 28 Hen. VIII., to Sir Anthony Denny.

At Clothale. An Hospital of ancient foundation; valued at 4*l.* 2*s.* 8*d.* yearly, now worth 82*l.* 13*s.* 7*d.* ; granted 2 James I.

At De la Praye. A Benedictine Nunnery, founded, in the year 1190, by Garinus, Abbot of St. Alban's; granted, 32 Henry VIII., to Ralph Rawlet, Esq.

At TEMPLE DYNNESLEY. A Preceptory of Templars, richly endowed in lands, in the time of King Stephen, by Bernard de Balliol; granted, by King Henry VIII., to Sir Ralph Sadler.

At FLAMSTED. A Benedictine Nunnery, founded, in the time of Stephen, by Roger de Toney. Yearly value 46*l.* 16*s.* 1½*d.*, now worth 936*l.* 2*s.* 6*d.*; granted, 31 Henry VIII., to Sir Richard Page.

At HERTFORD. A Benedictine Abbey, founded, in the time of William the Conqueror, by Ralph de Limesie; value yearly 86*l.* 14*s.* 8*d.*, now worth 1,734*l.* 13*s.* 4*d.*; granted, 29 Henry VIII., to Sir Anthony Denny, and to his wife.

At HITCHIN. A Gilbertine Nunnery, founded, at some early period; value yearly, at the suppression, 15*l.* 11*s.* 1*d.*, now worth 301*l.* 18*s.* 4*d.*; granted, 36 Henry VIII., to John Cock.

A Dominican Friary, founded, at the end of this town, by King Edward, about 1316; yearly value 4*l.* 9*s.* 4*d.*, now worth 89*l.* 6*s.* 8*d.*; granted, 38 Henry VIII., to Edward Watson and H. Hendson.

At KING'S LANGLEY. A Friary, founded, near the royal palace here, by Roger Helle, an English Baron, but endowed by Edward I., Edward II., Edward III., and Edward IV., so that it exceeded all houses of the order in England; yearly value 150*l.* 14*s.* 8*d.*, now worth

3,014*l.* 13*s.* 4*d.* ; granted, 16 Elizabeth, to Edward Grimston.

At REDBURN. A Benedictine Cell, subservient to St. Alban's, founded, before 1195 ; granted, 31 Henry VIII., to John Cock.

At ROYSTON. An Augustine Monastery, founded, in the time of Henry II., by Eustace de Merc; yearly value 106*l.* 3*s.* 1*d.*, now worth 3,123*l.* 1*s.* 8*d.* ; granted, 32 Henry VIII., to Robert Slete, Esq.

St. John's Hospital, founded, in the time of Henry III. ; valued at 5*l.* 6*s.* 10*d.*, now worth 106*l.* 8*s.* 4*d.* ; granted, 5 James I., to Roger Aston.

At ROWHEING, or ROWNAY. A Benedictine Nunnery, founded, 10 Henry II., by Conan, Duke of Britain; valued, at the dissolution, 13*l.* 10*s.* 9*d.*, now worth 270*l.* 15*s.*

At SOPEWELL. A Benedictine Nunnery, built by Jeffrey, sixteenth Abbot of St. Alban ; yearly revenues 68*l.* 8*s.*, now worth 1,368*l.* ; granted, 30 Henry VIII., to Sir Richard Lee.

At STANDON. An Hospital of Knights Hospitalers, endowed with 140 acres of lands, by Richard de Clare, before 1180; granted, 36 Hen. VIII., to Sir Ralph Sadler.

At WARE. An Alien Priory, endowed by

Hugo de Grentemaisnil, before 1081; granted by Henry VIII.

At WYMONDESLEY PARVA. An Augustine Hospital, built in the time of Henry III., by Richard Argentein; yearly value 37*l.* 10*s.* 6½*d.*, now worth 750*l.* 10*s.* 10*d.*; granted, 29 Henry VIII., to James Nedeham, surveyor of the king's works.

HUNTINGDON (COUNTY).

At HINCHINGBROOKE, near Huntingdon. A Benedictine Nunnery, founded by King William the Conqueror; value yearly 19*l.* 9*s.* 2*d.*, now worth 389*l.* 3*s.* 4*d.*; granted, 29 Henry VIII., to Sir Richard Cromwell, alias Williams.

At HUNTINGDON. An Augustine Monastery, founded, outside the town, by Eustace de Luvetot, in the time of King Stephen; yearly value 232*l.* 7*s.*, now worth 4,647*l.*; granted, 33 Hen. VIII., to Sir Richard Cromwell, alias Williams.

At ST. IVES, *olim* Slepe. A Benedictine Cell, founded, by Ednoth, Abbot of Ramsey, in honour of St. Ivo, whose relics were found here in the year 1001; granted, 36 Henry VIII., to Sir Thomas Audley.

At ST. NOET'S. A Benedictine Priory, founded by Noet, but was destroyed in the subsequent wars, and restored in the year 1113;

yearly value 256*l.* 13*s.,* now worth 5,125*l.* 5*s.;* granted, 33 Hen. VIII., to Sir Richard Cromwell, alias Williams.

At RAMSEY. A Benedictine Abbey, founded, 969, by Ailwine, Earl of East Angles; yearly value 983*l.* 15*s.* 3¼*d.,* now worth 19,675*l.* 5*s.* 10*d.;* granted, 31 Henry VIII., to Sir Richard Cromwell, alias Williams.

At SALTREY. A Cistercian Abbey, founded, 1146, by Simon, Earl of Northampton; yearly value 199*l.* 11*s.* 8*d.,* now worth 3,991*l.* 13*s.* 4*d.;* granted, 29 Henry VIII., to Sir Richard Cromwell, alias Williams.

At STONELEY. An Augustine Priory, founded 1180, by William Mandeville; yearly value 62*l.* 12*s.* 3½*d.,* now worth 1,252*l.* 5*s.* 10*d.;* granted, 36 Henry VIII., to Oliver Leder.

KENT (COUNTY).

At AYLESFORD. A Carmelite Friary, founded, 1240, by Richard Lord Grey; granted, 33 Hen. VIII., to Sir Thomas Wyat.

At BILSINGTON. An Augustine Priory, founded, 1253, by John Mansell; valued yearly 81*l.* 1*s.* 6*d.,* now worth 1,621*l.* 10*s.;* granted, 30 Hen. VIII., to the Archbishop of Canterbury.

At BOXLEY. A Cistercian Abbey, founded, 1146, by William de Ipre, Earl of Kent, who afterwards became a Monk himself, at Laon in France; valued at 218*l.* 19*s.* 10*d.*, now worth 4,379*l.* 18*s.* 4*d.*; granted, 32 Henry VIII., to Sir Thomas Wyat.

At BRADGARE. A College, founded, 16 Rich. II., by Mr. Robert, pastor of the town, and seven gentlemen; granted, 29 Henry VIII., to the Archbishop of Canterbury.

At BRADSOLE, near Dover. A Premonstratensian Abbey, founded, 1191, by King Richard I.; yearly value 142*l.* 8*s.* 9*d.*, now worth 2,848*l.* 15*s.*; granted, by Henry VIII., to the Archbishop of Canterbury.

At BURNE, or PATRICKSBURN. An Alien Priory, founded, 1200; granted, 4 Edward VI., to Sir Thomas Cheiney.

At CANTERBURY. A Cathedral Church, and Benedictine Priory, founded, by King Ethelbert, on his conversion to Christianity, in the year 600. The Cathedral was built by Lanfranc, in the year 1080. Besides the great offerings at Thomas à Becket's shrine, the yearly revenues, at the dissolution, made 2,489*l.* 4*s.* 9*d.*, now worth 49,784*l.* 16*s.*

St. Augustine's Monastery, founded, by the same Convert, Ethelbert, King of Kent, by the advice of St. Augustine, who was buried here. The yearly revenues 1,274*l.* 0*s.* 10½*d.*, are now worth 29,480*l.* 17*s.* 6*d.*

St. Gregory's Hospital, founded, in the year 1084, by Archbishop Lanfranc ; yearly revenues 166*l.* 4*s.* 5½*d.*, now worth 3,328*l.* 9*s.* 2*d.* ; granted, 28 Henry VIII., to the Archbishop of Canterbury.

St. Sepulchre's Nunnery, founded, 1100, by Archbishop Anselm, in the south east of the city ; revenues 38*l.* 19*s.* 7½*d.*, now worth 779*l.* 12*s.* 6*d.* ; granted, 38 Henry VIII., to James Hale.

Eastbridge Hospital, founded, as some say, by Lanfranc ; or, as others think, by St. Thomas the Martyr, for the entertainment of pilgrims ; yearly value 23*l.* 18*s.* 9½*d.*, now worth 478*l.* 15*s.* 10*d.*

St. Laurence's Hospital, founded, south east of this town, in the year 1137, by Hugh, the Abbot of St. Augustine's ; yearly revenues 31*l.* 10*s.* 7*d.*, now worth 630*l.* 11*s.* 8*d.* ; granted to Sir John Parrot.

St. Margaret's Hospital, founded, 1243, by Simon de Langton, Archdeacon of Canterbury, for poor infirm priests ; yearly value 10*l.* 13*s.* 8*d.*, now worth 213*l.* 13*s.* 4*d.*; granted, 13 Elizabeth, to the Mayor, &c., and is now a Bridewell.

An Augustine Friary, founded, in the reign of Edward I., by Richard French, baker ; granted, 33 Henry VIII., to G. Harper.

A Dominican Friary, founded, about 1221, by King Henry III.; granted, 2 Elizabeth, to Thomas Wiseman, and then to John Harrington.

A Franciscan Monastery, founded, 1270, by John Diggs, an Alderman of the city; granted, 31 Henry VIII., to Thomas Spilman.

At CUMBWELL, in the Parish of Goudhurst. An Augustine Priory, founded, by Robert de Turneham, in the reign of Henry II.; yearly value, 80*l*. 17*s*. 6½*d*., now worth 1,617*l*. 10*s*. 10*d*.; granted, 29 Henry VIII., to Thomas Culpepper, and, 34 Henry VIII., to Sir John Gage.

At DAVINGTON. A Benedictine Nunnery, founded, 1153, by Fulk de Newenham; yearly value 21*l*. 13*s*. 10*d*., now worth 433*l*. 8*s*. 4*d*.; granted, 38 Henry VIII., to Sir Thomas Cheiney.

At DARTFORD. An Augustine Nunnery, founded, 1355, by King Edward III.; value, at the dissolution, 408*l*., now worth 8,160*l*.; granted, 36 Henry VIII., to Edm. Mervyn, and finally became the property of the Earl of Salisbury.

At DOVER. A Benedictine Priory, founded, 640, within the Castle, by King Eadbald, removed down into the town, 696; yearly value 232*l*. 1*s*. 5½*d*., now worth 4,641*l*. 9*s*. 2*d*.

At GREENWICH. A Dominican Friary, founded, 1376, by King Edward III. and Sir John Norbury. The religious were restored by Queen Mary twenty years after they were expelled by her father, but were finally expelled by Elizabeth.

At HARBALDOWN. An Hospital, founded, about a mile from the west gate of Canterbury, for the poor, by Bishop Lanfranc; yearly value 109*l.* 7*s.* 2*d.*, now worth 2,187*l.* 3*s.* 4*d.*; suppressed in the reign of Edward VI.

At MONK's HORTON. A Cluniac Cell, founded, in the reign of Henry II., by Robert de Vere; yearly value 111*l.* 16*s.* 11½*d.*, now worth 2,236*l.* 19*s.* 2*d.*; granted, 30 Henry VIII., to Richard Tate, and after to —— Mantell.

At WEST LANGDON. A Premonstratensian Abbey, founded, 1192, by William de Auberville; yearly value 56*l.* 6*s.* 9*d.*. now worth 1,126*l.* 15*s.*; granted, 30 Henry VIII., to the Archbishop of Canterbury.

At LEEDES. An Augustine Priory, built, 1119, by Robert Crocheart, Knight; yearly value 362*l.* 7*s.* 7*d.*, now worth 7,247*l.* 11*s.* 8*d.*; granted, 4 Edward VI., to Sir Anthony St. Leger.

At LILLECHURCH, or HEYHAM. A Benedictine Nunnery, founded, 1151, by King Stephen; granted by Henry VIII., to Cambridge College.

At MAIDSTONE. A College, or Hospital, founded, 1260, by Boniface, Archbishop of Canterbury; valuation 159*l.* 7*s.* 10*d.* yearly, now worth 3,187*l.* 18*s.* 4*d.*; granted, 3 Edw. VI., to Lord Cobham.

At MALLING. A Benedictine Nunnery, founded, in the reign of William Rufus, by Gundulf, bishop of Rochester; yearly value 245*l.* 10*s.* 2$\frac{1}{2}$*d.*, now worth 4,910*l.* 4*s.* 2*d.*; granted, 12 Elizabeth, to Henry Cobham, alias Brook.

At MELTON. An Hospital, granted to Sir Henry Wyat.

At MUTTIDEN. A Friary, founded, 1224, by Sir Michael de Ponynges; yearly value 30*l.* 13*s.* 0$\frac{1}{2}$*d.*, now worth 613*l.* 0*s.* 10*d.*; granted, 30 Henry VIII., to Sir Anthony Aucher.

At OSPRINGE. An Hospital, founded, 1235, by King Henry III.; granted by Henry VIII.

At WEST PECKHAM. An Hospital of Hospitalers; yearly value 63*l.* 6*s.* 8*d.*, now worth 1,266*l.* 13*s.* 4*d.*; granted, 35 Henry VIII., to Sir Robert Southwell.

At PUCKESHALL. An Hospital, granted by King Henry VIII., to Lynch, his Physician; granted to Sir John Parrot.

At ROCHESTER. A Cathedral and Benedictine

Priory, founded, in the year 600, by King Ethelbert; yearly value 486*l.* 11*s.* 5*d.*, now worth 9,731*l.* 8*s.* 4*d.*

At SEVENOAKS. Two Hospitals, one founded in the year 1418, for twenty men and women, by William Sevenoke; another in the gift of the Archbishop of Canterbury; both granted, 31 Henry VIII., to Archbishop Cranmer.

At SHEPEY. A Benedictine Nunnery, founded, in the year 675, by Sexburg, widow of Ercombert, King of Kent; yearly value 122*l.* 14*s.* 6½*d.*, now worth 2,454*l.* 10*s.* 10*d.*; granted, 29 Henry VIII., to Sir Thomas Cheiney.

At NEWWORK, near Rochester. An Hospital, founded, in the year 1194, by Bishop Glanville of Rochester, for the reception of poor travellers, and other indigent persons; granted, 33 Henry VIII.

At SWINGFIELD, near Dover. An Hospital of Sister Hospitalers, founded, in the year 1190, by Sir Robert de Clotingham, Arnulf Cade, and others; yearly value 88*l.* 3*s.* 3½*d.*, now worth 1,763*l.* 5*s.* 10*d.*; granted, 33 Hen. VIII., to Sir Thomas Aucher.

At TANINGTON. An Hospital, founded, in the reign of Henry II.; yearly value 33*l.* 11*s.* 1*d.*, now worth 671*l.* 1*s.* 8*d.*; granted, 5 Edw. VI., to Robert Dartnall.

At THURLEGH. An Alien Priory, bestowed, 22 Henry II., to the Abbey of St. Bertin at St. Omers.

At WENGHAM. A College, founded, in the year 1286, by John Peckham, Archbishop of Canterbury; yearly revenues 33*l.* 6*s.* 8*d.*, now worth 666*l.* 13*s.* 4*d.*; granted, 7 Edward VI., to Sir Thomas Palmer.

At WESTWOOD. An Augustine Priory, founded, in the year 1178, by Richard de Lucy, Viceroy here from the King, who was absent in France; next year he quitted his great palaces, took the religious habit, and died in this house; yearly revenues 186*l.* 9*s.*, now worth 7,329*l.*; granted, 28 Henry VIII., to Sir Ralph Sadler.

At WYE. A College, founded, in the year 1431, by John Kempt, Archbishop of York; yearly value 93*l.* 2*s.* 0½*d.*, now worth 1,862*l.* 0*s.* 10*d.*; granted, 36 Henry VIII., to Walter Buckler.

LANCASTER (COUNTY).

At BURSCOUGH. An Augustine Priory, founded, in the reign of Richard I., by Robert Fitz Henry, Lord of Latham; yearly value 129*l.* 1*s.* 10*d.*, now worth 2,581*l.* 16*s.* 8*d.*

LANCASTER.

At COCKERSAND. A Premonstratensian Abbey, founded, in the reign of Henry II., by William Lancastre; yearly value 282*l.* 7*s.* 7½*d.*, now worth 5,647*l.* 12*s.* 6*d.*; granted, 35 Henry VIII., to John Kechin.

At CONISHEVED. An Augustine Priory, founded, in the reign of Henry II., by Gabriel Pennington; yearly value 124*l.* 2*s.* 1*d.*, now worth 2,482*l.* 1*s.* 8*d.*

At FURNES. A Cistercian Abbey, founded, in the year 1127; yearly value 966*l.* 7*s.* 10*d.*, now worth 19,327*l.* 16*s.* 8*d.*

At HOLAND. A Benedictine Priory, founded, in the year 1319, by Walter, Bishop of Litchfield; yearly value 78*l.* 12*s.*, now worth 1,572*l.*; granted, 37 Henry VIII., to John Holcroft.

At HORNEBY. A Premonstratensian Abbey, founded, by the ancestors of Sir Thomas Stanley; valuation 26*l.* yearly, now worth 520*l.*; granted, 36 Henry VIII., to Lord Monteagle.

At KERSHALL. A Cluniac Cell, bestowed by Henry II. to the monastery of Lenton, Nottinghamshire; granted, 32 Henry VIII., to Baldwin Willoughby.

At KERTMEL. An Augustine Priory, founded, in the year 1188, by William Mareschall, Earl of Pembroke; yearly value 212*l.* 11*s.* 10*d.*;

now worth 4,251*l*. 16*s*. 8*d*. ; granted, 32 Henry VIII., to John Holcroft.

At LANCASTER. An Alien Priory, founded, in the year 1094, by Earl Roger of Poictiers; yearly value 90*l*., now worth 1,600*l*.

A Dominican Friary, founded 44 Henry III., by Sir Hugh Harrington; granted, 3 Henry VIII., to John Holcroft.

At LYTHOM. A Benedictine Cell, founded, by Richard Fitz Rogers, in the reign of Richard I.; yearly value 53*l*. 15*s*. 10*d*. ; now worth 1,075*l*. 16*s*. 8*d*. ; granted to Sir Thomas Holcroft.

At MANCHESTER. A College, founded, 9 Hen. V., by Thomas de la Ware, Pastor of the town ; yearly value 213*l*. 10*s*. 11*d*., now worth 4,270*l*. 18*s*. 4*d*.

At PENWORTHAM. A Benedictine Priory, founded, in the reign of William the Conqueror, by the bounty of Warine Bussel ; yearly value 114*l*. 16*s*. 9*d*., now worth 2,296*l*. 15*s*. ; granted, 34 Henry VIII., to John Fleetwood.

At PRESTON. A Friary, founded, on the north-west of this town, by Edmond, Earl of Lancaster, son of Henry III. ; granted, 32 Henry VIII., to Thomas Holcroft.

At WARRINGTON. An Augustine Friary, built

at the end of the bridge, in the year 1379 ; granted, 32 Henry VIII., to Thomas Holcroft.

At WHALLEY. A Cistercian Abbey, founded, in the year 1296 ; valued at 551*l.* 4*s.* 6*d.* yearly, now worth 11,024*l.* 10*s.*; granted, 7 Edward VI., to Richard Aston and John Braddyll.

LEICESTER (COUNTY).

At BELTON. An Augustine Nunnery, founded, in the reign of Henry III., by Rosia de Verdon ; yearly value 101*l.* 8*s.* 2½*d.*, now worth 2,028*l.* 4*s.* 2*d.* ; granted, 30 Henry VIII., to Humphrey Foster.

At BRADDLEY. An Augustine Priory, founded, in the time of King John, by Robert Bundy ; valued at 20*l.* 15*s.* 7*d.* yearly, now worth 415*l.* 11*s.* 8*d.*; granted, 29 Henry VIII., to Thomas Newell, Esq.

At BREDON. An Augustine Cell, founded, in the year 1144, by Robert Ferrers, Earl Nottingham ; valued at 25*l.* 8*s.* 1*d.* yearly, now worth 508*l.* 1*s.* 8*d.*; granted, 7 Edward VI., to John, Lord Grey.

At BURTON LAZARS. An Hospital, founded, in the time of King Stephen, by Roger de Moubray; valued at 265*l*. 10*s*. 2½*d* yearly, now worth 5,310*l*. 4*s*. 2*d*.; granted, 36 Henry VIII., to John Dudley, Lord Lisle.

At CHORLEY and ULVESCROFT. An Augustine Priory, founded, in the time of Henry II., by Blanchmain's, Earl of Leicester; valued at 101*l*. 3*s*. 10½*d*. yearly, now worth 2,023*l*. 17*s*. 6*d*.; granted to Frideswide, widow.

At CROXTON. A Premonstratensian Abbey, founded, in the year 1162, by William Porcarius; valuation, at the suppression, 458*l*. 19*s*. 1½*d*. yearly, now worth 9,179*l*. 19*s*. 2*d*.; granted, 30 Henry VIII., to Thomas, Earl of Rutland.

At DALBY. An Hospital of Knights Templars, founded, it is thought, by Robert Bossu, Earl of Leicester, in the reign of Henry III.; yearly value 103*l*. 16*s*. 7½*d*., now worth 2,076*l*. 12*s*. 6*d*.; granted, 35 Henry VIII., to Sir Andrew Nowell.

At CASTLE DONINGTON. An Hospital, founded, in the reign of Henry II., or sooner, by John Lacy, Constable of Chester; yearly value 5*l*. 13*s*. 4*d*., now worth 113*l*. 6*s*. 8*d*.

At GERONDON. A Cistercian Abbey, founded, in the year 1133, by Robert Bossu, Earl of Leicester; yearly value 186*l*. 15*s*. 2½*d*., now worth 3,735*l*. 4*s*. 2*d*.; granted, 32 Henry VIII., to Thomas, Earl of Rutland.

At HETHER. An Hospital of Knights Hospitallers, founded, in the reign of King John; yearly value 39*l*. 1*s*. 5*d*., now worth 781*l*. 8*s*. 4*d*.

At HINKLEY. An Alien Priory, founded, in the year 1173, by Robert Blanchmaines, Earl of Leicester; granted, 34 Henry VIII., to the Dean and Chapter of Westminster.

At KERKBEY ON THE WRETHEK. An Augustine Priory, founded, 9 Edward II., by Roger Beller; yearly value 178*l*. 7*s*. 10½*d*., now worth 3,567*l*. 17*s*. 6*d*. ; granted, 35 Henry VIII., to Charles Blount, Lord Mountjoy.

At LANDA. An Augustine Priory, founded, in the reign of Henry I., by Richard Basset and Maud his wife ; yearly value 510*l*. 16*s*. 5½*d*., now worth 10,216*l*. 9*s*. 2*d*.; granted, 31 Henry VIII., to Thomas, Lord Cromwell.

At LANGLEY. A Benedictine Nunnery, founded, in the reign of Henry II., by William Pontulf; yearly value 32*l*. 6*s*. 2*d*., now worth 646*l*. 3*s*. 4*d*.; granted, 35 Henry VIII., to Thomas Grey.

At LEICESTER. An Augustine Monastery, founded near the town, in the year 1143, by Robert Bossu, Earl of Leicester; yearly value 1,062*l*. 0*s*. 4½*d*., now worth 21,240*l*. 7*s*. 6*d*.; granted, 4 Edward VI., to William, Marquis of Northampton.

The College of St. Mary the Less, founded, in the year 1107, by Robert, Earl of Mallent and Leicester; yearly value 23*l.* 12*s.* 11*d.*; now worth 472*l.* 18*s.* 4*d.*

The College of St. Mary the Greater, founded, in the year 1330, by Henry Earl of Leicester; yearly value 595*l.* 7*s.* 4*d.*, now worth 11,907*l.* 6*s.* 8*d.*; granted, 2 Edward VI., to John Beaumont and William Guyse.

St. John's Hospital, founded, prior to 1235, which was converted into a gaol, 31 Elizabeth.

An Augustine Friary, granted to John Bellew and John Broxholm.

A Dominican Friary, founded, in the reign of Henry III., by the Earl of Leicester; granted, 38 Henry VIII., to Henry, Marquis of Dorset.

A Franciscan Friary, founded, in the year 1265, by Simon de Montfort, Earl of Leicester; granted 37 Henry VIII., to John Bellow and John Broxholm.

At LUTTERWORTH. An Hospital, founded, in the reign of King John, by Roise de Verdon and her son; yearly value 26*l.* 9*s.* 5*d.*, now worth 529*l.* 8*s.* 4*d.*

At MELTON MOUBRAY. A Cluniac Cell, subject to the Monastery of Lewes in Sussex;

granted, 29 Henry VIII., to Thomas, Lord Cromwell.

At MOUSELEY. A College, founded, 2 Edward I., by Sir Anketine de Martival; yearly value 87*l.* now worth 340*l.*

At OSULVESTON. An Augustine Priory, founded, in the reign of Henry II., by Sir Robert Grimbald; yearly value 173*l.* 18*s.* 9*d.*, now worth 3,478*l.* 15*s.*; granted, 30 Henry VIII., to Sir John Harrington.

At ROTHELEY. An Hospital of Knights Templars, endowed by Henry III.; yearly value 231*l.* 7*s.* 10*d.*, now worth 4,627*l.* 16*s.* 8*d.*; granted, 35 Henry VIII., to Henry Cartwright.

LINCOLN (COUNTY).

At ALVINGHAM. A Gilbertine Priory, founded, in the reign of King Stephen, by Robert Cheiney, Bishop of Lincoln; yearly value 141*l.* 15*s.*, now worth 2,835*l.*; granted, 5 Edward VI., to Edward, Lord Clinton.

At ASLAKEBY. An Hospital of Templars, founded, in the reign of Richard I., by John le Mareschal; granted, 35 Henry VIII., to Edward, Lord Clinton.

LINCOLN.

At BARDNEY. A Benedictine Abbey, founded, about the year 697, by the bounty of Ethelred, King of Mercia, who resigned his crown and became a Monk here, and afterwards an Abbot, until his death ; valuation 429*l.* 7*s.*, now worth 8,587*l.* ; granted to Sir Robert Tirwhit.

At BARLINGS. A Premonstratensian Abbey, founded, in the year 1154, by Ralph de Haye ; yearly value 307*l.* 16*s.* 6*d.* ; now worth 6,556.*l* 10*s.* 0*d.* ; granted to Charles Duke of Suffolk.

At BELVOIR. A Benedictine Cell, founded, in the reign of William the Conqueror, by Robert de Belvedere ; yearly value 129*l.* 17*s.* 6*d.*, now worth 2,597*l.* 10*s.* 0*d.* ; granted, to Thomas, Earl of Rutland, and to Robert Tirwhit.

At LONG BENYGTON. An Alien Priory, founded, in the year 1175, by Ralph de Filgeries ; granted, 34 Henry VIII.

At BOSTON. An Augustine Friary, founded by King Edward II. ; granted, 37 Henry VIII., to the Mayor and Burgesses of the town.

A Dominican Monastery, founded prior to the year 1288 ; granted, 32 Henry VIII., to Charles, Duke of Suffolk.

A Franciscan Monastery, founded by the

Esterling Merchants, at an early period; granted, 37 Henry VIII., to the Mayor and Burgesses.

A Carmelite Friary, founded, in the year 1300, to the west of the river, by Sir—— Orreby, Knight; granted, 37 Henry VIII., to the Mayor and Burgesses of the town.

At BOURN. An Augustine Priory, founded, in the year 1138, by Baldwin Fil. Gilsberti; yearly value 200*l.*, now worth 4,000*l.*; granted, 30 Henry VIII., to Richard Cotton.

At TEMPLE BRUER. An Hospital of Knights Templars, founded, prior to the year 1185; granted, 33 Henry VIII., to Charles, Duke of Suffolk; yearly value 195*l.* 2*s.* 2½*d.*, now worth 3,902*l.* 4*s.* 2*d.*

At BULLINGTON. A Gilbertine Priory, founded, in the reign of King Stephen, by Simon Fitzwilliam; yearly value 187*l.* 7*s.* 9*d.*, now worth 3,747*l.* 15*s.*; granted, 30 Henry VIII., to Charles Duke of Suffolk.

At BURWELL. An Alien Priory, founded by the Lords of Kyme; granted, 36 Henry VIII., to Charles, Duke of Suffolk.

At CAMERINGHAM. An Alien Priory, founded, in the reign of Henry II., by Richard de Haya and Maud his wife ; granted, 37 Henry VIII., to Robert Tirwhit.

At CATTELEY. A Gilbertine Priory, founded, in the reign of King Stephen, by Peter de Belingey ; yearly value 38*l.* 13*s.* 8*d.*, now worth 773*l.* 13*s.* 4*d.* ; granted, 31 Henry VIII., to Robert Carr of Sleford.

At COTHAM. A Cistercian Nunnery, founded in the reign of Henry I., by Alan Muncel ; yearly value 46*l.* 17*s* 7*d.*, now worth 937*l.* 11*s.* 8*d.* ; granted, 32 Henry VIII., to Edward Shipwith.

At CROWLAND. A Benedictine Abbey, founded, in the year 716, by Ethelbald, King of Merica. After the Religious were murdered, and the Monastery burned, by the Danes, in the year 870, King Edred restored the lands, in the year 948, and rebuilt the house. Yearly value 1,217*l.* 5*s.* 11*d.*, now worth 24, 345*l.* 18*s.* 4*d.* ; granted, 4 Edward VI., to Edward, Lord Clinton.

At DEPING. A Benedictine Cell, founded, in the year 1139, by Baldwin Fil. Gilsberti ; granted, 32 Henry VIII., to the Duke of Norfolk.

At EGLE. An Hospital of Knights Templars, founded by King Stephen ; yearly value 144*l.* 18*s.* 10*d.*, now worth 2,898*l.* 16*s.* 8*d.* ; granted,

33 Henry VIII., to Thomas Earl of Rutland, and
Robert Tirwhit.

At ELLESHAM, or AILESHAM. An Augustine
Priory, founded in the year 1166, by Beatrix de
Amundeville, for several poor brethren ; yearly
value 83*l.* 17*s.* 10*d.*, now worth 1,677*l.* 16*s.*
4*d.* ; granted, 30 Henry VIII., to Charles Duke
of Suffolk.

At the PRIORY IN THE WOOD, near Epp-
worth, in the Isle of Axholm. A Carthusian
Priory, founded, 19 Richard II., by Thomas
Moubray, Earl of Nottingham ; yearly value
290*l.* 11*s.* 7*d.*, now worth 5,811*l.* 12*s.* 6*d.* ;
granted, 32 Henry VIII., to Mr. John Candish.

At FOSSE. A Benedictine Nunnery, founded,
in the reign of John, by the inhabitants of
Torkeysy ; yearly value 8*l.* 5*s.* 4*d.*, now worth
165*l.* 6*s.* 8*d.* ; granted, 5 Edward VI., to Edward,
Lord Clinton.

At GOKWELLE. A Cisterican Nunnery,
founded in the year 1185, by William de Alta
Ripa ; yearly value 19*l.* 18*s.* 6d., now worth
398*l.* 10*s.* ; granted, 30 Henry VIII., to sir William Tirwhit.

At GRANTHAM. A Franciscan Friary, built in
the year 1290; granted, 33 Henry VIII., to
Robert Bocher, and David Vincent.

At GREENFIELD. A Cistercian Nunnery, founded, in the year 1153, by Eudo de Greinesby, and Ralph his Son ; yearly value 79*l*. 15*s*. 1*d*., now worth 1,595*l*. 1*s*. 8*d*. ; granted, 12 Elizabeth, to Sir Henry Stanley and Lord Strange.

At GRIMESBY. A Benedictine Nunnery, founded before the year 1185 ; yearly value 12*l*. 3*s*. 7*d*., now worth 243*l*. 11*s*. 8*d*. ; granted 34 Henry VIII.

An Augustine Friary, founded prior to the year 1304 ; granted, 34 Henry VIII., to Augustine Porter and John Bellew.

A Franciscan Friary, founded, in the reign of Edward II. ; granted, 38 Henry VIII., to John Bellew and Robert Brokesby.

At HAGH. An Alien Priory, founded, in the year 1164, by Henry II. ; granted, 33 Henry VIII., to John, Lord Russell.

At HAGHAM. An Alien Priory, founded, by Hugh Earl of Chester ; granted, 37 Henry VIII., to John Bellew and J. Broxholm.

At HAGNEBY. A Premonstratensian Abbey, founded, in the year 1175, by Herbert de Orreby, and Lady Agnes, his wife ; yearly value

98*l.* 7*s.* 4*d.*; now worth 1,967*l.* 6*s.* 8*d.* ; granted, 30 Henry VIII., to John Freeman, of London.

At HAVERHOLM. A Gilbertine Priory, founded, in the year 1137, by the Bishop of Lincoln, Alexander ; yearly value 88*l.* 5*s.* 5*d.*, now worth 1,765*l.* 8*s.* 4*d.* ; granted, 30 Henry VIII., to Lord Clinton.

At HEYNINGES. A Cistercian Nunnery, founded, in the year 1180, by Reyner Evermere ; yearly value 58*l.* 13*s.* 4*d.*, now worth 1,173*l.* 6*s.* 8*d.* ; granted, 31 Henry VIII., to Sir Thomas Heneage.

At HOLLANDBRIDGE. A Gilbertine Priory, founded, in the reign of King John, by Godwin, a citizen of Lincoln ; yearly value 5*l.* 1*s.* 11*d.*, now worth 101*l.* 18*s.* 4*d.* ; granted, 33 Henry VIII., to Edward, Lord Clinton.

At HUMBERSTEYN. A Benedictine Monastery, founded, in the reign of Henry II., by William Hermeri ; yearly value 42*l.* 11*s.* 3*d.*, now worth 851*l.* 5*s.* ; granted, 5 Edward VI., to John Cheke, Esq.

At HYRST. An Augustine Cell, founded, in the reign of Henry I., by Nigel de Albini ; yearly value 7*l.* 11*s.* 8*d.*, now worth 151*l.* 13*s.* 4*d.* ; granted, 1 Edward VI., to John, Earl of Warwick.

LINCOLN.

At IRFORD. A Premonstratensian Nunnery, founded, in the reign of Henry II., by Ralph de Albini; yearly value 14*l.* 13*s.* 4*d.*; now worth 293*l.* 6*s.* 8*d.*; granted, 31 Henry VIII., to Robert Tirwhit.

At KIRKSTED. A Cistercian Abbey, founded, in the year 1139, by Hugh Britto; yearly value 338*l.* 13*s.* 11½*d.*, now worth 6,673*l.* 19*s.* 2*d.*; granted, 30 Henry VIII., to Charles, Duke of Suffolk.

At KYME. An Augustine Priory, founded, in the reign of Henry II., by Philip de Kyme; yearly value 138*l.* 9*s.* 4*d.*, now worth 2,769*l.* 6*s.* 8*d.*; granted, 33 Henry VIII., to Thomas, Earl of Rutland and Robert Tirwhit.

At LEKEBURN. A Cistercian Nunnery, founded, in the year 1150, by Robert Fitz Gilbert; yearly value 57*l.* 13*s.* 5½*d.*, now worth 1,153*l.* 9*s.* 2*d.*; granted, 32 Henry VIII., to Thomas Heneage.

At LEMBURGH MAGNA. An Alien Priory, founded, in the reign of Henry II., by Richard de Humet; granted, 36 Henry VIII., to John Bellew and others.

At LINCOLN. A Cathedral, founded, in the reign of William the Conqueror, by Remigius, Bishop of Dorchester; the Bishop's revenue,

1,962*l.* 17*s.* 4½*d.* ; the Chapter's, 575*l.* 8*s.* 2*d.* ; both sums would make now 50,765*l.* 10*s.* 10*d.*

A Gilbertine Priory, in the south-west suburbs; yearly value 270*l.* 1*s.* 3*d.,* now worth 5,401*l.* 5*s.*; granted, 30 Henry VIII., to Charles, Duke of Suffolk.

A Benedictine Cell, founded by Hen. II.; yearly value 26*l.* 1*s.* 3*d.,* now worth 521*l.* 5*s.* ; granted, 37 Henry VIII., to John Bellew and John Broxholm.

The Holy Innocent's Hospital, founded, by Remigius, Bishop of Lincoln, for leprous persons; granted, 7 Edward VI., to Sir William Cecil.

An Augustine Monastery, founded, prior to the year 1291, on the south side of the city; granted, 37 Henry VIII., to John Bellew and John Broxholm.

A Dominican Friary, in the east of the city; granted, 37 Henry VIII., to John Bellew and John Broxholm.

A Franciscan Friary, founded, in the year 1230, by William de Beningworth; granted, 36 Henry VIII., to J. Pope.

The White Friary, in High-street, founded by Odo of Kilkenny, Ireland, in the year 1269; granted, 36 Henry VIII., to John Broxholm.

At LOUTH PARK. A Cistercian Abbey, founded, in the year 1139, by Alexander, Bishop of Lincoln; yearly value 169*l.* 5*s.* 6½*d.*, now worth 3,385*l.* 10*s.* 10*d.*; granted, 12 Elizabeth, to Sir Henry Stanley.

At Markeby. An Augustine Priory, founded, in the reign of John, by Ralph Fitz Gilbert; yearly value 163*l.* 17*s.* 6*d.*, now worth 3,277*l.* 10*s.*; granted, 30 Henry VIII., to Charles, Duke of Suffolk.

At Minting. An Alien Priory, founded, in the year 1129, by Ranulph de Meschines; granted 34 Henry VIII.

At Neubo. A Premonstratensian Abbey, founded, in the year 1198, by Richard de Malebisse: yearly value 115*l.* 11*s.* 8*d.*, now worth 2,211*l.* 13*s.* 4*d.*; granted, 29 Henry VIII., to Sir John Markam.

At Neus, or Newhouse. A Premonstratensian Abbey, founded, in the year 1143, by Peter de Gousel; yearly value 114*l.* 1*s.* 4½*d.*, now worth 2,281*l.* 7*s.* 6*d.*; granted, 30 Hen. VIII., to Charles, Duke of Suffolk.

At Newstede on Alcolm. A Gilbertine Priory, granted, within the bounds of Cadney, by Henry II.; yearly value 55*l.* 1*s.* 8*d.*, now worth 1,101*l.* 13*s.* 4*d.*; granted, 31 Hen. VIII., to Robert Heneage.

At NEWSTEDE. An Augustine Priory, founded, in the reign of Henry III., by William de Albini; yearly value 42*l*. 1*s*. 3*d*., now worth 841*l*. 5*s*.; granted, 31 Henry VIII., to Richard Manners.

At NOCTON. An Augustine Priory, founded, in the reign of King Stephen, by Rob. D'Arcey; yearly value 52*l*. 19*s*. 2½*d*., now worth 1,059*l*. 4*s*. 2*d*.; granted, 30 Henry VIII., to Charles, Duke of Suffolk; and 12 Elizabeth, to Sir John Stanley.

At NORTHOMERSBY. A Gilbertine Priory, founded, in the reign of King Stephen, by William, Earl of Albemarle; yearly value 98*l*., now worth 1,960*l*.; granted, 31 Henry VIII., to Robert Heneage.

At REVESBY. A Cistercian Monastery, founded, in the year 1142, by William, Earl of Lincoln; valued at 349*l*. 4*s*. 10*d*. yearly, now worth 6,988*l*. 18*s*. 4*d*.; granted, 30 Henry VIII., to Charles, Duke of Suffolk.

At SEMPRINGHAM. A Gilbertine Priory, founded, in the year 1139, by Sir Gilbert, of Sempringham; valued at 359*l*. 12*s*. 7*d*. yearly, now worth 7,192*l*. 11*s*. 8*d*.; granted, 30 Henry VIII., to Edward, Lord Clinton.

At SIXHILL. A Gilbertine Priory, founded, by —— Grelle; valued at 170*l*. 8*s*. 9*d*. yearly,

now worth 3,408*l*. 15*s*.; granted, 30 Hen. VIII.,
to Thomas Heneage.

At Skirbeke. An Hospital, founded for ten
poor persons, in the year 1130, by Sir John
Multon ; the Knights Hospitalers settled there ;
granted, 33 Henry VIII., to Charles, Duke of
Suffolk.

At Spalding. A Benedictine Monastery,
founded, by Thorold de Buckenhale, in the
year 1052; valued at 878*l*. 18*s*. 3*d*. yearly, now
worth 17,578*l*. 5*s*.; granted, 3 Edward VI., to
Sir John Cheke.

At Spillesbey. A College, founded, 12 Edward III., by Sir John Willoghby; granted,
4 Edward VI., to the Duchess of Suffolk.

At Stanfeld. A Benedictine Nunnery,
founded, in the reign of Henry II., by Henry
Percy ; valued at 112*l*. 5*s*. yearly, now worth
2,245*l*.; granted, 29 Henry VIII., to Robert
Tirwhit.

At Stanford. A Benedictine Cell, or Nunnery, founded, in the reign of Henry II., by
William, Abbot of Peterburgh ; valued at 78*l*.
18*s*. 10½*d*. yearly, now worth 1,578*l*. 17*s*. 6*d*.;
granted, 32 Henry VIII., to Richard Cecil.

Benedictine Cell, dedicated to St. Leonard ; valued at 37*l*. 17*s*. yearly, now worth

757*l.* ; granted, 5 Edward VI., to Sir William Cecil ; it is now a farm-house belonging to the Earl of Exeter, under the name of St. Cuthbert's fee.

Augustine Friary, in the west of the town, founded, before the year 1340, by the Archdeacon of Richmond ; granted, 6 Edward VI., to Edward, Lord Clinton.

Dominican Friary, founded on the east of the town, before the year 1240 ; granted, 33 Henry VIII., to Robert Bocher and David Vincent.

Franciscan Convent, founded, 48 Edward III. ; granted, 32 Henry VIII., to Charles, Duke of Suffolk.

At STYKESWOLD. A Cistercian Nunnery, founded, in the reign of King Stephen, by the Countess Lucy ; valued at 163*l.* 1*s.* 2½*d.* yearly, now worth 3,261*l.* 4*s.* 2*d.* ; granted, 32 Henry VIII., to Robert Dighton.

At SWINSHED. A Cistercian Monastery, founded, in the year 1134, by Robert de Griesley ; valued at 175*l.* 19*s.* 10*d.* yearly, now worth 3,519*l.* 16*s.* 8*d.*; granted, 6 Edward VI., to Edward, Lord Clinton.

At TATESHALE. A College, founded, 17 Hen. VI., by Sir Ralph Cromwell ; valued at 348*l.* 5*s.* 11*d.* yearly, now worth 6,965*l.* 18*s.* 4*d.* ;

granted, 36 Henry VIII., to Charles, Duke of Suffolk.

At THORNETON UPON THE HUMBER. An Augustine Priory, founded, in the year 1139, by William, Earl of Albemarle; valued at 730*l.* 17*s.* 2½*d.* yearly, now worth 14,617*l.* 4*s.* 2*d.*; granted, 1 Edward VI., to the Bishop of Lincoln.

At THORNHOLM. An Augustine Priory, founded by King Stephen; valued at 155*l.* 19*s.* 6*d.* yearly, now worth 3,119*l.* 10*s.*; granted, 30 Henry VIII., to Charles, Duke of Suffolk.

At TORKESEY. An Augustine Priory, built by King John; valued at 27*l.* 2*s.* 8*d.* yearly, now worth 542*l.* 13*s.* 4*d.*; granted, 35 Henry VIII., to Sir Philip Hoby.

At TUPHOLM. A Premonstratensian Monastery, founded, in the reign of Henry II., by Alan de Nevill and Gilbert his brother; valued at 119*l.* 2*s.* 8*d.* yearly, now worth 2,382*l.* 13*s.* 4*d.*; granted, 30 Henry VIII., to Sir Thomas Heneage.

At VAUDEY. A Cistercian Monastery, founded, in the year 1147, by William, Earl of Albemarle; valued at 177*l.* 15*s.* 7½*d.* yearly, now worth 3,555*l.* 12*s.* 6*d.*; granted, 30 Hen. VIII., to Charles, Duke of Suffolk.

At WELLOW. An Augustine Priory, founded,

by King Henry I.; valued at 152*l*. 7*s*. 4*d*. yearly, now worth 3,047*l*. 6*s*. 8*d*.; granted, 36 Henry VIII., to Sir Thomas Heneage.

At WILLESFORD. An Alien Priory, founded, in the reign of King Stephen, by Hugh de Evermue; granted, 30 Henry VIII., to Charles, Duke of Suffolk.

At WILEKETONE. An Hospitaler's House, founded, in the reign of King Stephen, by Roger de Buslei; valued at 174*l*. 11*s*. 1½*d*. yearly, now worth 3,491*l*. 2*s*. 6*d*.; granted, 37 Henry VIII., to John Cock and John Thurgood.

At WITHAM. A Templar's Hospital, founded, in the year 1164, by Hubert de Ria and Margaret de Perci; granted, 5 Elizabeth, to Stephen Holford.

MIDDLESEX (COUNTY).

At HERMONDESWORTH. An Alien Priory; granted, 1 Edward VI., to Sir William Paget.

At HOUNSLOW. A Trinitarian Friary, founded, for the redemption of captives, 3 Edward I.; valued at 80*l*. 15*s*. 0½*d*. yearly, now worth 1,615*l*. 0*s*. 10*d*.; granted to William, Lord Windsor.

At KYLBURN. A Benedictine Nunnery, founded, in the reign of Henry I., by the Convent of Westminster; valued at 121*l*. 16*s*. yearly, now worth 2,436*l*.; granted, 1 Edward VI., to John, Earl of Warwick.

In LONDON. St. Paul's Cathedral, founded, in the year 604, by Bishop Mellitus: rebuilt, 961, by Ælfstan; burnt, 1666; rebuilt, 1675; yearly revenues, 1,855*l*. 15*s*. 11½*d*., now worth 17,115*l*. 19*s*. 2*d*.

St. Bartholomew's Priory, founded, in the year 1123, by Rayere; valued at 757*l*. 8*s*. 4½*d*. yearly; now worth 15,148*l*. 7*s*. 6*d*.; granted, 1 Elizabeth, to Lord Rich.

Charter-House, founded, in the year 1349, by Sir Walter de Manny, without West Smithfield Bars; valued at 736*l*. 2*s*. 7*d*. yearly, now worth 14,722*l*. 11*s*. 8*d*.; granted, 36 Henry VIII., to Sir Thomas Audley.

Christ Church, within Aldgate, founded, by Queen Maud, in the year 1108; granted, 23 Henry VIII., to Sir Thomas Audley, Speaker of the House of Commons.

Clerkenwell Monastery, founded, in the year 1100, by Robert, a Priest; valued at 282*l*. 16*s*. 5*d*. yearly, now worth 5,656*l*. 8*s*. 4*d*.; granted, 37 Henry VIII., to Walter Hanley, and John Williams, Knight.

Eastminster, New Abbey, founded, east

of the Tower of London, by King Edward III., in the year 1349; revenues at the dissolution, 602*l*. 11*s*. 10½*d*., now worth 12,051*l*. 17*s*. 6*d*.; the site granted, 34 Henry VIII., to Sir Arthur Darcy, on which Tower-hill now stands.

At ELSING SPITTLE, near Cripplegate. A College, founded, in the year 1329, by William Elsing, of London; valued at 239*l*. 13*s*. 11*d*. yearly, now worth 4,793*l*. 18*s*. 4*d*.; granted, 31 Henry VIII., to John Williams, master of the King's jewels; but it was burnt on the following Christmas eve, as he was living in it.

At HALIWELL. A Benedictine Nunnery, founded, in the year 1127, by Robert Fitz More; yearly revenues 347*l*. 1*s*. 3*d*., now worth 6,941*l*. 5*s*.; granted, 36 Henry VIII., to William Webb.

At ST. HELEN's. A Benedictine Nunnery, founded, in the year 1210, by William Fitz Williams; revenues yearly 376*l*. 6*s*. now worth 7,526*l*.; granted, 33 Henry VIII., to Sir Richard Cromwell.

St. James's Chapel on the Wall, founded near the wall, as early as the time of Richard I., corner of Monkwell-street; granted, 34 Henry VIII., to William Lamb, cloth-maker, from whom it was called Lamb's Chapel.

St. John of Jerusalem, founded, near

West Smithfield, by Jordan Briset, in the year 1100; valued at 2,385*l.* 12*s.* 8*d.* yearly, now worth 47,712*l.* 13*s.* 4*d.*; suppressed 1 Elizabeth.

The Minories, or Nunnery of the ladies of St. Clare, founded, by Blanch, Queen of Navarre, in the year 1293, in the street leading from the Tower to Aldgate; yearly revenues 342*l.* 5*s.* 10½*d.*, now worth 6,845*l.* 18*s.* 4*d.*; granted, 6 Edward VI., to Henry, Duke of Suffolk.

Barking Chapel, within the Church of Allhallows, Barking, founded, by King Richard I.; suppressed, 2 Edward VI.

Holmes' College, founded, by Chancellor Holmes, in the year 1395, near the north door of the Cathedral of St. Paul; granted, 2 Edward VI., to John Hulson and W. Pendred.

London, or Guild Hall College, founded, in the Chapel of St. Mary Magdalen, by Adam Francis and Henry Frowick, in the year 1368; yearly revenues 12*l.* 18*s.* 9*d.*, now worth 258*l.* 15*s.*; granted, 4 Edw.VI., to the Mayor and Corporation of London.

St. Martin-le-Grand, within Aldersgate, founded, about the year 700, by Victred, or Wicthred, King of Kent; granted, 34 Henry VIII., to the Dean and Chapter of Westminster.

St. Michael, Crooked-lane, founded, about the year 1380, by William Walworth, Mayor of London; granted to George Cotton and Thomas Reeves.

Poultney College, founded, in the year 1332, by Sir John Poultney; yearly revenues 97l., now worth 1,940l.; granted, 1 Edward VI., to John Cheke, and Osbert Mountford, and Thomas Gawdy.

Whitingdon College, or Hospital, in the Church of St. Michael Royal, founded, in the year 1424, by Sir Richard Whitingdon, Mayor of London; yearly revenues, 20l. 1s. 8d., now worth 401l. 13s. 4d.; granted, 2 Edward VI., to Armigel Wade.

St. Anthony's Hospital, on the west of Threadneedle-street, given, by King Henry III., to the Brethren of St. Antony; yearly revenues 55l. 6s. 8d., now worth 1,106l. 13s. 4d.

St. Bartholomew's Hospital, founded, in Smithfield, by a Courtier of King Henry I., for sick persons and women in labour, and for the maintenance of the orphans, until the age of seven, whose mothers died in the Hospital; yearly revenues 371l. 13s. 2d., now worth 7,433l. 3s. 4d.

St. Giles' College, for leprous persons, founded, by the charitable Maud, Queen of Henry I.; granted, 36 Henry VIII., to John, Lord Dudley.

MIDDLESEX.

St. Catherine's Chapel, near the Tower, founded in the year 1148, by Maud, Queen of King Stephen; yearly revenues 315*l.* 14*s.* 2*d.*, now worth 6,314*l.* 3*s.* 4*d.*

St. Mary Spittle, without Bishopgate, a Priory, founded, in the year 1197, by Walter Fitz Ealdred; yearly revenues 557*l.* 14*s.* 10*d.*, now worth 11,154*l.* 17*s.* 6*d.* ; granted, 34 Henry VIII., to Stephen Vaughan.

Rouncivall Hospital, on the south side of the Strand, between York-buildings and Northumberland house, founded, by William Mareschall, Earl of Pembroke, in the time of Henry III.; granted, 3 Edward VI., to Sir Thomas Cawarden.

Savoy Hospital, near the Strand, founded, by Henry VII., in the year 1505, for 100 poor people; yearly revenues 529*l.* 5*s.* $7\frac{1}{2}d.$ now worth 10,585*l.* 12*s.* 6*d.* ; suppressed 7 Edward VI.

Almshouses in Staining-lane, ten in number, founded near Haberdasher's Hall, by Thomas Huntlow, for the poor of that Company, in the year 1539.

St. Thomas of Acon, an Hospital, founded on the north side of Cheapside, by Thomas Fitz Theobald and his wife, sister to St. Thomas, in the reign of Henry II.; yearly revenues 300*l.* now worth 6,000*l.* ; granted, 33 Henry VIII., to the Mercers' Company.

MIDDLESEX.

Augustine Monastery, founded on the west side of Broad-street, London, by Humphry Bohun, Earl of Hereford, in the year 1253; valued at 57*l.* 0*s.* 5*d.* yearly now worth 1,140*l.* 8*s.* 4*d.*; granted, in the year 1550, to John a Lasco, as a preaching-house for his congregation of Walloons, and still continues a Dutch house.

Black Friar's Monastery, founded about the year 1221, near Holborn, in Chancery-lane; yearly revenues 104*l.* 15*s.* 7*d.*, now worth 2,095*l.* 11*s.* 8*d.*; granted to Thomas Cawarden.

Grey Friars, or Franciscan Abbey, founded near Newgate, about the year 1224, by John Ewin and others; yearly revenues 32*l.* 19*s.* 10*d.*, now worth 659*l.* 17*s.* 6*d.*; granted 38 Henry VIII.

Carmelite Friary, founded, on the south side of Fleet-street, between the New Temple and Salisbury-court, by Sir Richard Gray; yearly revenue 62*l.* 7*s.* 3*d.*, now worth 1,247*l.* 5*s.*; granted, 32 Henry VIII., to Richard Moresyne and William Butts.

Holy Cross Friary, founded near Tower-hill, in the year 1298, by Ralph Hosier and William Soberns; yearly revenue 52*l.* 13*s.* 4*d.*, now worth 1,053*l.* 6*s.* 8*d.*; granted, 32 Henry VIII., to Sir Thomas Wyat.

At RISELIPP. An Alien Priory, founded, in

the reign of William the Conqueror, by Ernulph de Heding; yearly revenue 18*l.*, now worth 360*l.*; granted, 16 Henry VIII.

At STRATFORD. A Benedictine Nunnery, founded, in the reign of William the Conqueror, by William, Bishop of London; yearly revenue 121*l.* 16*s.*, now worth 2,436*l.*; granted, 32 Henry VIII., to Ralph Sadler.

At SYON. A Brigitine Nunnery, founded, in the year 1414, by King Henry V.; yearly revenue 1,944*l.* 11*s.* 8½*d.*, now worth 38,891*l.* 14*s.* 2*d.*; granted, 7 Edward VI., to John, Duke of Northumberland.

Syon, or Brentford Hospital, founded in the east end of the town, 25 Henry V., by John Summerset, Chancellor of the Exchequer; granted, 1 Edward VI., to Edward, Duke of Summerset.

At WESTMINSTER. A Benedictine Abbey, founded, on the ruins of the Temple of Apollo, by King Lucius; rebuilt in the year 610, by the Saxon King, Sebert; destroyed in the Danish wars; restored by King Ethelbert; and Dunstan, Bishop of London, in the year 958; and largely endowed by King Edward the Confessor; yearly revenue 3,977*l.* 6*s.* 4½*d.*, now worth 79,546*l.* 7*s.* 6*d.*

St. Stephen's Chapel, founded, in the year 1347, by King Edward III.; rents

1,085*l.* 10*s.* 5*d.*, now worth 21,710*l.* 8*s.* 4*d.*; granted, 6 Edward VI., to Sir John Gate.

St. James' Hospital, founded, before the conquest, for 14 leprous women; on or near it is built St. James' Palace; yearly value 100*l.*, now worth 2,000*l.*

MONMOUTH (County).

At ABERGAVENNY. A Benedictine Priory, founded, in the reign of William the Conqueror, by Hamelin Baylon; rents 59*l.* 4*s.*, now worth 1,184*l.*; suppressed.

At GOLDCLIFF. An Alien Priory, founded, in the year 1113, by Robert de Chandos; valued at 144*l.* 18*s.* 1*d.* yearly, now worth 2,898*l.* 1*s.* 8*d.*

At GRACE-DIEU, or STOW. A Cistercian Abbey, built in the year 1226, by sir John of Monmouth; rents 26*l.* 1*s.* 4*d.*, now worth 521*l.* 6*s.* 8*d.*; granted, 37 Henry VIII., to Thomas Herbert and William Bretton.

At ST. KENMERCY. A Priory, founded, prior to 1291; valued at 8*l.* 4*s.* 8*d.*, now worth 164*l.* 13*s.* 4*d.*

At LLANHODENEI, or LANTONY. An Augustine Priory, founded, before the year 1108, by Hugh Lacy; valued at 71*l.* 3*s.* 2*d.* yearly, now worth 1,423*l.* 3*s.* 4*d.*; granted, 38 Henry VIII., to Nicholas Arnold.

At LLANGKYWAN. An Alien Priory, founded, in the year 1183; granted, 37 Henry VIII., to John Doyley and John Scudamore.

At LLANTARNAM. A Cistercian Monastery, with the yearly revenue of 71*l.* 3*s.* 2*d.*, now worth 1,423*l.* 3*s.* 4*d.*; granted, 31 Henry VIII., to John Parker.

At MALPAS. A Cluniac Cell, founded, in the reign of Henry I., by Winebald de Baeluna; rents 15*l.* 6*s.* 8*d.*, now worth 306*l.* 13*s.* 4*d.*; granted, 1 Edward VI., to Sir William Herbert.

At MONMOUTH. A Benedictine Priory, founded, in the reign of Henry I., by Wihenoc of Monmouth; rents 56*l.* 1*s.* 11*d.*, now worth 1,121*l.* 18*s.* 4*d.*; granted to Richard Price and Thomas Perry.

At NEWPORT. A Friary stood by the Key, beneath the Bridge; granted, 35 Henry VIII., to Sir Edward Carn.

At STROGUIL. An Alien Priory, founded in the reign of King Stephen, stood here; rents, at the dissolution, 32*l.* 4*s.*, now worth 644*l.*

At TINTERN. A Cistercian Abbey, founded, in the year 1131, by Walter de Clare ; rents 256*l.* 11*s.* 6*d.*, now worth 5,131*l.* 10*s.* ; granted, 28 Henry VIII., to Henry, Earl of Worcester.

At USK. A Benedictine Nunnery, founded, before the year 1236 ; rents 69*l.* 9*s.* 8*d.*, now worth 1,389*l.* 13*s.* 4*d.* ; granted, 36 Henry VIII., to Roger Williams.

————————

NORFOLK (COUNTY).

At ALDEBY. A Benedictine Cell, founded, in the reign of Henry I., by Bishop Herbert.

At ATTELBURGH. A College, founded, 7 Henry IV., by Sir Robert Mortimer ; rents 21*l.* 16*s.* 0½*d.*, now worth 436*l.* 0*s.* 10*d.* ; granted, 33 Henry VIII., to Robert, Earl of Sussex.

At BEESTON. An Augustine Priory, founded, in the reign of Henry III., by Lady Margery de Cressy; yearly value 50*l.* 6*s.* 4½*d.*, now worth 1,006*l.* 7*s.* 6*d.*; granted 37 Henry VIII., to Sir Edmond Windham and Giles Seafoule.

At BEK HOSPITAL. An Hospital, founded, in the reign of Henry I., by William de Bek, on the great road from Norwich to Walsingham, with thirteen beds and night's lodging for poor travellers ; granted to Sir John Parrot.

At St. Bennet's of Hulme. A Benedictine Abbey, founded, in the year 800, by Prince Horn, in this solitary place, for Hermits ; yearly value 677*l.* 9*s.* 8½*d.*; now worth 13,549*l.* 14*s.* 2*d.* ; granted, 27 Henry VIII., to the Bishop of Norwich.

At Binham. A Benedictine Cell, founded, in the reign of Henry I., by the Nephew of William the Conqueror ; yearly value 160*l.* 1*s.*, now worth 3,201*l.* ; granted, 33 Henry VIII., to Thomas Paston, Esq.

At Blackborough. A Benedictine Nunnery, founded, in the reign of Henry II., by Roger de Scales ; yearly value 76*l.* 3*s.* 9½*d.*, now worth 1,523*l.* 15*s.* 10*d.* ; granted, 4 Edward VI., to the Bishop of Norwich and his successors.

At Blakeney. A Carmelite Monastery, founded, 24 Edward I., by Richard Stomer and others ; granted, 33 Henry VIII., to William Rede.

At Bromehill. An Augustine Priory, founded, about the year 1528, granted to the Fellows of Christ's College, Cambridge, by Edward VI.

At Bromholm. A Cluniac Priory, founded, in the year 1113, by William de Glanvill ; yearly value 144*l.* 19*s.* 0½*d.,* now worth 2,899*l.* 0*s.* 10*d.* ; granted, 37 Henry VIII. to Thomas Woodhouse.

At Oldbuckenham. An Augustine Priory, founded, in the reign of King Stephen, by William de Albini, Earl of Chichester ; rents 131*l.* 11*s.,* now worth 2,631*l.*; granted, to Sir Thomas Lovell.

At Burnham Nortan. A Carmelite Monastery, founded, in the year 1241, by Sir Ralph de Hemenhale ; yearly value 2*l.* 5*s.* 4*d.,* now worth 85*l.* 6*s.* 8*d.* ; granted, 33 Henry VIII., to William, Lord Cobham.

At Carbroke. A House of Knights Hospitalers, founded, in the reign of Henry II., by Maud, Countess of Clare ; yearly value 65*l.* 2*s.* 11*d.,* now worth 1,302*l.* 18*s.* 4*d.* ; granted, 35 Henry VIII., to Sir Richard Gresham and Sir Richard Southwell.

At Castleacre. A Cluniac Priory, founded, before the year 1085, by William Warren, Earl of Surrey ; yearly value 324*l.* 17*s.* 5½*d.,* now worth 6,497*l.* 9*s.* 2*d.* ; granted, 29 Henry VIII., to Thomas, Duke of Norfolk.

At Costre, by Yarmouth. A College, founded, in the reign of Edward I., by Sir John

Falstaff; yearly value 2*l*. 13*s*. 4*d*.; now worth 53*l*. 6*s*. 8*d*

At CHOSELL. A Lazarite Monastery, founded, before the time of Edward I., by Earl Giffard; yearly value 13*l*. 18*s*. 2*d*., now worth 276*l*. 3*s* 4*d*.; granted, 36 Henry VIII., to Sir John Dudley, Viscount Lisle.

At COKESFORD. An Augustine Canons, established in the reign of King Stephen, by William Cheiny; yearly value 153*l*. 7*s*. 1*d*., now worth 3,067*l*. 1*s*. 8*d*.; granted, 29 Henry VIII., to Thomas Duke, of Norfolk.

At CRABHOUSE. An Augustine Nunnery, founded, in the south of the parish of Wigenhale, in the year 1181, by the Convent of Reynham; yearly value 31*l*. 16*s*. 7*d*., now worth 636*l*. 11*s*. 8*d*.; granted to Sir John Gage.

At WEST DEREHAM. A Premonstratensian Abbey, founded, in the year 1188, by Hubert, Bishop of Salisbury; yearly value 252*l*. 12*s*. 11½*d*., now worth 5,052*l*. 19*s*. 2*d*.; granted, 31 Henry VIII., to Thomas Dereham.

At FIELDALLYNG. An Alien Priory, built in the reign of Henry II., by Maud de Harscolye; granted to Martin Hastings and James Borne.

At FLITCHAM. An Augustine Cell, given in the reign of Richard I., to Dametta de Flicham;

yearly value 62*l.* 10*s.* 6½*d.*, now worth 1,250*l.* 10*s.* 10*d.*; granted, 30 Henry VIII., to Edward, Lord Clinton.

At HAMPTON. An Augustine Priory, founded, in the time of Henry I., by Roger de St. Martins ; rents 39*l.* 0*s.* 9*d.*, now worth 780*l.* 15*s.* ; granted, 37 Henry VIII., to Sir William Fermer.

At HERINGLEY. An Hospital de Dieu founded, in the year 1475, by Hugh Attefenne ; yearly value 23*l.* 6*s.* 5*d.*, now worth 466*l.* 8*s.* 4*d.* ; granted, 37 Henry VIII., to Sir Thomas Clere.

At HICKLING. An Augustine Priory, founded, in the year 1185, by Theobald de Valentia ; yearly value 137*l.* 0*s.* 1½*d.*, now worth 2,740*l.* 2*s.* 6*d.* ; granted, 37 Henry VIII., to the Bishop of Norwich, and his successors.

At HITCHAM. A Cluniac Cell, founded, in the time of William Rufus, by William Warren, Earl of Surrey ; granted, 29 Henry VIII., to Thomas, Duke of Norfolk.

At HORSHAM. A Benedictine Priory, founded, in the year 1105, by Robert Fitzwalter ; rents 193*l.* 2*s.* 3½*d.*, now worth 3,864*l.* 5*s.* 10*d.* ; granted, 35 Henry VIII., to Sir Edward Elrington.

NORFOLK.

At INGHAM. A College for the redemption of Captives, founded, in the year 1360, by Sir Miles Stapleton ; yearly value 74*l*. 2*s*. 7½*d*., now worth 1,482*l*. 12*s*. 6*d*. ; granted, 36 Henry VIII., to the Bishop of Norwich.

At LANGLEY. A Premonstratensian Abbey, built in the year 1198, by Robert Fitz Roger ; rents 128*l*. 19*s*. 9½*d*. ; now worth 2,579*l*. 15*s*. 10*d*. ; granted, 38 Henry VIII., to John Berney.

At LYNN. A Benedictine Cell, founded, in the year 1100, by Bishop Herbert.

St John's Hospital, founded, in the reign of Edw. I. ; yearly value 7*l*. 6*s*. 11*d*., now worth 146*l*. 18*s*. 4*d*.

St. Mary Magdalen's Hospital founded 1145.

An Augustine Monastery, founded, in the reign of Edward I. ; granted, 36 Henry VIII., to John Eyer ; yearly value 1*l*. 4*s*. 6*d*., now worth 24*l*. 10*s*.

A Dominician Friary, founded, 21 Edward I., by Thomas Gedney ; valued at 18*s*. yearly, now worth 18*l*. ; granted, 36 Henry VIII., to John Eyer.

A Carmelite Friary, founded, in the year 1264, by Thomas de Feltsham ; granted to John Eyer. The steeple stands as a sea mark.

NORFOLK.

White Friar's House, founded, in the year 1269, by some Noblemen; yearly value 1*l.* 15*s.* 8*d.*, now worth 35*l.* 13*s.* 4*d.*

At MARHAM. A Cistercian Nunnery, endowed in the year 1251, by the Countess of Arundel; yearly value 42*l.* 4*s.* 7½*d.*, now worth 844*l.* 12*s.* 6*d.*; granted, 38 Henry VIII., to Sir Nicholas Hare and Robert Hare.

At MASSINGHAM MAGNA. An Augustine Priory, founded, in the year 1260, by Nicholas de Syre; granted to Sir Thomas Gresham.

At MODNEY. A Benedictine Cell, in the parish of Helgay; granted, 35 Henry VIII., to Robert Hogan.

At MONTE JOVIS, or MOUNTJOY. An Augustine Priory, founded, in the reign of King John, by William de Gisnetto.

At NEWBRIDGE. A Hermit's Chapel, built in the year 1373; rents 3*l.* 7*s.* 6*d.*; now worth 67*l.* 10*s.*

At NORWICH. A Cathedral and Benedictine Priory, built, in the year 1094, by Herbert, Bishop of Thetford. The revenues of the bishoprick were valued at 1,050*l.* 17*s.* 6*d.*, and of the convent 1,061*l.* 14*s.* 3½*d.* yearly; both sums now worth 42,251*l.* 15*s.* 10*d.* The estates granted, 27 Henry VIII., to the Bishops of

Norwich, but instead of the estates, they got the revenues of some monasteries.

St. Leonard's Benedictine Cell, founded, on a hill near the city, by Bishop Herbert; granted, 5 Elizabeth, to Thomas, Duke of Norfolk.

Kairo, or Carow. A Benedictine Nunnery, endowed, in the year 1146, by King Stephen; yearly value 84*l.* 12*s.* 1½*d.*, now worth 1,692*l.* 2*s.* 6*d.*; granted, 30 Henry VIII., to John Shelton, Knight.

Chapel in the Fields, built, in the year 1250, by John Brown, Priest; rents 86*l.* 16*s.* 0½*d.*, now worth 1,736*l.* 0*s.* 10*d.*; granted, 37 Henry VIII., to Doctor Miles Spenser.

St. Giles's Hospital, founded, in the year 1249, by Walter, Bishop of Norwich; rents 90*l.* 12*s.*; now worth 1,812*l.*

Lazar's Houses, several of them founded here for the poor; granted to Edmond Newport.

An Augustine Friary, settled here in the time of Edward I.; granted, 2 Edward VI., to Sir Thomas Heneage and to William Lord Willoughby.

The Black Friary, founded, by Sir Thomas Gelham, in the year 1226; granted, 32 Henry VIII., to the Mayor and Citizens.

The House of Grey Friars, founded in

the year 1226, by John de Hastingford; granted, 30 Henry VIII., to the Duke of Norfolk.

The White, or Carmelite, Friary, founded, in the year 1256, by Philip Cougate of Norwich; granted, 34 Henry VIII., to Richard Andrews and Leonard Chamberlayne.

At PENTNEY. An Augustine Priory, founded, in the reign of William the Conqueror, by Robert de Vallileus; yearly value 215*l*. 18*s*. 8*d*., now worth 4,318*l*. 13*s*. 4*d*.; granted, 30 Henry VIII., to Thomas Mildmay.

At PETERSTONE. An Augustine Priory, founded before the year 1200; granted 4 Edw. VI.

At RUSHWORTH. A College, founded, in the year 1342, by Sir Edmond de Gonville, Priest; yearly value 85*l*. 15*s*. 0½*d*., now worth 1,715*l*. 0*s*. 10*d*.; granted, 33 Henry VIII., to Henry, Earl of Surrey; and after that to Sir John Cheke.

At SHOULDHAM. A Cistercian Priory, founded, in the reign of Richard I., by Jeffrey Fitz Piers, Earl of Essex; rents 171*l*. 6*s*. 8*d*., now worth 3,426*l*. 13*s*. 4*d*.; granted, 7 Edward VI., to Thomas Mildmay.

At SLEVESHOLM. A Cluniac Cell, in the parish of Methwold, by William Earl, Warren, in the year 1222; granted, 23 Elizabeth, to Osbert Mundeford.

At SPORLE. An Alien Priory, granted, 1 Elizabeth, to Eaton College.

At THETFORD. A Cluniac Priory, founded, in the year 1104, by Roger Bigod, Nobleman; yearly value 418*l*. 6*s*. 3*d*., now worth 8,369*l*. 5*s*.; granted, 32 Henry VIII., to Thomas, Duke of Norfolk.

A Benedictine Nunnery, founded, about the year 1160, by Hugh de Norwold, Abbot; rents 50*l*. 9*s*. 8*d*., now worth 1,009*l*. 13*s*. 4*d*.; granted, 30 Henry VIII., to Richard Fulmerston, Esq.

A College, or Guild, founded, in the reign of Edward I., by Gilbert de Pykenham; rents 5*l*. 9*s*. 7*d*., now worth 109*l*. 11*s*. 8*d*.; granted, 7 James I., to Francis Morice and Francis Philips, Esqrs.

St. John's Hospital, founded for lepers; granted, 32 Henry VIII., to Richard Fulmerstone, Esq.

St. Mary Magdalen's Hospital, founded, by John de Warren, Earl of Surrey, and he endowed it with 864 acres of land; yearly value 1*l*. 13*s*. 6*l*. only, now worth 33*l*. 10*s*.; granted to Sir Richard Fulmerstone.

An Augustine Friary, granted, 32 Henry VIII., to Sir Richard Fulmerstone.

At THOMESTON. A College, founded, 23 Edward III., by Sir Thomas de Shardelau and his brother; yearly value 52*l.* 15*s.* 7½*d.*, now worth 1,055*l.* 12*s.* 6*d.*; granted, 32 Henry VIII., to Sir Edmond Knyvet.

At WABURN. An Augustine Priory, founded, in the reign of Henry II., by Sir Ralph Meyngaryn; yearly value 28*l.* 7*s.* 2*d.*, now worth 567*l.* 3*s.* 4*d.*; granted to Richard Heydon, 37 Henry VIII.

At WALSINGHAM. An Augustine Priory, built, in the year 1061, by the widow of Richoldis de Favarches; yearly value 446*l.* 14*s.* 4½*d.*, now worth 8,934*l.* 7*s.* 6*d.*; granted, 31 Henry VIII., to Thomas Sidney.

A Franciscan Friary, founded, about the year 1346, by Elizabeth de Burgo, Countess of Clare; value yearly 3*l.*, now worth 60*l.*; granted, 36 Henry VIII., to John Eyer.

At WELLES. An Alien Priory, founded, in the time of William the Conqueror, by William de Streis; granted, 2 Edward VI., to the Bishops of Ely.

At WENDLING. A Premonstratensian Monastery, founded, 50 Henry III., by the Rev. William de Wendling; valuation 55*l.* 18*s.* 4½*d.*, now worth 1,118*l.* 7*s.* 6*d.*; granted, 16 Elizabeth, to Edward Dyer and H. Cressener.

NORFOLK.

At WESTACRE. An Augustine Priory, founded, in the time of William Rufus, by Oliver, the parish priest; value 308l. 19s. 11½d. yearly, now worth 6,179l. 19s. 2d.; granted, 7 Edward VI., to Thomas Gresham.

At WEYBRIDGE. An Augustine Priory, founded early, by the Bigod family; value 7l. 13s. 4d. yearly, now worth 153l. 6s. 8d.; granted, 30 Henry VIII., to Richard Fulmerstone.

At WIRHAM. An Alien Priory, founded, by the Earls of Clare, in the time of Richard I.; value 7l. 16s. yearly, now worth 156l.; granted to Thomas Guibon and William Mynn.

At WORMGAY. An Augustine Priory, founded, in the time of Richard I., by William de Warren; granted, 4 Edward VI., to the Bishop of Norwich.

At WYMONDHAM. A Benedictine Monastery, founded, in the year 1107, by William de Albini; yearly value 72l. 5s. 4d., now worth 1,445l. 6s. 8d.; granted, 37 Henry VIII., to Sir Walter Hadden.

An Hospital, founded, by William de Albini, in the year 1146; granted to the Corporation of Norwich.

At YARMOUTH. A Benedictine Cell, built, in the year 1101, by Herbert, Bishop of Norwich; now belongs to the Cathedral of Norwich.

St. Mary's Hospital, built in the time of Edward I., by Thomas Falstaff; the chapel and rooms are now a grammar school, and workhouse for the poor.

A Dominican Friary, built, 55 Henry III., by Sir William Garbridge; granted, 34 Henry VIII., to Richard Andrews and Leonard Chamberlayne.

A Grey Friary, founded in the time of Henry III., by Sir William Garbridge; granted, 33 Henry VIII., to Sir Richard Cromwell, alias Williams.

A Carmelite Friary, founded, in the year 1278, by King Edward I.; granted, 36 Henry VIII., to Thomas Denton and Richard Nottington.

NORTHAMPTON (County).

At CANON'S ASHBY. An Augustine Priory, founded, in the time of John; valuation 127l. 19s. yearly, now worth 2,559l.; granted, 29 Henry VIII., to Sir Francis Bryan.

At BARNACKE. A College, granted, 6 Edward VI., to David Vincent.

At CHACOMB. An Augustine Priory, founded, in the time of Henry II., by Hugh de Chacomb;

value 93*l*. 6*s*. 3½*d*. yearly, now worth 1,866*l*. 5*s*. 10*d*.; granted, 35 Henry VIII., to Michael Fox.

At COTHERSTOKE. A College, founded, in the year 1336, by the Rev. John Gifford; granted, 1 Edward VI., to Sir Robert Kirkham.

At DAVENTREE. A Cluniac Priary, built in the time of William the Conqueror, by Hugh de Leicester; value 236*l*. 7*s*. 6*d*. yearly, now worth 4,727*l*. 10*s*.; granted, by Henry VIII., to Christ-Church, in Oxford.

At ST. DEWES, or ST. DAVID'S, near Northampton. An Hospital, founded, in the year 1200, by Walter the Prior of St. Andrew's; value 24*l*. 6*s*. 1*d*. yearly, now worth 486*l*. 1*s*. 8*d*.

At DINGLEY. A House of Hospitalers, built in the time of Stephen; rents 108*l*. 13*s*. 5½*d*., now worth 2,173*l*. 9*s*. 2*d*.; granted, 35 Henry VIII., to Edward Griffith.

At FODRINGHEY. A College, founded, in the year 1411, by King Henry IV.; value 419*l*. 11*s*. 10½*d*. yearly, now worth 8,391*l*. 17*s*. 6*d*; granted to James Crew.

At HIGHAM FERRERS. A College, founded, in the time of Henry V., by the most Reverend and munificent Henry Chicheley, Archbishop of Canterbury; value 156*l*. 2*s*. 7½*d*. yearly, now worth 3,124*l.* 12*s.* 6*d.* ; granted, 6 Elizabeth, to John Smith and Richard Duffield.

At CASTLE HYMEL. An Augustine Priory, founded, in the reign of John, by Richard Engain, Lord of Blatherwike ; value 62*l.* 16*s.* yearly, now worth 1,256*l.* ; granted, 33 Henry VIII., to John, Lord Russell.

At IRTELINGBURGH. A College, founded, in the time of Edward III., by the Executrix of John Pyel ; value 64*l.* 12*s.* 10½*d.* yearly, now worth 1,292*l.* 17*s.* 6*d.* ; granted, 23 Elizabeth, to Edward Downing and P. Ashton.

At KATEBI, or KATESBY. A Benedictine Nunnery, built in the time of Richard I., by Robert de Esseby ; value 145*l.* 0*s.* 6*d.* yearly, now worth 2,900*l.* 10*s.* ; granted, 28 Henry VIII., to John Onley.

At LUFFIELD. A Benedictine Priory, founded, 24 Henry I., by Robert Bossu Earl of Leicester ; yearly value 19*l.* 19*s.* 2*d.*, now worth 399*l.* 3*s.* 4*d.* ; granted, 5 Edward VI., to Sir Nicholas Throkmorton.

At NORTHAMPTON. A Cluniac Priory, founded, in the year 1076, by Simon Seinliz, Earl of Huntingdon ; value 344*l.* 13*s.* 7*d.* yearly, now worth 6,893*l.* 11*s.* 8*d.* ; granted, 4 Edward VI., to Sir Thomas Smith.

NORTHAMPTON.

An Augustine Priory, founded, in the year 1112, by William Peverell, natural son of William the Conqueror; value 213*l.* 17*s.* 2*d.* yearly, now worth 4,377*l.* 3*s.* 4*d.*; granted, 37 Henry VIII., to Nicholas Giffard.

A Cluniac Nunnery de Pratis, founded, in the time of Stephen, by Simon Seinliz, Earl of Northampton; value 119*l.* 9*s.* 7½*d.* yearly, now worth 2,389*l.* 12*s.* 6*d.*; granted, 34 Henry VIII., to John Mershe.

A College, founded, 38 Henry VI., value 1*l.* 19*s.* 4*d.* yearly; now worth 39*l.* 6*s.* 8*d.*; granted, 2 Edward VI., to William Ward and Richard Venebles.

St. John's Hospital, for the sick, founded, in the year 1137, by Walter, Archdeacon of Northampton; value 25*l.* 6*s.* 2½*d.* yearly, now worth 516*l.* 4*s.* 2*d.*; granted 26 Hen. VIII.

St. Leonard's Hospital, in East Cotton, founded, outside the town, by William the Conqueror; value 11*l.* 6*s.* 8*d.* yearly, now worth 226*l.* 13*s.* 4*d.*

An Augustine Friary, founded, in the year 1322, by John Longville; granted, 32 Henry VIII., to Robert Dighton.

A Black Friary, founded, in the year 1240, by John Dabington; value 5*l.* 7*s.* 10*d.* yearly, now worth 107*l.* 18*s.* 4*d.*; granted, 36 Henry VIII., to William Ramesden.

A Grey Friary, founded, about the year 1224; revenues 6*l*. 13*s*. 4*d*., now worth 133*l*. 6*s*. 8*d*. ; granted, 36 Henry VIII., to Richard Taverner.

A Carmelite Friary, built in the year 1271, by Thomas Chetwood and Simon Montford; value 10*l*. 10*s*. yearly, now worth 230*l*.; granted, 36 Henry VIII., to William Ramesden.

At OXNEY. A Benedictine Cell, founded before the time of Richard I.; granted, 33 Henry VIII., to Roger Horton.

At PETERBURGH. A Benedictine Abbey, begun in the year 655, by Peada, King of Mercia; but afterwards it underwent many changes during the wars; Ethelwold, Bishop of Winchester, assisted by King Edgar, rebuilt it magnificently, in the year 970; income 1,972*l*. 7*s*. 0½*d*. yearly, now worth 39,447*l*. 0*s*. 10*d*.

At PIKEWELL. A Cistercian Abbey, founded, in the year 1143, by William de Boutwylein; value 347*l*. 8*s*. 0½*d*. yearly, now worth 6,948*l*. 0*s*. 10*d*.; granted, 1 Edward VI., to William, Marquis of Northampton.

At ROTHWELL. An Augustine Nunnery, supposed to have been founded by the Clare family; value 10*l*. 10*s*. 4*d*. yearly, now worth 210*l*. 6*s*. 8*d*. ; granted, 37 Henry VIII., to Henry Lee.

At SEWARDESLEY. A Cistercian Nunnery, founded, in the time of Henry II., by Richard de Lestre; yearly value 18*l*. 11*s*. 2*d*., now worth 371*l*. 3*s*. 4*d*.; granted, 4 Edward VI., to Richard Fermer.

At SULBEY. A Premonstratensian Abbey, founded, about the year 1155, by William de Wideville; rents 305*l*. 8*s*. 5½*d*., now worth 6,108*l*. 3*s*. 2*d*.; granted, 10 Elizabeth, to Sir Christopher Hatton.

At TOWCESTER. A College, founded, in the time of Henry VI., by William Sponne, D. D., pastor of the town; rents 19*l*. 6*s*. 8*d*., now worth 386*l*. 13*s*. 4*d*.; granted, 4 Edward VI., to Richard Heybourn and William Dalby.

At WYRTHORP. A Benedictine Nunnery, founded, in the time of Henry I.; granted, 32 Henry VIII., to Richard Cecil.

NORTHUMBERLAND (County).

At ALNWICK. A Premonstratensian Abbey, founded, in the year 1147, by Eustace Fitz John; value 194*l*. 7*s*. yearly, now worth 388*l*. 7*s*.; granted, 4 Edward VI., to Ralph Sadler and Laurence Winnington.

At BLANCA LANDA. A Premonstratensian Abbey, founded, in the year 1165, by Walter de Bolebec ; yearly value 44*l*. 9*s*. 1½*d*., now worth 889*l*. 2*s*. 6*d*. ; granted, 37 Henry VIII., to John Bellew and John Broxholm.

At BREKENBURNE. An Augustine Priory, founded in the reign of Henry I., by Osbertus Colutarius ; yearly value 77*l*., now worth 1,540*l*.; granted, 4 Edward VI., to John, Earl of Warwick.

At HAMBURGH. An Augustine Cell, founded by Henry I. ; yearly value 124*l*. 15s. 7*d*., now worth 2,495*l*. 11*s*. 8*d*. ; granted, 37 Henry VIII., to John Foster.

At HEXHAM. A Cathedral Church, Abbey, and Augustine Priory. St. Wilfrid and St. Etheldreda the Queen of Egfrid, King of Northumberland, founded, in the year 674, a Church and Monastery of the finest architecture ever seen in these parts of Europe. The Priory was founded in the reign of William the Conqueror, by Archbishop Thomas ; revenues at the dissolution, 138*l*. 1*s*. 9*d*., now worth 2,761*l*. 15*s*. ; granted, 30 Henry VIII., to Sir Reginald Carnaby.

An Hospital, founded, in the time of John, it is thought, by the Archbishop of York ; granted, 30 Henry VIII., to Sir Reginald Carnaby.

At HOLM. A Carmelite Friary, founded, in the year 1240, by John Lord Vesci ; granted, 6 Elizabeth, to Thomas Reve, and William Ryvet.

At LINDISFARNE. A Cathedral Church and Benedictine Cell. King Oswald gave this Island, in the year 635, to St. Aidan, who came from Scotland to plant Christianity in Northumbria, and there fixed his see. The Cell was founded, in the year 1082 ; yearly value 60*l*. 5*s*., now worth 1,205*l*. ; granted, 33 Henry VIII., to the Dean and Chapter of Durham.

At LAMBLEY UPON THE TYNE. A Benedictine Nunnery, founded, by King John, in honour to St. Patrick ; yearly revenue 5*l*. 15*s*. 8*d*., now worth 115*l*. 13*s*. 4*d*. ; granted, 7 Edward VI., to John, Duke of Northumberland.

At NESSEHAM. A Benedictine Nunnery, founded, it is thought, by Lord Dacres ; yearly value 26*l*. 9*s*. 9*d*., now worth 529*l*. 15*s*.; granted, 32 Henry VIII., to James Lawson.

At NEWCASTLE. A Benedictine Nunnery, built in the reign of William the Conqueror ; yearly value 37*l*. 4*s*. 2*d*., now worth 744*l*. 3*s*. 4*d*. ; granted, 36 Henry VIII., to William Barentine and others.

St. Catherine's Hospital, built in the

reign of Henry IV., by Roger Thornton ; yearly income 8*l.* 0*s.* 1*d.*, now worth 160*l.* 1*s.* 8*d.*

St. Mary the Virgin's Hospital, built in the reign of Henry III. ; yearly value 26*l.* 13*s.* 4*d.*, now worth 533*l.* 6*s.* 8*d.*

St. Mary the Virgin's Hospital, the second of that name, founded, in the reign of Henry I.

St. Mary Magdalen Hospital, founded, by Henry I. ; yearly value 9*l.* 11*s.* 4*d.*, now worth 191*l.* 6*s.* 8*d.*

An Augustine Friary, founded by Lord Ross ; granted, 5 Edward VI., to John, Duke of Northumberland.

A Black Friary, founded, in the year 1260, by Sir Peter and Sir Nicholas Scot ; granted, 35 Henry VIII., to the Mayor and Burgesses of the town.

A Carmelite Friary, founded, by Richard I. ; granted 37 Henry VIII., to Richard Gresham and Richard Billingford.

A Trinitarian Friary for the redemption of Captives, founded by William Wakefield, the master ; granted, 37 Henry VIII., to Richard Gresham and Richard Billingford.

At NOVUM MONASTERIUM, near MORPETH.
A Cistercian abbey, founded, by Ranulph de

Merlay, in the year 1138 ; yearly value 140*l.*
10*s.* 4*d.,* now worth 2,810*l.* 6*s.* 8*d.* : granted 7
James I., to Robert Brandling.

At OVINGHAM. An Augustine Cell, founded,
by Mr. Ufranville ; rents 13*l.* 4*s.* 8*d.,* now worth
268*l.* 13*s.* 4*d.*

At TINMOUTH. A Benedictine Cell, founded,
by St. Oswald, the first Christian King of Northumberland. St. Herebald was Abbot here in
the beginning of the eighth century. Yearly
value 511*l.* 4*s.* 1*d.,* now worth 10,224*l.* 1*s.* 8*d.* ;
granted, 5 Edward VI., to John, Duke of Northumberland.

NOTTINGHAM (COUNTY).

At BEAUVALE. A Carthusian Priory, founded,
17 Edward III., by Nicholas de Cantilupo ;
valued at 227*l.* 8*s.* yearly, now worth 4,548*l.* ;
granted 4 Edward VI., to Richard Morison.

At BLYTH. A Benedictine Priory, founded,
in the year 1088, by Roger de Builly ; rents
126*l.* 8*s.* 2½*d.* yearly, now worth 2,528*l.* 4*s.* 2*d.* ;
granted, 35 Henry VIII., to Richard Andrews
and William Ramesden.

NOTTINGHAM.

An Hospital, founded, for the sick, by William de Cressy, Lord of Hodesac; yearly value 8*l*. 14*s*., now worth 174*l*.

At Brodholm. A Premonstratensian Nunnery, founded in the reign of Stephen, by Agnes de Camvile; yearly revenue 16*l*. 5*s*. 2*d*., now worth 325*l*. 3*s*. 4*d*.; granted, 6 Elizabeth, to John Caniers and William Haber.

At Clifton. A College, founded, in the year 1156, by Ralph Brito; rents 61*l*. 4*s*. 8*d*., now worth 1,224*l*. 13*s*. 4*d*.; granted to Anthony Strelly.

At Fiskarton. An Augustine Cell, founded, by Ralph de Ayncourt; granted to Edward Fynes, Lord Clinton, and Thomas Morison.

At Lenton. A Cluniac Priory, founded, by William Peverell, in the reign of Henry I.; rents 417*l*. 19*s*. 3*d*. now worth 8,359*l*. 5*s*.; granted, 5 Elizabeth, to John Harrington.

At Marshe. A Benedictine Cell; valued yearly at 63*l*. 6*s*. 8*d*., now worth 1,266*l*. 13*s*. 4*d*.

At Mattersey. A Gilbertine Priory, founded, in the year 1192, by Robert de Maresey; granted, 31 Henry VIII., to Anthony Neville, Esq.

At Newark. An Hospital, founded, by

NOTTINGHAM.

Alexander Bishop of Lincoln, in the reign of Henry I.; yearly revenue 17*l*. 1*s*. 9½*d*., now worth 341*l*. 15*s*. 10*d*.

An Augustine Friary; granted, 35 Henry VIII., to John Andrews.

At NEWSTEAD. An Augustine Priory, built by Henry II. in the year 1170; yearly revenue 219*l*. 18*s*. 8½*d*., now worth 4,398*l*. 14*s*. 2*d*.; granted, 32 Henry VIII., to Sir John Byron.

At NOTTINGHAM. St. Jones' Hospital, for the sick poor, founded before the time of John; rents 4*l*. 13*s*. 4*d*.; now worth 93*l*. 6*s*. 8*d*.

Plumtree's Hospital, founded, 16 Richard II., by John Plumtree, for poor old widows; rents 11*l*. 1*s*., now worth 221*l*.

A House of Grey Friars, founded, Henry III., in the year 1250; granted, 2 Edward VI., to Thomas Heneage.

A Carmelite Friary, founded about the year 1276, by Lord Grey, of Wilton, and Sir John Shirley; granted, 33 Henry VIII., to James Hurley.

At RODINGTON. A College, founded, by William Babington, Esq., in the time of Henry VI., rents 30*l*. now worth 600*l*.

At RUFFORD. A Cistercian Abbey, founded, in the year 1148, by Gilbert, Earl of Lincoln ; value 254*l.* 6*s.* 8*d.*, yearly, now worth 5,086*l.* 13*s.* 4*d.* ; granted to George, Earl of Shrewsbury.

At SHELFORD. An Augustine Priory, founded, in the time of Henry II., by Ralph Hanselyn ; rents 151*l.* 14*s.* 1*d.*, now worth 3,034*l.* 1*s.* 8*d.* ; granted, 31 Henry VIII., to Michael Stanhope.

At SIBTHORP. A College, founded, in the time of Edward II., by Geffrey le Scrop ; rents 25*l.* 18*s.* 8*d.*, now worth 518*l.* 13*s.* 4*d.*; granted, 37 Henry VIII., to Richard Whalley and Thomas Magnus.

At SOUTHWELL. A College, founded, in the year 630, by Paulinus Archbishop of York ; worth, at the valuation of 26 Henry VIII., 516*l.* 1*s.* 6½*d.*, now worth 10,321*l.* 10*s.* 10*d.*

At STOKE, by Newark. An Hospital for Sick persons, founded, very early ; valued at 9*l.* yearly, now worth 180*l.* ; granted, 18 Elizabeth, to John Mersh and Francis Greneham.

At THURGARTON. An Augustine Priory, founded, in the year 1130, by Ralph de Ayncourt ; yearly value 359*l.* 15*s.* 10*d.*, now worth 7,195*l.* 16*s.* 8*d.* ; granted, 30 Henry VIII., to William Cooper.

At WALLINGWELLS. A Benedictine Nunnery, founded, in the reign of Stephen, by Ralph de Cheurolcourt ; yearly income 87*l.* 11*s.* 6*d.*, now worth 1,751*l.* 10*s.* ; granted, 6 Elizabeth, to Richard Pype and Francis Boyer.

At WELBECK. A Premonstratensian Abbey, founded, in the year 1153, by Thomas Jocei ; yearly income 298*l.* 4*s.* 8*d.*, now worth 5,964*l.* 13*s.* 4*d.* ; granted, 30 Henry VIII., to Richard Whalley.

At WIRKESOP, or RADFORD. An Augustine Priory, founded, 3 Henry I., by William de Luvetol ; yearly value 302*l.* 6*s.* 10*d.*, now worth 6,046*l.* 16*s.* 8*d.* ; granted, 33 Henry VIII., to Francis, Earl of Shrewsbury.

OXFORD (COUNTY.)

At BANBURY. A College ; yearly income 48*l.* 6*s.* now worth 966*l.*

An Hospital for several sick persons, founded, in the reign of John ; yearly value 15*l.* 1*s.* 10*d.* now worth 301*l.* 6*s.* 8*d.*

At BRUERIA, or BRUERNE. A Cistercian Abbey, founded, in the year 1147, by Nicholas Basset; yearly value 124*l.* 10*s.* 10*d.*, now worth 2,490*l.* 16*s.* 8*d.*; granted, 8 James I., to Sir Anthony Coke.

At BURCESTER. An Augustine Priory, founded, in the year 1182, by Gilbert Basset, Baron of Hedington; yearly value 167*l.* 2*s.* 10*d.*, now worth 3,342*l.* 16*s.* 8*d.*; granted, 30 Henry VIII., to Charles, Duke of Suffolk.

At BURFORD. An Hospital; valued at 13*l.* 6*s.* 6*d.*, now worth 266*l.* 10*s.*; granted, 35 Henry VIII., to Edward Herman.

At CAVERSHAM. An Augustine Cell, founded in the year 1162.

At CHARLETON. An Alien Priory, founded, in the year 1081, by Hugh Grentemoisnil; granted to Sir Thomas White and others.

At CLATTERCOTE. A Gilbertine Priory, founded in the time of King John; yearly value 34*l.* 19*s.* 11*d.*, now worth 699*l.* 18*s.* 4*d.*; granted, 2 Elizabeth, to Thomas Lee.

At CROWMERSH. An Hospital, built before the year 1248; granted to Thomas Gratewick and Anselm Lamb.

At DORCHESTER. An Augustine Priory,

founded, in the year 1140, by Alexander, Bishop of Lincoln; yearly value 219*l*. 12*s*. 0½*d*., now worth 4,392*l*. 0*s*. 10*d*.; granted, 36 Henry VIII., to Edmond Ashfield.

At EGNESHAM. A Benedictine Abbey, founded, in the year 1005, by Ailmer, Earl of Cornwall; yearly value 441*l*. 16*s*. 1*d*., now worth 8,836*l*. 1*s*. 8*d*.; granted, 35 Henry VIII., to Sir Edward North and William Darcy.

At EWELME. An Hospital for the Poor, founded, in the year 1437, by William de la Pole, Earl of Suffolk; yearly value 20*l*., now worth 400*l*.

At GODESTON. A Benedictine Nunnery, founded, by Editha, a religious woman, in the reign of Henry I.; yearly value 319*l*. 18*s*. 8*d*.; now worth 6,398*l*. 13*s*. 4*d*.; granted, by Henry VIII., to his Physician, Doctor George Owen.

At GORING. An Augustine Nunnery, founded in the time of Henry II.; yearly value 60*l*. 5*s*. 6*d*., now worth 1,205*l*. 10*s*.; granted, 30 Henry VIII., to Charles, Duke of Suffolk, and afterwards to Sir Thomas Pope.

At GOSFORD. A House of Hospitalers, founded, in the year 1180, by Robert D'Oily; granted 34 Henry VIII., to Anthony Stringer and John Williams.

At LITTLEMORE. A Benedictine Nunnery, founded in the reign of Henry II.; yearly value 33*l*. 6*s*. 8*d*., now worth 666*l*. 13*s*. 4*d*.; granted, 38 Henry VIII., to William Owen and John Bridges.

At NORTON. An Augustine Priory, founded, in the reign of Henry II., by William Fitz Alan; yearly value 50*l*., now worth 1000*l*.; granted to the Brazen Nose College, Oxford.

At ASENEY. An Augustine Priory, built, in the year 1129, by Robert D'Oily, on an island in the river, near the Castle of Oxford; yearly value 755*l*. 18*s*. 6½*d*., now worth 15,118*l*. 10*s*. 10*d*.

At OXFORD. St. Frideswide's, now Christ Church. King Didanus built this as a Nunnery, in the year 730; his own daughter Frideswide, who was afterwards canonized, had presided there. It became, in the course of time, a Priory, which was suppressed by virtue of a Bull from Pope Clement VII. dated April 3, 1525; and the site and lands granted to Cardinal Wolsey, who founded there a noble College for a Dean, Sub-dean, one hundred Canons, thirteen Chaplains, professors of the Canon and Civil Law, Physic, and of all the Arts and Sciences, and other persons, to the number of 186 in the whole. The revenues were valued at 224*l*. 4*s*. 8*d*., now worth 4,484*l*. 13*s*. 4*d*. It supports now a Dean, eight Canons, one hundred and one

Students, eight Chaplains, eight Clerks, eight Choristers, twenty-four Almsmen, &c.

St. George's College, founded, in the year 1149, on the ruins of an ancient Monastery, which was built by Robert D'Oily and Roger Tueri.

All Soul's College, founded, in the year 1438, by Henry Chicheley, Archbishop of Canterbury, for a Warden and forty Fellows, with Chaplains, Clerks, and Choristers; yearly value 392*l*. 2*s*. 3*d*., now worth 7,842*l*. 5*s*.

Baliol College, built by the widow of Sir John Baliol, in the year 1284, for poor Scholars; yearly value 74*l*. 3*s*. 4*d*., now worth 1,483*l*. 6*s*. 8*d*.; it now consists of a Master, 12 Fellows, and 14 Scholars.

St. Bernard's College, founded, in the year 1436, by Henry Chicheley, Archbishop of Canterbury, for monastic Students; the revenues and buildings were converted, in the year 1555, to support what is called St. John the Baptist.

Brazen Nose College, built by William Smith, Bishop of Lincoln, and Sir Richard Sutton, in the year 1511, for a Master and several Students.

Canterbury College, founded, in the year 1349, by the most Reverend Simon de Islip, Archbishop of Canterbury, to repair the chasm which was made in the Clergy by the pestilence ; he purchased some lands and built on it this, under the name of Canterbury Hall, for Students in the Canon and Civil Laws. It was made, 38 Henry VIII., a part of Christ Church College

Corpus Christi College, built, in the year 1513, by Richard Fox, Bishop of Winchester, and Hugh Oldham, Bishop of Exeter, for Augustine Students ; yearly value 382*l*. 8*s*. 9*d*., now worth 7,648*l*. 15*s*.; supports at present a Superior, twenty Fellows, twenty Scholars, two Chaplains, and two Clerks, &c.

Durham College, founded, in the year 1290, by the Convent of Durham, for their Students ; increased afterward in buildings, revenues and books, by Hugh de Bury, the learned Bishop of that see ; yearly value 115*l*. 4*s*. 4*d*., now worth 2,304*l*. 6*s*. 8*d*.; now called Trinity College.

Exeter College, or Stapleton Hall, founded, in the year 1314, by Walter Stapleton, Bishop of Exeter, for his Students, where Hart Hall now stands ; revenues 81*l*. 9*s*. yearly, now worth 1,629*l*. Supports now a Rector, twenty-two Fellows, and some Scholars.

Glocester Hall, or College ; the site was given, in the year 1283, by Sir John Giffard, to the Benedictine Friars, to build a habitation in the University; called now Worcester College.

Lincoln College, founded, in the year 1427, by Richard Fleming, Bishop of Lincoln, and the Archbishop of York and others; yearly value 101*l*. 8*s*. 10*d*., now worth 2,028*l*. 16*s*. 8*d*. Supports a Rector, twelve Fellows, and some Scholars.

London College, founded, in the year 1421, by Richard Clifford, Bishop of London, for secular and regular Students of Civil Law; suppressed in the reign of Henry VIII

Magdalen College. William Patten, Bishop of Winchester, founded, in the year 1448, a Hall for Students; and in the year 1458 a fine College, for a President, forty Fellows, thirty Scholars, four Chaplains, eight Clerks, sixteen Choristers, &c.; yearly value 1,076*l*. 5*s*. 2*d*., now worth 21,525*l*. 3*s*. 4*d*.

St. Mary College, founded, by Thomas Holden, Esq., in the year 1435, for the Augustine Students; granted, 38 Hen. VIII., to William Ramesden and Richard Vavasor.

Merton College, founded, in the year 1267, by Walter de Merton, Lord Chancellor of England, and afterwards Bishop of Rochester, for Chaplains and Students;

yearly value 354*l*. 2*s*. 6*d*., now worth 7,082*l*. 10*s*. Supports a Warden, twenty-four Fellows, fourteen Post Masters, &c.

New College, or Winchester College, founded, and amply endowed by William of Wykeham, Bishop of Winchester, in the year 1386, for a Warden, seventy Scholars, ten Chaplains, three Clerks, and sixteen Choristers ; yearly value 487*l*. 7s. 8*d*., now worth 9,747*l*. 13*s*. 4*d*.

Oriel, or St. Mary College, built, in the year 1324, by King Edward III., and Adam de Brom, Almoner to King Edward II., for students ; valued at 182*l*. 8*s*. 6*d*., yearly, now worth 3,684*l*. 10*s*. This supports now a Provost, 18 Fellows, &c.

Queen's College, founded, in the year 1340, by Robert de Eglesfield, Chaplain to Queen Philippa ; yearly value 302*l*. 2*s*. 10*d*., now worth 6,042*l*. 16*s*. 8*d*. It supports now a provost, 16 Fellows, two Chaplains, some Bachelors, two Clerks, and 19 undergraduate Scholars.

University College. King Alfred founded in this city three Societies or Halls ; one for students in grammar ; the second for philosophy ; and the third for divinity : but it is certain that this University was either rebuilt or enlarged by the bounty of William Archdeacon of Durham, Walter Skirlaw, Bishop of Durham, and some Noblemen, in the year 1249, valued, 26 Henry VIII., at 78*l.* 14*s.* 7*d.*, now worth 1,574*l.* 11*s.* 8*d.*; supports now a master, 12 Fellows, 13 Scholars, &c.

St. Bartholomew's College, half a mile east of the town, supposed to have been founded by King Henry I.

Carmelite Friary, settled in the royal palace of Beaumont, by King Edward II.; granted, 33 Henry VIII., to Edward Powel.

Trinity House, for the redemption of Captives, founded, in the year 1291, by Edmund, Earl of Cornwall.

At REWLEY. A Cistercian Abbey, founded, in the year 1280, by the executors of Richard King of the Romans, to pray for his soul ; yearly value 174*l.* 3*s.* 0$\frac{1}{2}$*d.*, now worth 3,483*l.* 0*s.* 10*d.* ; granted, 38 Henry VIII., to the Dean and Chapter of Christ Church, Oxford.

At SAUNFORD. A Templar's Hospital, founded by Maud, Queen of King Stephen, granted, 33 Henry VIII., to Edward Powel.

At STODELEY. A Benedictine Nunnery, built in the reign of Henry II., by Bernard de St. Walerico ; yearly value 102*l.* 6*s.* 7$\frac{1}{2}$*d.*, now worth 2,046*l.* 12*s.* 6*d.* ; granted, 31 Henry VIII., to John Croke.

At TAME. A Cistercian Abbey, founded, in

the year 1137, by the bounty of Alexander Bishop of Lincoln ; yearly value 256*l.* 13*s.* 7½*d.*, now worth 5,133*l.* 12*s.* 6*d.* ; granted, 1 Edward VI., to Edward, Duke of Somerset.

At WROXTON. An Augustine Priory founded, in the reign of Henry III., by Mr. Michael Belet; yearly value 78*l.* 14*s.* 3*d.*, now worth 1,574*l.* 5*s.* ; granted, 36 Henry VIII., to Sir Thomas Pope, who gave a part to Trinity College, Oxford.

RUTLAND (COUNTY).

At BROOKE. An Augustine Priory, founded, by Hugh Ferrers in the reign of Richard I. ; yearly value 43*l.* 13*s.* 4*d.*, now worth 873*l.* 6*s.* 8*d.* ; granted, 28 Henry VIII., to Anthony Coope.

At EDITH WESTON. An Alien Priory, built in the reign of Henry I., by William de Tankerville ; granted, 4 Edward VI., to William, Marquis of Northampton.

A College, founded, 25 Edward III., by William Wade and John Wade, Chaplain ; yearly value 22*l.* 18*s.* 6*d.*, now worth 458*l.* 10*s.* ; granted, 1 Elizabeth, to John Lord St. John.

At OKEHAM. A College for poor people, built in the year 1398, by William Dalby of Exton; yearly value 26*l*. 13*s*. 4*d*., now worth 533*l*. 6*s*. 8*d*.; granted, 26 Henry VIII., to Richard Flower, of Whitwell.

SALOP (COUNTY).

At BATTLEFIELD. A College, a mile north of Shrewsbury, founded, in the year 1403, by Henry IV.; yearly value 54*l*. 1*s*. 10*d*., now worth 1,081*l*. 16*s*. 8*d*.

At BILDEWAS. A Cistercian Abbey, founded, in the year 1135, by Roger Bishop of Chester; yearly value 129*l*. 6*s*. 10*d*., now worth 2,586*l*. 16*s*. 8*d*.; granted, 29 Henry VIII., to Edward, Lord Powis.

At BREWOOD. A Cistercian Nunnery, founded, prior to the reign of King John; yearly value 31*l*. 14*s*., now worth 621*l*. 6*s*. 8*d*.; granted, 31 Henry VIII., to William Whorwood.

At BRIDGENORTH. A College, founded, in the reign of William Rufus, by Robert, Earl of Shrewsbury; ganted, 21 Elizabeth, to Sir Christopher Hatton.

Hospital, founded, in the reign of

Richard I., by Ralph le Strange-; granted, 31 Henry VIII., to Leonard Edwards.

At BROMFIELD. A Benedictine Cell, built about the time of Henry I., ; yearly value 77*l*. 18*s*. 3*d*., now worth 1,558*l*. 5*s*. ; granted to Charles Fox.

At BURFORD. A Collegiate Church, founded in the reign of Edward I. ; granted, 13 Elizabeth, to William James and John Grey.

At CHIRBURY. An Augustine Priory, founded 11 Henry III. ; yearly value 87*l*. 7*s*. 4*d*., now worth 1,747*l*. 6*s*. 8*d*. ; granted, 37 Henry VIII., to Edward Hampton.

At HAGHMON. An Augustine Priory, founded, in the year 1110, by William Fitz Alan, of Clun ; yearly value 294*l*. 12*s*. 9*d*., now worth 5,892*l*. 15*s*. ; granted, 32 Henry VIII., to Edmund Littleton.

At HALES. A Premonstratensian Abbey, founded, 16 John, by Peter de Rupibus, bishop of Winchester ; yearly value 337*l*. 15*s*. 6½*d*., now worth 6,755*l*. 10*s*. 10*d*. ; granted 30 Henry VIII., to Sir John Dudley.

At HALSTONE. A Templars' Hospital ; yearly value 160*l*. 14*s*. 10*d*., now worth 3,214*l*. 16*s*. 8*d*. ; granted, 5 Elizabeth to William Horne.

SALOP.

At LILLESHULL. An Augustine Priory, built in the year 1145; yearly value 327*l*. 10*s*., now worth 6,550*l*. granted, 31 Henry VIII., to James Leveson.

At LUDLOW. An Hospital, built in the reign of John; yearly value 27*l*. 16*s*.10*d*., now worth 556*l*. 16*s*.8*d*. ; granted, 1 Edward VI., to John, Earl of Warwick.

    Augustine Priory, built about the year 1282 ; granted to George Cotton and William Man.

    Carmelite Friary, founded, in the year 1349, by Lawreance of Ludlow ; granted, 2 Elizabeth, to Richard Hacket and Thomas Trentham.

At MORFIELD. A Benedictine Cell, founded, and endowed by the Earl of Shrewsbury ; yearly value 15*l*., now worth 300*l*. ; granted, 37 Henry VIII., to Henry, Lord Lisle.

At NEWPORT. A College, founded, 20 Henry VI., by Thomas Draper ; granted, 13 Elizabeth, to Edmond Dowing and Peter Ashton.

PONSBURY. A College built before the reign of Edward I. ; yearly value 40*l*. 17*s*. 3*d*., now worth 817*l*. 5*s*.

SALOP.

At RATTLINGCOPE. An Augustine Cell, built in the reign of John ; granted 37 Henry VIII., to Robert Long.

At SHREWSBURY. A Benedictine Monastery, founded, in the year 1083, by Roger de Montgomery, Earl of Arundel ; yearly value 615*l.* 4*s.* 3*d.*, now worth 12,304*l.* 5*s.* ; granted, 33 Henry VIII., to Edward Watson and Henry Herdson.

St. Chadd's College, founded, before the time of William the Conqueror; yearly value 14*l.* 14*s.* 4*d.*, now worth 294*l.* 6*s.* 8*d.* ; granted, 3 Edward VI., to John Southcott and John Chadderton.

St. Michael's College, founded, prior to the time of Edward the Confessor; rents and tythes made 13*l.* 1*s.* 8*d.*, now worth 261*l.* 13*s.* 4*d.* ; granted to Thomas Reeve and George Cotton.

St. Chadd's Hospital for poor persons, founded by the society of Mercers in the town.

St. John's Hospital, built prior to the time of Edward II. ; rents 4*l.* 10*s.* 4*d.*, now worth 90*l.* 6*s.* 8*d.*

An Augustine Friary, founded, by the

Staffords ; granted, 53 Henry VIII., to Richard Andrews and Nicholas Temple.

A House of Black Friars, founded by Lady Geneville ; granted, 35 Henry VIII., to Richard Andrews and Nicholas Temple.

A House of Grey Friars, founded, in the reign of Henry III., by Hawise, Countess of Powis ; granted, 35 Henry VIII., to Richard Andrews and Nicholas Temple.

At TONGE. A College, founded, in the year 1410, by Isabel, Widow of Sir Fulk Pembroke and the Reverend William Swan, and the Rev. William Mosse ; valued yearly at 22*l.* 8*s.* 1*d.*, now worth 448*l.* 1*s.* 8*d.* ; granted, 1 Edward VI., to Sir Richard Manners.

At WENLOCK. A Cluniac Priory, founded, 14 William the Conqueror, by Roger of Montgomery, Earl of Arundel and Chichester, on the ruins of a Nunnery, founded, in the year 680, by St. Milburga, daughter of King Merwald ; yearly value 434*l.* 1*s.* 2½*d.*, now worth 8,681*l.* 4*s.* 2*d.* ; granted, 36 Henry VIII., to Augustino de Augustinis.

At WOMBRIDE. An Augustine Priory, founded, in the reign of Henry I., by William Fitz Alan ; revenues at the dissolution, 72*l.* 15*s.* 8*d.*, now worth 1,455*l.* 13*s.* 4*d.* ; granted, 31 Henry VIII., to James Leveson.

At Woodhouse. An Augustine Monastery, given to that Order by the Tuberville family, in the year 1250 ; granted to Thomas Reeves and George Cotton.

SOMERSET (County).

At Athelney. A Benedictine Abbey, founded, in the year 888, by King Alfred ; yearly value 209*l.* 0*s.* 3*d.*, now worth 4,180*l.* 5*s.* ; granted, 36 Henry VIII., to John Clayton.

At Barlinch. An Augustine Priory, built in the reign of Henry II., by William Say ; yearly value 98*l.* 14*s.* 8*d.*, now worth 1,974*l.* 13*s.* 4*d.* ; granted, 30 Henry VIII., to Sir John Wallop.

At Bath. A Cathedral, founded, in the reign of Henry I., by John Bishop of Wells, on the ruins of a Benedictine Abbey, which was originally built, 676, by King Osric, but destroyed and rebuilt several times afterwards ; yearly value 695*l.* 6*s.* 1½*d.* now worth 13,806*l.* 2*s.* 6*d.* ; granted, 34 Henry VIII., to Humphry Colles.

SOMERSET.

St. John's Hospital, near the Cross and Hot Baths, founded, in the year 1180, by Reginald Bishop of Bath, for poor strangers; yearly value 22*l.* 16*s.* 9*d.*, now worth 456*l.* 15*s.*; granted, by Elizabeth, to the Mayor and Corporation.

At BEARWE, or BORROW GURNEY. A Benedictine Nunnery, founded, in the year 1200, by——Gurney, Lord of Stoke Hamden; yearly value 29*l.* 6*s.* 8*d.*, now worth 586*l.* 13*s.* 4*d.*; granted, 36 Henry VIII., to William Clerke.

At BRIDGE WATER. St. John's Hospital, founded, before 15 John, by William Bruer, for Secular Clergy, under condition of keeping hospitality for the poor Natives, and for strange Pilgrims; yearly value 120*l.* 19*s.* 1½*d.*, now worth 2,419*l.* 2*s.* 6*d.*; granted, 34 Henry VIII., to Humphry Colles.

At BRUTON. An Augustine Priory, founded, in the year 1005, by Algar, Earl of Cornwall; yearly value 480*l.* 17*s.* 2*d.*, now worth 9,617*l.* 3*s.* 4*d.*; granted, 37 Henry VIII., to Maurice Berkely.

At MINCHIN BUCKLAND. A Nunnery and Hospital of Hospitalers, founded, about the year 1180, by Henry II.; yearly value 223*l.* 7*s.* 4*d.*, now worth 4,467*l.* 6*s.* 8*d.*; granted, 36 Henry VIII., to Alexander Popham and William Halley.

SOMERSET.

At BERKELY. An Augustine Priory, built in the year 1199, by William of Edingdon ; yearly value 6*l*. 5*s*. 2½*d*., now worth 125*l*. 4*s*. 2*d*. ; granted, 7 Edward VI., to John and James Bisse.

At CANYNGTON. A Benedictine Nunnery, founded, in the reign of King Stephen, by Robert de Courcey ; yearly value 39*l*. 15*s*. 8*d*., now worth 795*l*. 13*s*. 4*d*. ; granted, 30 Henry VIII., to Edward Rogers.

At CLYVE, cr CLIFF. A Cistercian Abbey, founded, in the year 1188, by William de Romare, Earl of Lincoln ; yearly value 155*l*. 9*s*. 5*d*., now worth 3,109*l*. 8*s*. 4*d*. ; granted, 33 Henry VIII., to Thomas, Earl of Sussex.

At TEMPLE COMB. A House of Hospitalers, founded, in the year 1185, by Serlo Odo ; yearly value 128*l*. 7*s*. 6*d*., now worth 2,567*l*. 10*s*. ; granted, 34 Henry VIII., to Richard Andrews and Leonard Chamberlayne.

At DUNSTER. A Benedictine Cell, founded, in the time of William the Conqueror, by Sir William de Mahun ; yearly value 37*l*. 4*s*. 8*d*., now worth 744*l*. 13*s*. 4*d*. ; granted, 34 Henry VIII., to Humphry Colles.

At GLASTONBURY. A Benedictine Monastrey, founded, as historians say, by Joseph of Arimathea. The first congregation of Monks, they

say, were brought together by a disciple of St.
Patrick, in the year 435. Yearly value 3,508*l.*
13*s.* 4½*d*., now worth 70,173*l.* 7*s* 6*d.* ; granted,
1 Edward VI., to Edward, Duke of Somerset,
and 1 Elizabeth, to Sir Peter Carew.

At KEYNSHAM. An Augustine Priory, founded, in the year 1170, by William, Earl of Gloucester; yearly value 450*l.* 3*s.* 6*d.*, now worth
9,003*l.* 10*s.* granted, 6 Edward VI., to Thomas
Bridges, Esq.

At MICHELNEY. A Benedictine Monastery,
founded, in the year 939, by King Athelstan;
yearly value 498*l.* 16*s.* 3½*d.*, now worth 9,976*l.*
5*s.* 10*d.* ; granted, 29 Henry VIII., to Edward,
Earl of Hertford.

At MARTOCK. A Priory, granted, 34 Henry
VIII., to Humphry Colles.

At CHARTERHOUSE ON MENDIP. A Cell,
granted, 36 Henry VIII., to Robert May.

At MONTECUTE, OLIM MONS ACUTUS. A
Cluniac Priory, founded, by William the Conqueror; yearly value 524*l.* 11*s.* 8*d.*, now worth
10,491*l.* 13*s.* 4*d.* ; granted, 16 Elizabeth, to
Robert, Earl of Leicester.

At SLAVERDALE. An Augustine Priory, built
by Sir William Zouch; granted, 36 Henry
VIII., to John, Earl of Oxford.

SOMERSET.

At STOKE CURCY. An Alien Priory, founded, in the reign of Henry II.; valued at the dissolution at 58*l*., now worth 1,160*l*.

At STOKE. A College, founded, in the year 1304, by Sir John de Bello Campo; granted, 2 Elizabeth, to Cuthbert Vaughan.

At TAUNTON. An Augustine Priory, built in the reign of Henry I., by William Giffard, Bishop of Winchester; yearly value 438*l*. 9*s*. 10*d*., now worth 8,769*l*. 16*s*. 8*d*.; granted, 36 Henry VIII., to Mathew Colehurst.

At WELLS. A Cathedral Church, built in the year 704, by King Ina; enlarged afterwards by different Bishops; revenues of the Bishop were valued at 1,843*l*. 19*s*. 4*d*., and of the Canons 897*l*. 5*s*. 11*d*., both sums now worth 54,825*l*. 5*s*.

Mauntery College, built in the year 1401, by Ralph Erghum, Bishop of Bath and Wells, for the Clergy of the Cathedral; yearly value 11*l*. 18*s*. 8*d*., now worth 238*l*. 13*s*. 4*d*.; granted, 2 Edward VI., to John Aylworth and John Lacy.

Vicar's College, began by Walter de Hull, Canon; enlarged, in the year 1347, by Rad. de Salopia, Bishop of Wells: yearly value 72*l*. 10*s*. 9½*d*., now worth 1,450*l*. 15*s*. 10*d*.

Brigstreet Hospital, founded, for twenty-four poor persons, by Nicholas Buthwith, Bishop of Bath, about the year 1424, but maintains now, they say, only twenty.

St. John's Hospital, founded, in the reign of King John, by Hugh of Wells, afterwards Bishop of Lincoln ; yearly value 41*l.* 3*s.* 6½*d.*, now worth 823*l.* 10*s.* 10*d.* ; granted, 13 Elizabeth, to Christopher Hatton.

At WITHAM. A Carthusian Priory, built and endowed by King Henry II. ; yearly value 227*l.* 1*s.* 8*d.*, now worth 4,541*l.* 13*s.* 4*d.* ; granted, 36 Henry VIII., to Ralph Hopton.

At WORSPRING. A Regular Priory, founded, in the year 1210, by William de Courtney; yearly value 110*l.* 18*s.* 4½*d.*, now worth 2,218*l.* 7*s.* 6*d.* ; granted, 2 Elizabeth, to William and John Lacy.

At BRISTOL. A Benedictine Priory, built by Robert, son of Henry I., in the north east of the city ; granted, 35 Henry VIII., to Henry Brayne.

Great St. Augustine's, now Holy Trinity and Cathedral, founded, in the year 1148, by Robert Fitzharding ; yearly value 767*l.* 15*s.* 3*d.*, now worth 15,355*l.* 5*s.*

St. Mary Magdalen Nunnery, founded, by Eva, wife to Robert Fitzharding, in the reign of Henry II., yearly value 21*l.* 11*s.* 3*d.*, now worth 431*l.* 5*s.*; granted, 31 Henry VIII., to Henry Brayn and John Marsh.

St. Bartholomew's Hospital, granted by Henry VIII., to the executors of Robert Thorn and Sir Thomas West; is now a grammar school.

St. Catherine's Hospital, founded, 4 Henry III., by Robert de Berkele; yearly value 21*l.* 15*s.* 8*d.*, now worth 435*l.* 13*s* 4*d.*,

Gaunts, or Billeswyke Hospital, built in the year 1229, by Maurice de Gaunt, for one hundred poor people; yearly value 140*l.*, now worth 2,800*l.*; granted, 33 Hen. VIII., to the Mayor and Citizens; is now an Orphan Hospital.

St. John's Hospital, built by John, Earl of Moreton, afterwards King of England, for the sick; yearly value 51*l.* 10*s.* 4*d.* now worth 1,030*l.* 6*s.* 8*d.*; granted, 36 Henry VIII., to G. Owen.

St. Lawrence's Hospital, founded, before 8 Henry III.; granted, 35 Henry VIII., to Sir Ralph Sadleyr.

Lyons, or Lewin's Mede-street Hospital, founded, in the year 1460, by William Spenser.

St. Michael's-hill Almshouse, founded, in the year 1501, by John Foster, for one priest, eight poor men, and five poor women, is yet in being.

Radcliff-hill Almshouse, built in the year 1442, by William Cannings, is still in being, though having no endowment.

Temple-street Hospitals. Under Tucker's Hall is one founded by the Tucker's Company; under the Weaver's Hall is another founded at a very early period.

Temple Gate Hospital, built by Roger Magdalen of Nonney.

Trinity Hospital, founded, 4 Henry V., by John Barstable, merchant of the town; granted, 20 Elizabeth, to the Mayor and Corporation; is still in being.

An Augustine Friary, built in the reign of Edw. II., by Sir Simon and Sir William Montacute; granted 35 Henry VIII., to Maurice Dennis.

The Black Friary, founded by Sir Maurice Gaunt; granted, 31 Henry VIII., to William Chester.

The Grey Friars' House, founded in the year 1234; granted, 33 Henry VIII., to the Mayor and Citizens.

STAFFORD (County).

At BLYTHBURY. A Benedictine Nunnery, founded, in the reign of Henry I., by Hugh Malveysin.

At BRIWERNE, or, the BLACK LADIES OF BREWOOD, founded, prior to the time of Richard I. ; yearly value 11*l.* 1*s.* 6*d.*, now worth 221*l.* 10*s.* ; granted, 30 Henry VIII., to Thomas Gifford.

At BURTON-UPON-TRENT. A Benedictine Abbey, founded, in the year 1004, by Walfric Spot ; yearly value 356*l.* 16*s.* 3½*d.*, now worth 7,136*l.* 5*s.* 10*d.*; granted, by Henry VIII., to Sir William Paget.

At CALWICK. A Benedictine Priory, built in the year 1142, by Geva, daughter of Hugh, Earl of Chester ; yearly value 25*l.* 10. 3*d.* now worth 510*l.* 5*s.*

At CHOTES. A Cistercian Abbey, founded, in the year 1176, by Bertram de Verdun ; yearly value 103*l.* 6*s.* 7*d.*, now worth 2,066*l.* 11*s.* 8*d.*; granted, 36 Henry VIII., to Jeffrey Foljamb.

At DIEULACRES. A Cistercian Abbey, founded, in the year 1214, by Randal de Blunderville, Earl of Chester ; value 243*l.* 3*s.* 6*d.* yearly, now worth 4,863*l.* 10*s.*; granted, 6 Edward VI., to Ralph Bagnall.

At DUDLEY. A Cluniac Cell, founded, in the year 1161, by Ralph Painell, lord of the manor, in pursuance of his father's will; value 33*l*. 1*s*. 4*d*. yearly, now worth 661*l*. 6*s*. 8*d*.; granted, 32 Henry VIII., to Sir John Dudley.

At GNOUSHALL. A College, founded in the time of Henry I.; rents 54*l*. now worth 1,080*l*.; granted, 1 Edward VI., to the Bishop of Lichfield and his successors.

At HULTON. A Cistercian Abbey, founded in the year 1223, by Henry Audley; value 76*l*. 14*s*. 11½*d*. yearly, now worth 1,534*l*. 19*s*. 2*d*.; granted, 34 Henry VIII., to Sir Edward Aston.

At LAPPELE. An Alien Priory, founded, in the time of Edward the Confessor, by Algar, Earl of Chester or Mercia; granted, 1 Edward VI., to Sir Richard Mannors.

At LICHFIELD. A Cathedral Church, built in the year 656, by King Oswy; underwent many changes and repairs since that time; revenues 703*l*. 5*s*. 2*d*.; and of the Chapter 275*l*. 13*s*. 2*d*.: make together now 19,578*l*. 6*s*. 8*d*.

Vicar's Choral, that is, the Sub-chanter, Sachrist and Clerks, of this Cathedral, had a separate Establishment; value 199*l*. 10*s*. 7*d*. yearly, now worth 3,990*l*. 11*s*. 8*d*.

St. John's Hospital; value 46*l*. 18*s*. 1*d*., now worth 938*l*. 1*s*. 8*d*.; it continues to this day.

STAFFORD.

A Grey Friary, founded in the year 1229, by Alexander, Bishop of Lichfield; granted, 36 Henry VIII., to Richard Crumbilthorn.

At PENKRIDGE. A College, or Free Chapel; granted, 17 John, by Mr. Hugh House, to the Archbishop of Dublin and his successors; value 106*l.* 15*s.* yearly, now worth 2,135*l.*; granted, 2 Edward VI., to John Earl of Warwick.

At ROUCESTER. An Augustine Priory, built in the year 1146, by Richard Bacoun; rents 111*l.* 11*s.* 7*d.*, now worth 2,231*l.* 11*s.* 8*d.*; granted, 31 Henry VIII., to Richard Trentham.

At SANDWELL. A Benedictine Priory, founded, in the time of Henry II., by William Guy, of Ophani; rents made 26*l.* 8*s.* 7*d.*, now worth 528*l.* 11*s.* 8*d.*

At DE SARTIS, or RONTON. An Augustine Priory, founded, in the time of Henry II., by Robert Noeli; value 102*l.* 11*s.* 1*d.* yearly, now worth 2,031*l.* 1*s.* 8*d.*; granted 30 Henry VIII., to John Wiseman.

At STAFFORD. A College or Free Chapel; granted, by King Stephen, to the Bishop and Chapter of Lichfield; value 38*l.* yearly, now worth 760*l.*; granted, 14 Elizabeth, to the Burgesses of Stafford.

An Augustine Priory, built in the year 1180, by Richard Peche, Bishop of Coventry and Lichfield; value 198*l*. 0*s*. 9½*d*. yearly, now worth 3,960*l*. 15*s*. 10*d*.; granted, 31 Henry VIII., to Doctor Rowland Lee, Bishop of Coventry and Lichfield.

St. John's Hospital, for poor brethren.

St. Leonard's Spytell, or Free Chapel; value 4*l*. 12*s*. 4*d*. yearly, now worth 92*l*. 6*s*. 8*d*.

A Franciscan Friary, founded 10 Edward I.; valued at 35*l*. 13*s*. 10*d*., now worth 713*l*. 16*s*. 8*d*.; granted, 31 Henry VIII., to James Leveson.

An Augustine Monastery, founded in the year 1344, by Ralph, Lord Stafford; granted to Thomas Neve and Giles Isam.

At Stone. An Augustine Priory, built originally by Wolphere, King of Mercia, for the salvation of his two sons Wolfadus and Rufinus, whom he murdered before his conversion to Christianity, in the year 670. Rents 119*l*. 14*s*. 11½*d*., now worth 2,394*l*. 19*s*. 2*d*.; granted, 30 Henry VIII., to George Harpur.

At Tamworth. A College; St. Editha, daughter of King Edgar, founded here a Convent, which became a College afterwards, and valued at 42*l*. 2*s*. 4*d*., now worth 842*l*. 6*s*. 8*d*.; granted, 23 Elizabeth, to Edward Downing and Peter Ashton.

An Hospital, founded, 15 Edward I., by Philip Marmion, for the Premonstratensian Friars; and he gave them in Ashfield pasture for four oxen and two horses, under condition of praying for his soul; yearly value 3*l*. 6*s*. 8*d*., now worth 66*l*. 13*s*. 4*d*.

At TETENHALL. A College, founded, in King Edgar's reign; value 21*l*. 6*s*. 8*d*., yearly, now worth 426*l*. 13*s*. 4*d*.; granted, 3 Edward VI., to Walter Wrottesley.

At TRICKINGHAM. An Augustine Priory, founded, in the time of Henry I., on the ruins of a convent, founded, in the year 680, by King Ethelred, for his daughter, St. Werburgh, who died there an Abbess; value 106*l*. 3*s*. 10*d*. yearly, now worth 2,123*l*. 16*s*. 8*d*.; granted, 30 Henry VIII., to Charles, Duke of Suffolk.

At TUTBURY. A Benedictine Priory, founded, in the year 1080, by Henry de Ferrers; rents 244*l*. 16*s*. 8*d*., now worth 4,896*l*. 13*s*. 4*d*.; granted, 6 Edward VI., to Sir William Cavendish.

At WOLVERHAMPTON. A College, or Monastery, built in the year 996, and amply endowed by a pious widow, Wulfruna; underwent many alterations in after times, and finally became one of the King's Free Chapels; the Deanery valued, 26 Henry VIII., at 38*l*. yearly; and five Prebends 28*l.*; both sums would make now 1,320*l.*; granted, 7 Edward VI., to John, Duke of Northumberland.

SUFFOLK (County).

At ALENSBORNE. An Augustine Priory, founded, before the year 1466 ; granted, 33 Henry VIII., to Sir John Wingfield.

An Hospital of Templars, founded, in the time of Henry II. ; rents 53*l.* 10*s.*, now worth 1,070*l.* ; granted, 35 Henry VIII., to Sir Richard Gresham.

At BLIBURGH. An Augustine Priory, settled by Henry I. ; rents 48*l.* 8*s.* 10*d.*, now worth 968*l.* 16*s.* 8*d.* ; granted, 30 Henry VIII., to Sir Arthur Hopton.

At BRUSYARD. A Nunnery of Minoresses, founded, at Ash, by Maud, Countess of Ulster, in the year 1354 ; yearly value 56*l.* 2*s.* 1*d.*, now worth 1,122*l.* 1*s.* 8*d.* ; granted, 30 Henry VIII., to Nicholas Hare.

SUFFOLK.

At BUNGAY. A Benedictine Nunnery, founded, in the time of Henry II., by Roger de Glanville; value 62*l.* 2*s.* 1½*d.* yearly, now worth 1,242*l.* 2*s.* 6*d.* ; granted, 29 Henry VIII., to Thomas, Duke of Norfolk.

At BURY ST. EDMOND. A Benedictine Abbey, founded, in the year 633, by Segebert, King of the East Angles, who, quitting his crown, became a religious there. The place took its name from the body of St. Edmond, King, that was translated thither, in the year 903 ; valued, at the dissolution, at 2,336*l.* 16*s.* 0½*d.*, now worth 46,736*l.* 0*s.* 10*d.* ; granted, 2 Elizabeth, to John Eyer.

A College, founded, in the time of Edward IV. ; granted, 2 Edward VI., to Richard Corbet.

St. Nicholas Hospital, founded by an Abbot of the town ; valued at 6*l.* 19*s.* 11*d.*, now worth 139*l.* 18*s.* 4*d.*

St. Peter's Hospital, founded, in the time of Henry I., by Abbot Anselm, for the maintenance of aged and sick Priests ; value 10*l.* 18*s.* 10½*d.* yearly, now worth 218*l.* 17*s.* 6*d.*

St. Saviour's Hospital, founded, in the year 1184, by Abbot Samson and his Convent, for the support of a warden, twelve chaplans, six clerks, twelve poor gentlemen and twelve poor women; granted, 34 Henry VIII., to Antony Stringer and John Williams.

A Grey Friary, founded, about the year 1256; granted, 33 Henry VIII., to Antony Harvey.

At BUTLEY. An Augustine Priory, founded, in the year 1171, by Ranulph de Glanville, the famous lawyer; income 318*l.* 17*s.* 2½*d.*, now worth 6,377*l.* 4*s.* 2*d.*; granted, 36 Henry VIII , to William Forth.

At CAMPESS. An Augustine Nunnery, founded, 6 Richard I., by Jane and Agnes, daughters of Theobald de Valoins, on a piece of ground which he gave them for that purpose; income 182*l.* 9*s.* 5*d.*, now worth 3,649*l.* 8*s.* 4*d.*; granted 35 Henry VIII., to Sir William Willoughby.

At CLARE. An Augustine Monastery, built in the year 1248, by Richard de Clare, Earl of Gloucester; granted, 31 Henry VIII., to Richard Friend.

At DODNASH. An Augustine Priory, founded, in the time of Edward I., by the ancestors of the noble family of Norfolk; yearly value 42*l.* 18*s.* 8½*d.*, now worth 858*l.* 14*s.* 2*d.*; granted, by Henry VIII., to Thomas Alverde.

SUFFOLK.

At DUNWICH. A House of Knights Templars; granted, 4 Elizabeth, to Thomas Andrews.

St. James's Hospital; founded in the time of Richard I.; revenues 26*l.* now worth 520*l.*

A Black Friary, granted, 36 Henry VIII., to John Eyre.

A Grey Friary, founded, in the time of Henry III., by Robert Fitz John granted to John Eyre.

At EYE. A Benedictine Priory, founded in the time of William the Conqueror, by Robert Malet; yearly value 184*l.* 9*s.* 7½*d.*, now worth 3,689*l.* 12*s.* 6*d.*; granted, 28 Henry VIII., to Charles, Duke of Suffolk.

At FLIXTON. An Augustine Priory, built in the year 1258, by Margery Harnes, widow of Bartholomew de Clerk; value 23*l.* 4*s.* 1*d.* yearly, now worth 468*l.* 1*s.* 8*d.*; granted, 26 Henry VIII., to John Tasburgh.

At GISELINGHAM. A Preceptory of Templars, founded, before the time of Richard I., by Sir Robert de Burgate; granted, 7 Edward VI., to John Grene and Robert Hall.

At GORLESTON. An Augustine Priory, built

in the time of Edward I., by William Woderove; granted, 36 Henry VIII., to John Eyre.

At HERINGFLEET. An Augustine Priory, founded, in the time of Henry III., by Roger Fitz Osbert ; rents 49*l.* 11*s.* 7*d.*, now worth 991*l.* 11*s.* 8*d.* ; granted, 38 Henry VIII., to Henry Jerningham.

At HOXON. A Benedictine Cell, founded, about the year 950, by Theodred, Bishop of London ; and richly endowed with lands, in the year 1130, by Maurice of Windsor and Egidia his Wife, for supporting there Monks, in order to pray for the soul of Ralph Dapifer ; rents 18*l.* 1*s.*, now worth 351*l.* ; granted, 38 Henry VIII., to Richard Gresham.

At IPSWICH. An Augustine Priory, built before the year 1177, by Norman Eadnothi ; rents 88*l.* 6*s.* 9*d.*, now worth 1,766*l.* 15*s.* ; granted, 36 Henry VIII., to Sir Thomas Pope.

St. Peter and Paul, another Priory of Augustine Canons, founded, in the time of Henry II., by Thomas Lacy ; granted, 9 James I., to Richard Percival and Edmund Duffield.

St. Mary Magdalen and St. James' Hospital, founded, in the time of King John.

Dandy's Almshouse, founded, in the year

1515, by Edmund Dandy, for the poor; granted by Edward VI.

An Augustine Friary, founded, in the time of Henry III., by Henry de Manesby and others; granted, 33 Henry VIII., to William Sabyne.

A Carmelite Friary, built about the year 1279, by Sir Thomas de Loudham; granted, 36 Henry VIII., to John Eyre.

An Augustine Priory, built in the time of William the Conqueror, by Gilbert Blund; rents 280*l.* 9*s.* 5*d.*, now worth 5,609*l.* 8*s.* 4*d.*; granted, 30 Henry VIII., to Richard Codington.

At KERSEY. An Austin Priory, founded, before 3 Henry III.; granted, 25 Henry VIII., to the King's College in Cambridge.

At LETHERINGTON. An Austin Cell; yearly value 26*l.* 18*s.* 5*d.*, now worth 538*l.* 8*s.* 4*d.*; granted, 7 Edward VI., to Elizabeth Naunton, daughter of Sir Anthony Naunton of Wingfield.

At LEYESTONE. A Premonstratensian Abbey, founded, in the year 1182, by Ralph de Glanville; yearly value 181*l.* 17*s.* 1½*d.*, now worth 3,637*l.* 2*s.* 6*d.*; granted, 28 Henry VIII., to Charles, Duke of Suffolk.

At METINGHAM. A College, built 6 Richard II.; yearly value 202*l.* 7*s.* 5½*d.*, now worth

4,047*l.* 9*s.* 2*d.*; granted, 33 Henry VIII., to Thomas Denny.

At MINDHAM. A Cluniac Priory, founded, in the time of Stephen, on the island of Hurst, in this parish, by William of Huntingfield; granted, to Richard Freston.

At REDLINGFIELD. A Benedictine Nunnery, founded, in the year 1120, by Manasses, Earl of Ghisnes; yearly value 81*l.* 2*s.* 5½*d.*, now worth 1,622*l.* 9*s.* 2*d.*; granted, 28 Henry VIII., to Edmund Bedingfield.

At RUMBURGH. A Benedictine Cell, built about the time of the Conquest.

At SIBTON. A Cistercian Abbey, founded, in the year 1149, by William de Cheney; yearly value 250*l.* 15*s.* 7½*d.*, now worth 5,015*l.* 12*s.* 6*d.*; granted, 1 Edward VI., to Sir Antony Denny.

At SNAPE. A Benedictine Priory, built in the year 1155, by William Martel; yearly value 99*l.* 1*s.* 11½*d.*, now worth 1,981*l.* 19*s.* 2*d.*; granted, 34 Henry VIII., to Thomas, Duke of Norfolk.

At STOKE. A College, founded, in the year 1124, by Richard de Clare, Earl of Hertford; yearly value 324*l.* 4*s.* 1½*d.*, now worth 6,484*l.* 2*s.*

6*d.*; granted, 2 Edward VI., to Sir John Cheke and Michael Mildmay.

At SUDBURY. A College, founded, in the year 1374, by Simon, Bishop of London, on the ruins of a very ancient church; yearly value 122*l.* 18*s.* 3*d.*, now worth 2,458*l.* 5*s.* ; granted, 36 Henry VIII., to Sir Thomas Paston.

A Benedictine Cell, founded, in the reign of Henry II., by Wilfric; granted, 34 Henry VIII., to the Dean and Chapter of Westminster.

An Hospital, founded, in the time of John, by Amicia, Countess of Clare ; granted, 5 Edward VI., to John Cheke, Esq.

A Dominican Friary, founded, in the reign of Edward I., by Baldwin de Shipling; granted, 31 Henry VIII., to Thomas Eden, Esq.

At WANGFORD. A Cluniac Cell, founded before the year 1160, by Doudo Asini; yearly value 30*l.* 9*s.* 5*d.*, now worth 609*l.* 8*s.* 4*d.* ; granted, 32 Henry VIII., to Thomas, Duke of Norfolk.

At WILTON ST. FELIX. A Benedictine Cell, founded, in the reign of William Rufus, by Roger Bigod; granted, 19 Elizabeth, to Thomas Sexford.

At GREAT WELTHAM. A House of Crossed Friars, founded, 2 Edward I.; granted, 31 Henry VIII., to Antony Rouse.

At WICKHAM. A Monastery, built in the reign of King Stephen, by Robert de Salco Villa, Knight.

At WINGFIELD. A College, built in the year 1362, by Lady Alianor, relict of Sir John Wingfield; yearly value 69*l*. 14*s*. 5*d*., now worth 1,394*l*. 8*s*. 4*d*.; granted by Edward VI. to the Bishop of Norwich.

At WOODBRIDGE. An Austin Priory, founded, before the time of Edward II., by Ernaldus Ruffus; yearly value 50*l*. 3*s*. 5½*d*., now worth 1,003*l*. 9*s*. 2*d*.; granted, 19 Elizabeth, to Thomas Sexford, Master of Requests.

SURREY (County).

At ALDBURY. An Austin Priory, built in the reign of Richard I., by Rual de Calva; yearly value 294*l*. 18*s*. 4½*d*., now worth 5,898*l*. 7*s*. 6*d*.; granted, 36 Henry VIII., to Sir Antony Brown.

SURREY.

At BERMONDSEY. A Cluniac Abbey, built about the year 1089, by Aylwin Child, citizen of London; yearly income 548*l*. 2*s*. 5½*d*., now worth 10,962*l*. 9*s*. 2*d*.; granted, 33 Henry VIII., to Sir Richard Southwell.

At CHERTSEY. A Benedictine Abbey, built in the year 666, by Erkenwald, Bishop of London; destroyed, with the Abbot and ninety Monks killed, in the Danish wars; rebuilt by King Edgar; income 744*l*. 13*s*. 6½*d*. yearly, now worth 14,893*l*. 10*s*. 10*d*.; granted, 7 Edward VI., to Sir William Fitz Williams.

At LINGFIELD. A College, built in the time of Henry VI., by Reginald Cobham; income 79*l*. 15*s*. 10½*d*. yearly, now worth 1,595*l*. 17*s*. 6*d*.; granted, 38 Henry VIII., to Thomas Cawarden.

At MERTON. An Austin Priory, founded, in the year 1117, by Gilbert Norman, Sheriff of Surrey; yearly value 1,039*l*. 5*s*. 3*d*., now worth 20,785*l*. 5*s*.

At NEWINGTON. An Hospital, continued here until the year 1551, when their proctor, William Cleybroke, *had a protection or license to beg.*

At REIGATE. An Austin Priory or Hospital, founded, by William de Warren, Earl of Surrey; income 78*l*. 16*s*. 10*d*., now worth 1,576*l*.

16s. 8d. ; granted, 33 Henry VIII., to William, Lord Howard.

At SHENE. A Carthusian Priory, founded, in the year 1414, by Henry V., income 962l. 11s. 6d., now worth 19,251l. 10s. ; granted, 32 Henry VIII., to Edward, Earl of Hertford.

At SOUTHWARK. St. Mary Overy, Austin Priory, built on the ruins of an ancient Nunnery, that was founded, by Mary, and endowed with the profits of a ferry on the Thames; value 656l. 10s. 0½d., yearly, now worth 13,130l. 0s. 10d. ; granted, 36 Henry VIII., to Sir Antony Brown.

Overy Hospital, or St. Thomas's, founded, about the year 1228, by the Bishop of Winchester, Peter de Rupibus; value 309l. 1s. 11d., yearly, now worth 6,181l. 18s. 4d. ; contained, 30 Henry VIII., beds, food, and firing, for forty poor and sick persons, when it was given up.

At TANDRIDGE, or TANREGGE. An Austin Priory, founded, in the time of Richard I., and much contributed to by Odo de Dammartin; rents 86l. 7s. 6d., now worth 1,727l. 10s. ; granted, 29 Henry VIII., to John Rede.

At WAVERLEY. A Cistercian Abbey, founded,

in the year 1128, by William Giffard, Bishop
of Winchester; value 169*l.* 13*s.* 11*d.*, yearly,
now worth 3,933*l.* 18*s.* 4*d.*; granted, 28 Hen.
VIII., to Sir William Fitz Williams.

SUSSEX (County).

At ARUNDEL. An Alien Priory, founded, in
the time of William the Conqueror, by Roger
of Montgomery; became afterwards a College,
and valued at 263*l.* 14*s.* 9*d.*, yearly, now worth
5,274*l.* 15.; granted, 36 Henry VIII., to Hen.
Earl of Arundel.

An Hospital, built 18 Edward II., by Richard,
Earl of Arundel; rents 89*l.* 5*s.* 2½*d.*, now
worth 1,785*l.* 4*s.* 2*d.*; granted, to Sir Richard
Lee.

At BATTEL. A Benedictine Abbey, founded,
by William the Conqueror, on the spot where a
decisive battle was fought, Oct. 14, 1066, between King Harold and William, Duke of Normandy; value 987*l.* 0*s.* 10½*d.*, yearly, now worth
19,740*l.* 17*s.* 6*d.*; granted, 30 Henry VIII., to
Sir Antony Brown.

At Beigham. A Premonstratensian Abbey, founded, in the year 1200, by Robert de Turreham; value 152*l.* 9*s.* 4½*d.* yearly, now worth 3,049*l.* 7*s.* 6*d.*

At Bosanham. A College, originally founded, in the year 681, by St. Wilfrid; granted, 6 Elizabeth, to the Dean and Chapter of Chichester.

At Boxgrave. A Benedictine Priory, founded, in the time of Henry I., by Robert de Haya; income 145*l.* 10*s.* 2½*d.*, now worth 2,910*l.* 4*s.* 2*d.*; granted, 3 Elizabeth, to Henry, Earl of Arundel.

At Bramber. An Hospital, valued, 26 Hen. VIII., at 20*s.* yearly.

At Chichester. A Cathedral, founded, in the year 1075, by Bishop Stigand; valued at the dissolution at 677*l.* 1*s.* 3*d.* yearly; the Chapter's revenues made 601*l.* 7*s.* 10*d.*; both together would make now 25,589*l.* 1*s.* 8*d.*

A College of Vicars, had revenues 31*l.* 12*s.* 6*d.*, now worth 632*l.* 10*s.*

St. James's Hospital, founded, in the reign of King John; rents 4*l.* 3*s.* 9*d.*, now worth 83*l.* 15*s.*

St. Mary's Hospital, founded, for the poor;

value 11*l*. 11*s*. 6½*d*. yearly, now worth 231*l*. 10*s*. 10*d*.

An Augustine Friary, founded, in the time of Edward I., by Queen Alianor; granted, 32 Henry VIII., to Edward Millet.

A Dominican Friary, built in the reign of Henry III.; granted, 32 Henry VIII., to the Mayor and Citizens.

At DUREFORD. A Premonstratensian Abbey, founded, in the year 1169, by Robert Hoese; value 108*l*. 13*s*. 9*d*. yearly, now worth 2,173*l*. 15*s*.; granted, 29 Henry VIII., to Sir William Fitz Williams.

At EASEBORNE. A Benedictine Nunnery, founded, in the time of Henry III., by Sir John Bohun; yearly value 47*l*. 3*s*., now worth 943*l*.; granted, 28 Henry VIII., to Sir William Fitz Williams.

At HASTINGS. A College, built in the time of Henry I., by Hugh de Augo; value 41*l*. 13*s*. 5*d*. yearly, now worth 833*l*. 8*s*. 4*d*.; granted, 38 Henry VIII., to Sir Antony Brown.

An Austin Priory, founded, in the time of Richard I., by Sir Walter Bricet; value 57*l*. 1*s*. 9*d*. yearly, now worth 1,159*l*.; granted, 29 Henry VIII., to John Baker.

At LEWES. A Cluniac Priory, founded, in the year 1078, by Earl William de Warrenna; income 1,091*l.* 9*s.* 6½*d.*, now worth 21,829*l.* 10*s.* 10*d.*; granted, 2 Elizabeth, to Richard Baker and Richard Sackville.

At SOUTH MALLYNG. A College, founded, in the year 688, by Ceadwalla, King of the West Saxons; yearly value 45*l.* 12*s.* 5½*d.*, now worth 912*l.* 9*s.* 2*d.*

At MICHELHAM. Austin Canons, established in the time of Henry III., by Gilbert de Aquila; yearly income 191*l.* 19*s.* 3*d.*, now worth 3,839*l.* 5*s.*; granted, 33 Henry VIII., to William, Earl of Arundel.

At PLEYDONE. An Hospital, granted, 34 Henry VIII., to Andrew, Lord Windsor.

At PYNHAM. An Austin Priory, built in the time of Henry I., by his Queen Adeliza; income 43*l.* 0*s.* 10*d.*, now worth 860*l.* 16*s.* 8*d.*; granted, 5 James I., to Antony, Lord Montage.

At ROBERT'S BRIDGE. A Cistercian Abbey, built in the year 1176, by Alfred de St. Martino; yearly income 272*l.* 9*s.* 8*d.*, now worth 5,449*l.* 13*s.* 4*d.*; granted, 33 Henry VIII., to Sir William Sidney.

SUSSEX.

At RUSPUR. A Benedictine Nunnery, founded before the time of Richard I. ; income 39*l.* 13*s.* 7*d.*, now worth 793*l.* 11*s.* 8*d.* ; granted, 29 Henry VIII., to Sir Robert Southwell.

At SELE. An Austin Priory, built in the year 1075, by William de Braiosa ; valued at 26*l.* 9*s.* 9*d.* yearly, now worth 529*l.* 15*s.*; granted to the College of Oxford.

At SHOREHAM. St. James's Hospital ; valued at 1*l.* 6*s.* 8*d.*, now worth 26*l.* 13*s.* 4*d.* ; granted, 16 Elizabeth, to John Mersh

At TORTINGTON. An Austin Priory, founded, in the time of John, by Lady Hadwisa Corbet ; value 101*l.* 4*s.* 1*d.* yearly, now worth 2,024*l.* 1*s.* 8*d.* ; granted, 42 Elizabeth, to Sir John Spencer.

At WILMINGTON. An Alien Priory, built in the reign of William Rufus, by Robert, Earl of Morteton ; granted, 7 Elizabeth, to Sir Richard Sackville.

At WINCHELSEY. A Dominican Friary, granted, 36 Henry VIII., to William Clifford, and Michael Wildbore.

At WOLINCHMERE. An Austin Priory, founded by Ralph de Ardern ; income 79*l.* 15*s.* 6*d.*, now worth 1,595*l.* 10*s.* ; granted, 36 Henry VIII., to Antony Brown.

WARWICK (County).

At ALENCESTER. A Benedictine Abbey, founded, in the year 1140, by Ralph Pincerna ; yearly value 101*l*. 14*s*., now worth 2,024*l*. ; granted, 36 Henry VIII., to William and John Sewester.

At ASTLEY. A College. founded, 17 Edward III., by Sir Thomas de Astley ; rents 39*l*. 10*s*. 6*d*., now worth 790*l*. 10*s*. ; granted, 38 Henry VIII., to Henry, Marquis of Dorset.

At ATHERSTON. An Austin Friary, built 49 Edw. III., by Ralph, Lord Basset ; valued at 1*l*. 10*s*. 2*d*. yearly, now worth 30*l*. 3*s*. 4*d*. ; granted, 35 Henry VIII., to Henry Cartwright.

At AVECOTE. A Benedictine Cell, built in the year 1159, by William Burdett ; rents 28*l*. 6*s*. 2*d*., now worth 566*l*. 3*s*. 4*d*. ; granted, 34 Henry VIII., to Thomas, Lord Audley, and Sir Thomas Pope.

At BALSHALL. A House of Templars, built in the reign of Stephen, by Roger de Moubray ; granted, 8 Elizabeth, to Sir Robert Dudley.

WARWICK.

At BIRMINGHAM. An Hospital, founded before the time of Edward I. ; yearly value 8*l.* 5*s.* 3*d.*, now worth 165*l.* 5*s.*

At COMBE. A Cistercian Abbey, built in the year 1150, by Richard de Camvilla ; rents 343*l.* 0*s.* 5*d.*, now worth 6,860*l.* 8*s.* 4*d.* ; granted, 1 Edward VI., to John, Earl of Warwick.

At COVENTRY. A Cathedral, created out of a Monastery that was built in the year 1043, by Leofric, the good Earl of Mercia, on the ruins of a Nunnery built by the Saxons, before the year 1016; rents 499*l.* 7*s.* 4*d.*, now worth 9,987*l.* 6*s.* 8*d.* ; granted, 37 Henry VIII., to John Combes and Richard Stansfiel.

A Charter-House, founded, in the year 1381, by William, Lord Zouch ; rents 251*l.* 5*s.* 9*d.*, now worth 5,035*l.* 15*s.* ; granted, 34 Henry VIII. to Richard Andrews, and Leonard Chamberlayne.

Bablake-College, founded, before the year 1350, by the Burgesses ; yearly value 111*l.* 13*s.* 8*d.*, now worth 2,233*l.* 13*s.* 4*d.*

Bablake Hospital, founded, in the year 1506, by Thomas Bond, Draper : rents 49*l.* 11*s.* 7*d.*, now worth 991*l.* 11*s.* 8*d.*

WARWICK.

Grey Friars' Hospital, built in the year 1529, by William Ford, for five poor men and one poor woman.

St. John's Hospital, built in the reign of Henry II., by Edmund, Archdeacon of Coventry; yearly value 83*l*. 3*s*. 3*d*., now worth 1,663*l*. 5*s*.; granted, to John Hales, Esq.

Grey Friary, founded, in the year 1234, by Ralph, Earl of Chester; granted, 34 Henry VIII., to the Mayor and Bailiffs of the town.

Carmelite Friary, erected in the year 1342, by Sir John Poultney; yearly income 7*l*. 13*s*. 8*d*., now worth 153*l*. 13*s*. 4*d*.; granted, 36 Henry VIII., to Ralph Sadler.

At NUN EATON. A Nunnery, founded, in the reign of Henry II., by Robert Bossu, Earl of Leicester; income 290*l*. 5*s*. 0½*d*., now worth 5,805*l*. 0*s*. 10*d*.; granted, 32 Henry VIII., to Sir Marmaduke Constable.

At ERDBURY. An Augustine Priory, built in the reign of Henry III., by Ralph de Sudley; rents, 122*l*. 8*s*. 6*d*., now worth 2,448*l*. 10*s*.; granted, 30 Henry VIII., to Charles Brandon, Duke of Suffolk.

At HEANWOOD. A Benedictine Nunnery, built in the reign of Henry II., by Katelbern de Langdon ; income 21*l.* 2*s.* 0½*d.*, now worth 422*l.* 0*s.* 10*d.* ; granted, 31 Henry VIII., to John Higford.

At KENILWORTH. An Augustine Priory, built in the year 1122, by Jeffery de Clintone, Chamberlain to Henry I. ; income 538*l.* 19*s.*, now worth 10,779*l.* ; granted, by Henry VIII., to Sir Andrew Flamock.

At MONK'S KIRBY. An Alien Priory, founded, in the year 1077, by Gosfred de Wircha ; income 220*l.* 3*s.* 4*d.*, now worth 4,403*l.* 6*s.* 8*d.* ; granted, 37 Henry VIII., to Trinity College, Cambridge.

At KNOLL. A College, built 4 Henry V., by Lady Elizabeth Clinton, income 18*l.* 5*s.* 6*d ,* now worth 365*l.* 10*s.*

At MAXSTOKE. An Augustine Priory, built in the year 1336, by Sir William de Clinton, Earl of Huntingdon ; income 129*l.* 11*s.* 8½*d.*, now worth 2,591*l.* 4*s.* 2*d.* ; granted, 30 Henry VIII., to Charles, Duke of Suffolk.

At MEREVAL. A Cistercian Abbey, built in the year 1148, by Robert, Earl of Ferrers ; income 303*l.* 10*s.*, now worth 6,070*l.* granted, 32 Henry VIII., to Walter, Lord Ferrers.

At OLDBURY. A Benedictine Nunnery, built in the reign of William the Conqueror, by Walter de Hastings ; income 6*l.* 0*s.* 10*d.*, now worth 120*l.* 16*s.* 8*d.* ; granted, 33 Henry VIII., to Charles, Duke of Suffolk.

At PINLEY. A Cistercian Nunnery, built in the reign of Henry I., by Robert de Pilardinton ; yearly value 27*l.* 14*s.* 7*d.*, now worth 554*l.* 11*s.* 8*d.* ; granted 36 Henry VIII., to] William Wigston, Esq.

At POLLESWORTH. A Benedictine Nunnery, built by King Egbert for Modwenna, a holy woman lately come from Ireland ; here his own daughter, St. Editha presided ; income 87*l.* 16*s.* 3*d.*, now worth 1,756*l.* 5*s.* ; granted, 36 Henry VIII., to Francis Goodyere, Esq.

At STONELY. A Cistercian Abbey, built by King Henry II., in the year 1154 ; income 178*l.* 2*s.* 5½*d.*, now worth 3,562*l.* 9*s.* 2*d.*, ; granted, 30 Henry VIII., to Charles Brandon, Duke of Suffolk.

At STRATFORD. A College, founded, about the year 703 ; income 123*l.* 12*s.* 9*d.*, now worth 2,472*l.* 15*s.* ; granted, 4 Edward VI., to John, Earl of Warwick.

Hospital, built in the reign of Henry II.

At STUDLEY. An Augustine Priory, built in the reign of Henry II. ; rents 181*l.* 3*s.* 6*d.*, now worth 3,623*l*. ; granted, 30 Henry VIII., to Sir Edmund Knightly.

At THELESFORD. A Maturine Friary founded, in the reign of John, by William de Cherlecote ; income 23*l*. 10*s*., now worth 470*l*; granted, 35 Henry VIII., to William Whorwood, Esq., and William Walter.

At WARMINGTON. An Alien Priory, founded, in the reign of Henry I., by Paul de Prattelles; granted, 35 Henry VIII., to William and Francis Seldon, Esqrs.

At WARWICK. An Augustine Priory built, in the reign of Henry I., by Henry of Newburgh ; income 49*l*. 13*s*. 6*d*., now worth 993*l*. 10*s*. ; granted, 38 Henry VIII., to Thomas Hawkins.

Hospital of Templars, built in the reign of Henry I., by Roger, Earl of Warwick ; income 14*l*. 6*s*. 8*d*., now worth 286*l*. 13*s*. 4*d*.

St. James's College, built in the reign of Richard II.

St. Mary's College, built before the time of William the Conqueror ; income 247*l*. 13*s*. 0½*d*., now worth 4,953*l*. 0*s*. 10*d*.; granted, 37 Henry VIII., to the Burgesses of Warwick.

St. John's Hospital, built in the reign of Henry II., by William, Earl of Warwick, for the entertainment of travellers and strangers; income, 19*l.* 3*s.* 7*d.*, now worth 383*l.* 11*s.* 8*d.* ; granted, 27 Henry VIII., to Anthony Staughton.

St. Michael's Hospital, founded, in the reign of Henry I., by Roger, Earl of Warwick, for the sick; income 10*l.* 19*s.* 10*d.*, now worth 219*l.* 16*s.* 8*d.*

Black Friary, built in the reign of Hen. III., by the Botelers, Lords of Sudley; income 4*l.* 18*s.* 6*d.*, now worth 98*l.* 10*s.* ; granted, 5 Edward VI., to John, Duke of Northumberland.

Carmelite Friary, built 18 Edward III., by John Peyto, jun. granted, 4 Edward VI., to John, Earl of Warwick.

At WOLFRICHESTON. An Alien Priory, built soon after the conquest, by Roger de Montgomery; granted, 3 Edward VI., to Richard Fielde and Richard Woodward.

At WROXHALL. A Benedictine Nunnery, built in the reign of Henry I., by Hugh de Hatton ; yearly value 78*l.* 10*s.* 1½*d.*, now worth 1,570*l.* 2*s.* 6*d.*; granted, 36 Henry VIII., to Robert Burgoin and John Scudamore.

WESTMORELAND (County).

At BROUGH. An Hospital, founded, in the 16th century, by John Brunskill, with a chapel, and beds for travellers and other poor persons; yearly income 7*l.* 4*s.* 4*d.*, now worth 144*l.* 6*s.* 8*d.*

At HEPP. A Premonstratensian Abbey, built in the reign of Henry II., by Thomas Fitz Gospatrick; yearly value 166*l.* 10*s.* 6*d.*, now worth 3,330*l.* 10*s.*; granted, 36 Henry VIII., to Thos. Lord Wharton.

At KIRKLEY. An Hospital for lepers, built before the time of Henry II.; yearly income 6*l.* 4*s.* 5*d.*, now worth 124*l.* 8*s.* 4*d.*; granted, 38 Henry VIII., to Alan Bellingham, and Alan Wilson.

WILTS (County).

At AMESBURY. A Nunnery, built by Alfrida Queen of Edgar; income 558*l.* 10*s.* 2*d.*, now worth 11,170*l*. 3*s*. 4*d*.; granted, 32 Hen. VIII., to Edward, Earl of Hertford.

At Ansty. An Hospital of Hospitalers, built 12 John, by Walter de Turbelville; yearly income 81*l*. 8*s*. 5*d*., now worth 1,628*l*. 8*s*. 4*d*.; granted, 38 Henry VIII., to John Zouch.

At Avebury. An Alien Priory, built in the reign of Henry I., by William de Tancer-villa; granted, 2 Edward VI., to Sir William Sharington.

At Bradenstoke. An Augustine Priory, founded, in the year 1142, by Walter de Evreux; yearly value 270*l*. 10*s*. 8*d*., now worth 5,410*l*. 13*s*. 4*d*.; granted, 38 Henry VIII., to Richard Pexall.

At Mayden Bradeley. An Augustine Priory, founded, in the reign of Stephen, by Manasses Biset; yearly value 197*l*. 18*s*. 8*d*., now worth 3,958*l*. 13*s*. 4*d*.; granted, 29 Henry VIII., to Sir Edward Seymore.

At Caln. An Hospital, built in the reign of Henry III.; income 2*l*. 2*s*. 8*d*., now worth 42*l*. 13*s*. 4*d*.

At Charleton. An Alien Priory, built in the year 1187, by Reginald de Pavely; yearly income 22*l*., now worth 440*l*. ; granted, 2 Edw. VI., to Sir William Sharington.

At COSHAM. An Alien Priory, built in the reign of William the Conqueror ; yearly income 22*l*. 13*s*. 4*d*., now worth 453*l*. 6*s*. 8*d*.; granted, 6 James I., to Philip Moore.

AtCRICKLADE. An Hospital, built in the reign of Henry III.; yearly income 4*l*. 7*s*. 10½*d*., now worth 87*l*. 17*s*. 6*d*.

At EDINDON. Bonhommes, built about the year 1347 ; rents 521*l*. 12*s*. 5½*d*., now worth 10, 432*l*. 9*s*. 2*d*. ; granted, 33 Henry VIII., to William Pawlet, Lord St. John.

At ESTON. A Trinitarian Friary, founded, for the redemption of captives, in the reign of Hen. III., by Stephen, Archdeacon of Salisbury ; yearly income 55*l*. 14*s*. 4*d*., now worth 1,114*l*. 6*s*. 8*d*. ; granted, 6 James I., to Edward, Earl of Hertford.

At FARLEIGH. A Cluniac Priory, built in the year 1125, by Humphrey de Bohun ; yearly income 152*l*. 3*s*. 7*d*., now worth 3,043*l*. 11*s*. 8*d*. ; granted, 28 Henry VIII., to Sir Edward Seymore.

At HEYTESBURY. A College, built in the year

1300 ; yearly income 28*l*. 12*s*. 6*d*., now worth 572*l*. 10*s*.

Hospital, founded, about the year 1470, by Lady Margaret Hungerford, for twelve poor men and one poor woman ; yearly income 38*l*. 4*s*. 7*d*., now worth 764*l*. 11*s*. 8*d*. ; it stands to this day.

At TOY CHURCH. An Augustine Priory, built in the reign of Henry II.; yearly income 133*l*. 0*s*. 7½*d*., now worth 2,660*l*. 12*s*. 6*d*.; granted, 36 Henry VIII., to John Barwick.

At KEINTON. A Benedictine Nunnery, founded, 2 Henry II.; yearly income 38*l*. 3*s*. 10½*d*., now worth 763*l*. 17*s*. 6*d*. ; granted, 30 Henry VIII., to Sir John Long.

At KINGSWOOD. A Cistercian Abbey, built in the year 1139, by William de Berkly ; yearly income 254*l*. 11*s*. 3*d*., now worth 5,091*l*. 3*s*. 4*d*. ; granted, 2 Elizabeth, to Sir John Thynne.

At LACOCK. An Augustine Priory, built in the year 1232, by Ela, Countess of Salisbury ; yearly income 203*l*. 12*s*. 3*d*., now worth 4,072*l*. 5*s*. ; granted, 32 Henry VIII., to Sir William Sharington.

At LONGLEAT. An Augustine Priory, ; granted, 32 Henry VIII., to Sir John Thynne.

At MALMESBURY. A Benedictine Abbey, built in the year 675, in the place of an ancient Nunnery ; yearly income 803*l.* 17*s.* 7*d.*, now worth 16,077*l.* 11*s.* 8*d.* ; granted, 36 Henry VIII., to William Stump.

At MARLEBOROUGH. A Gilbertine Abbey, founded, in the reign of John ; yearly income 38*l.* 19*s.* 2*d.*, now worth 779*l.* 3*s.* 4*d.* ; granted to Anthony Stringer.

Hospital, St. John's, built 16 John, by Mr. Levenoth ; yearly income 6*l.* 18*s.* 4*d.*, now worth 138*l.* 6*s.* 8*d.*

Carmelite Friary, built in the year 1316, by John Godwin and William Ramesbesch ; granted, 34 Henry VIII., to John Pye and Robert Brown.

At PULTON. A Gilbertine Priory, built, 21 Edward III., by Sir Thomas Seymore ; yearly value 20*l.* 3*s.* 2*d.*, now worth 403*l.* 3*s.* 4*d.* ; granted, 36 Hen. VIII., to Sir Thomas Stroude, Walter Erle, and John Paget.

At TEMPLE ROCKLEY. An Hospital of Templars, built 2 Henry II., by John

Mareschall; granted, 32 Henry VIII., to Sir Edward Bainton.

At SALISBURY. A Cathedral Church, the building of which took forty years; was finished in the year 1258; the revenues of the Bishop made 1,367*l*. 11*s*. 6*d*., of the Chapter 601*l*. 12*s*.; both would now make 39,383*l*. 10*s*.

St. Edmond's College, founded, by Walter de la Wyle, Bishop of Salisbury, in the year 1270; revenues 94*l*. 5*s*., now worth 1,885*l*.; granted, 38 Henry VIII., to William St. Barbe.

College de Vaux, and possessions; granted, 35 Henry VIII., to Sir Michael Lister.

Vicar's College, incorporated 11 Henry IV.; revenues 47*l*. 18*s*. 0½*d*., now worth 958*l*. 0*s*. 10*d*.

Harnham College, founded, in the year 1220, by Bishop Poore; rents 25*l*. 2*s*. 2*d*., now worth 502*l*. 3*s*. 4*d*.; it was for the poor, and still continues.

Trinity College, founded for the sick, 17 Richard II., by John Chandeler.

Dominican Friary, founded, by King Edward I.; granted, 36 Henry VIII., to John Pollard, and William Byrte.

Franciscan Friary, built by a Bishop of the town ; granted, 36 Henry VIII., to John Wroth.

At STANLEGH. A Cistercian Abbey, built in the year 1154, by King Henry II., and his mother Maud ; rents 222*l.* 19*s.* 4*d.*, now worth 4,459*l.* 6*s.* 8*d.* ; granted, 28 Henry VIII., to Sir Edward Bainton.

At UPHAVEN. An Alien Priory, built in the reign of Henry I. ; granted, 4 James I., to Francis and A. Anderson.

At WILTON. A Benedictine Nunnery, built by King Edgar, in the year 871, on the ruins of an Abbey built 773, and destroyed by the Danes ; yearly revenues 652*l.* 11*s.* 5½*d.*, now worth 13,051*l.* 9*s.* 2*d.* ; granted, 35 Henry VIII., to Sir William Herbert.

St Giles' Hospital, built by Queen Adelicia, wife of Henry I ; yearly value 5*l.* 13*s.* 4*d.*, now worth 113*l.* 6*s.* 8*d.*

St. John's Hospital, built in the year 1217, for a Prior and poor brethren ; rents 14*l.* 13*s.* 10½*d.*, now worth 393*l.* 17*s.* 6*d.*

WORCESTER (County).

At Astley. An Alien Priory, built in the reign of William the Conqueror, by Ralph de Todenei ; granted, by King Henry VIII., to Sir Ralph Sadler.

At Bordesley. A Cistercian Abbey, built in the year 1138, by the Empress Maud ; rents 392*l*. 8*s*. 6*d*., now worth 7,848*l*. 10*s*. granted, 34 Henry VIII., to Andrew, Lord Windsor.

At Cokehill. A White Nunnery, built in the reign of Richard I., by Gervase of Canterbury ; rents 34*l*. 15*s*. 11*d*., now worth 695*l*. 18*s*. 4*d*. ; granted, 34 Henry VIII., to Nicholas Fortescue, whose posterity now inhabit the ancient Priory-house.

At Dodford. A Premonstratensian Cell, built by King Henry II. ; granted, 30 Henry VIII., to John Dudley, who sold it to John Fownes.

At Droitwich. An Hospital, built 13 Edward I., by William de Dovere, Pastor of Dodderhill ; rents 21*l*. 11*s*. 8*d*., now worth 431*l*. 13*s*. 4*d*.

At Elmely. A College, built in the reign

of Edward II., by Guy, Earl of Warwick; granted, 37 Henry VIII., to Sir Thomas Hobby.

At Evesham. A Benedictine Abbey, founded, and endowed 701, by Egwin, Bishop of Worcester; yearly value 1,268*l*. 9*s*. 9*d*., now worth 25,369*l*. 15*s*.; granted, 34 Henry VIII., to Philip Hobby, Esq.

At Malvern Major. A Benedictine Priory founded, by Edward the Confessor; rents 375*l*. 0*s*. 6½*d*., now worth 7,500*l*. 10*s*. 10*d*.; granted, 36 Henry VIII., to William Pynnok.

At Malvern Minor. A Benedictine Cell, founded in the year 1171, by Joceline and Edred, brothers, who were afterwards Priors there; rents 102*l*. 10*s*. 9½*d*., now worth 2,050*l*. 15*s*. 10*d*.; granted, 35 Henry VIII., to Richard Andrews and Nicholas Temple.

At Pershore. A Benedictine Abbey, founded, in the year 689, by Oswald, nephew of King Ethelred; rents 666*l*. 13*s*. now worth 13,333*l*.; granted, 36 Henry VIII., to William and Francis Sheldon.

At Westwood. A Fontevrauld Nunnery, built in the reign of Henry II., by Eustachia de Say; rents 75*l*. 18*s*. 11*d*., now worth 1,518*l*.

17*s.* 6*d.*; granted, 30 Henry VIII., to John Pakinton.

At WORCESTER. A Cathedral Church, built in the year 964, by Bishop Oswald, which became afterwards a Monastery; rents 1,290*l.* 10*s.* 6½*d.*, now worth 25,810*l.* 10*s.* 10*d.*

Whiston Nunnery, built by a Bishop of Worcester; rents 56*l.* 3*s.* 7*d.*, now worth 1,123*l.* 11*s.* 8*d.*; granted, 35 Henry VIII., to Richard Callowhile.

St. Oswald's Hospital, founded, by Bishop Oswald himself, before the year 1268, for the poor; with revenues 15*l.* 18*s.*, now worth 318*l.*; granted, by Henry VIII., to Christ Church, Oxford.

A Dominican Friary, founded, by Beauchamps of Powike; granted, 31 Henry VIII., to the Bailiffs and Citizens of Worcester.

A Franciscan Friary, built in the year 1268, by Charles of Warwick; granted, 31 Henry VIII., to the Bailiffs, &c. of Worcester.

YORK (County).

At NORTH ALLERTON. St James's Hospital, founded, in the reign of Henry II., by Hugh Pusar, Bishop of Durham, for the poor brethren; rents 56*l*. 2*s*. 2*d*., now worth 1,122*l*. 3*s*. 4*d* ; granted, 32 Henry VIII., to Christ Church, Oxford.

> Maison de Dieu, built in the year 1476, by Richard Moore, draper, for thirteen poor persons ; four only are now supported on it.

> A Carmelite Friary, built in the year 1354, by Thomas Hatfield, Bishop of Durham.

At NUN APPLETON. A Cistercian Nunnery, built in the reign of King Stephen, by Adeliz de St. Quintin ; rents 83*l*. 5*s*. 9*d*., now worth 1,665*l*. 15*s*. ; granted, 33 Henry VIII., to Robert Darknall.

At ARDEN. A Benedictine Nunnery, built in the year 1150, by Peter de Hotton ; rents 13*l*. 7*s*. 4*d*., now worth 267*l*. 6*s*. 8*d*. ; granted, 32 Henry VIII., to Thomas Culpeper.

At ARTHINGTON. A Benedictine Nunnery, built in the time of King Stephen, by Peter de

Ardington ; rents 19*l.*, now worth 380*l*, ; granted, 34 Henry VIII., to Cranmer, Archbishop of
Canterbury.

At NETHER AULCASTER. A College, found-
ed, by Robert Stillington ; rents 27*l*. 13*s*. 4*d*.,
now worth 553*l*. 6*s*. 8*d*. ; granted, 2 Edward
VI., to John Hulse and William Pendred.

At BAGBY. An Hospital for the sick and
poor.

At BASE DALE HOTON. A Cistercian Nunnery, built in the year 1162, by Ralph de
Neville ; yearly value 21*l*. 19*s*. 4*d*., now worth
439*l*. 6*s*. 8*d*. ; granted, 36 Henry VIII., to
Ralph Bulmer and John Thynde.

At BAWTREE. An Hospital, built in the year
1316, by Robert Moreton, Esq. for the poor ;
rents 6*l*. 6*s*. 8*d*., now worth 126*l*. 13*s*. 4*d*. ; yet
in being.

At BEGARE. An Alien Priory, built in the
reign of Henry III. ; granted to Eton college.

At BEVERLEY. A College, built in the year
700, by John, Archbishop of York. After various alterations, it supported, at the dissolution,
one Provost, eight Prebendaries, a Chancellor,
Precentor, seven Rectors, Choral, nine Vicars
Choral, many Chantry Priests, Clerks, Choris-

ters, officers and Servants. Revenues 345*l*. 13*s*. 2*d*., now worth 6,913*l*. 1*s*. 8*d*. ; granted, 2 Edward VI., to Michael Stanhope and John Bellew.

A House of Hospitalers, built in the year 1201, by Sibylla de Valoniis ; rents 167*l*. 10*s*., now worth 3,350*l*. ; granted, 36 Henry VIII., to William Barkely.

St. Giles's Hospital, built before the conquest by a Mr. Wulse ; rents 8*l*., now worth 160*l*. ; granted, 32 Henry VIII., to Thomas, Earl of Rutland.

St. Nicholas's Hospital, built before the year 1268 ; yearly value 5*l*. 14*s*. 6*d*., now worth 114*l*. 10*s*.

A Dominicals' Friary, founded, before the year 1241 ; granted, 36 Henry VIII., to John Pope and Anthony Foster.

A Franciscan Friary, founded, in the year 1297 by William Liketon and Henry Wighton ; granted, 32 Henry VIII., to Thomas Culpeper.

At BOLTON. An Augustine Priory, founded, in the year 1120, by William Meschines ; yearly, value 212*l*. 3*s*. 4*d*., now worth 4,243*l*. 6*s*. 8*d*. ; granted. 33 Henry VIII., to Henry, Earl of Cumberland.

YORK.

At MONK BRETTON. A Cluniac Priory, founded, in the reign of Henry II., by Adam Fitz Swain ; rents 323*l*. 8*s*. 2*d*., now worth 6,468*l*. 3*s*. 4*d*. ; granted, 32 Henry VIII., to William Blithman.

At BRUNNUM. A Benedictiue Nunnery, founded, in the reign of Henry III., by Roger de Merely, Lord Morpeth ; rents 10*l*. 3*s*. 3*d*., now worth 203*l*. 5*s*. ; granted, 33 Henry VIII., to Robert Tirwhit.

At BURLINGTON. An Augustine Priory, built in the reign of Henry I., by Walter de Gant ; rents 682*l*. 13*s*. 9*d*., now worth 13,653*l*. 15*s*.

At BYLAND. A Cistercian Abbey, built in the year 1143, by Roger de Mowbray ; rents 295*l*. 5*s*. 4*d*., now worth 5,905*l*, 6*s*. 8*d*. ; granted, 32 Henry VIII., to William Pykering.

At CORHAM. A Premonstratensian Abbey, built in the reign of Henry II., by Ralph Fitz Robert, Lord of Middleham ; rents 207*l*. 14*s*. 8*d*., now worth 4,154*l*. 13*s*. 4*d*.

At DONCASTER. A Franciscan Friary, erected before the year 1315 ; granted, 36 Henry VIII., to William Gifford and Michael Welbore.

At DRAX. An Augustine Priory, built before the

reign of Henry I., by William Paynel; rents
181*l*. 18*s*. 3½*d*., now worth 3,638*l*. 5*s*. 10*d*.,
granted, 30 Henry VIII., to Sir Marmaduke
Constable.

At EGLESTONE. A Premonstratensian Abbey,
founded, in the reign of Henry 11.; by Ralph de
Multon; rents 36*l*. 8*s*. 3*d*., now worth 728*l*. 5*s*.;
granted, 2 Edward VI., to Robert Shelley.

At ELRETON. A Cistercian Nunnery, built in
the reign of Henry II., by Warnerius Dapifer,
Earl of Richmond; rents 15*l*. 10*s*. 6*d*., now worth
310*l*. 10*s*.; granted, 33 Henry VIII., to John
Aske.

At ELRETON ON THE DERWENT. A Gilbertine Priory, built in the year 1212, by William
Fitz Peter, under condition that they would
maintain thirteen poor persons; rents 78*l*. 0*s*.
10*d*., now worth 1,560*l*. 16*s*. 8*d*.; granted, 33
Henry VIII., to John Aske.

At ESSEHOLT. A Cistercian Nunnery, founded
in the year 1172; rents 19*l*.; now worth 380*l*.;
granted, 1 Edward VI., to Henry Thompson.

At NORTH FERRY. An Augustine Priory, valued
yearly 95*l*. 11*s*. 7½*d*., now worth 1,911*l*. 12*s*. 6*d*.;
granted, 32 Henry VIII., to Thomas Culpeper.

At FOUNTAINS, in the Deanery of West
Riding. A Cistercian Abbey, built in the year

1132; rents 1,173*l.* 0*s.* 7½*d*, now worth 23,560*l.* 12*s.* 6*d.*; granted, 32 Henry VIII., to Sir Richard Gresham.

At GISEBURNE. An Augustine Priory, founded, in the year 1129, by Robert de Brus; rents 712*l.* 6*s.* 6*d.*, now worth 14,246*l.* 10*s.*; granted, 4 Elizabeth, to Sir Thomas Chaloner.

At GROSMONT. An Alien Priory, built in the reign of John, by Joanna, daughter of William Fossard; rents 14*l.* 2*s.* 8*d.*, now worth 282*l.* 13*s.* 4*d.*; granted, 35 Henry VIII., to Edward Wright.

At HALTEMPRICE. An Augustine Priory, founded, 15 Edward II., by Thomas, Lord Wake of Lyddel; yearly value 178*l.* 0*s.* 10½*d.*, now worth 3,560*l.* 17*s.* 6*d.*; granted, 32 Henry VIII., to Thomas Culpeper.

At HANDALE. A Benedictine Nunnery, founded, in the year 1133, by William Percy; rents 29*l.* 7*s.* 8*d.*, now worth 407*l.* 13*s.* 4*d.*; granted, 35 Henry VIII., to Ambrose Beckwith.

At HANEHOPE. A Cistercian Nunnery, founded, in the year 1170, by William de Clarefai; rents 85*l.* 6*s.* 11*d.*, now worth 1,706*l.* 18*s.* 4*d.*; granted, 6 Edward VI., to Francis Aislaby.

At HEDON. An Hospital, founded, in the time of King John, by Alan Ouberni; rents 11*l.* 18*s.*

$4d.$, now worth 238$l.$ 6$s.$ 8$d.$; granted, 7 Edward VI., to Robert Constable.

At HELAGH PARK. An Augustine Priory, founded, in the year 1218, by Berthram Haget; rents 86$l.$ 5$s.$ 9$d.$, now worth 1,725$l.$ 15$s.$; granted, 31 Henry VIII., to James Gage.

At HEMINGBURGH. A College, founded in the year 1426; rents 36$l.$ 1$s.$, now worth 721$l.$

At HOWDEN. A College, founded, in the year 1266, by Robert, Bishop of Durham; rents 13$l.$ 6$s.$, now worth 266$l.$

At TEMPLE HURSTE. An Hospital of Templars, founded, in the year 1152, by Ralph de Hostings ; granted to Lord Darcy.

At JOREVAL. A Cistercian Abbey, founded, about the year 1156, by Conan, Duke of Richmond ; yearly value 455$l.$ 10$s.$ 5$d.$, now worth 9,110$l.$ 8$s.$ 4$d.$; granted, 36 Henry VIII., to Matthew, Earl of Lenox.

At KELDON. A Cistercian Nunnery, founded, in the reign of Henry I., by Robert Stuteville ; rents 29$l.$ 6$s.$ 1$d.$, now worth 586$l.$ 1$s.$ 8$d.$; granted, 30 Henry VIII., to Ralph, Earl of Westmorland.

At NUN KELYNGE. A Benedictine Nunnery, built in the reign of King Stephen, by Agnes de Archis; rents 50*l.* 17*s.* 2*d.*, now worth 1,017*l.* 3*s.* 4*d.* ; granted, 32 Henry VIII., to Richard Gresham.

At KILLINGWOLDGROVE. An Hospital, founded for women before the year 1169; rents 12*l.* 3*s.* 4*d.*, now worth 243*l.* 6*s.* 8*d.*

At KINGSTON. A Cistercian Priory, built about the time of Richard III., by Michael de la Pole, Earl of Suffolk; rents 231*l.* 17*s.* 3*d.*, now worth 4,637*l.* 5*s.* ; granted, 6 Edward VI., to Edward, Lord Clinton.

Grigge's and Mariners' Hospitals; one for Priests and the other for Sailors; founded, by John Grigge; valued, 26 Henry VIII., at 10*l.*, now worth 400*l.* yearly. They are in being to this day.

Pole's Hospital, founded in the year 1384, by Michael de la Pole, for thirteen poor men and so many poor women; rents 10*l.*, now worth 200*l.*; still in being.

A Carmelite Friary, founded by King Edward I., or by some others; granted, 32 Henry VIII., to John Henneage.

A Dominican Friary, granted, 36 Henry VIII., to John Broxholm.

At KIRKHAM. An Augustine Priory, founded, in the year 1121, by Walter Espec; rents 300*l.*

15*s*. 6*d*., now worth 2,015*l*. 10*s*.; granted, 32 Henry VIII., to Henry Knyvet.

At KIRKLEGHES. A Cistercian Nunnery, founded, in the reign of Henry II., by Reynerus Flandersis; rents 20*l*. 7*s*. 8*d*., now worth 407*l*. 13*s*. 4*d*.; granted, 36 Henry VIII., to John Tasburgh and Nicholas Saville.

At KIRKSTALL. A Cistercian Abbey, built in the year 1147, by Henry de Lacy; rents 512*l*. 13*s*. 4*d*., now worth 10,253*l*. 6*s*. 8*d*.

At KNARESBURGH. A Trinitarian Friary, built in the reign of Henry III., by Richard, Earl of Cornwall, and King of the Romans; rents 35*l*. 10*s*. 11*d*., now worth 710*l*. 18*s*. 4*d*., granted, 7 Edward VI., to Francis of Shrewsbury.

At LAYSINGBY. A College, founded, 18 Edward I., by John de Lythegraynes; rents 9*l*. 6*s*. 8*d*., now worth 186*l*. 13*s*. 4*d*.

At OLD MALTON. A Gilbertine Priory, founded, in the year 1150, by Eustace Fitz John; rents 257*l*. 7*s*. now worth 5,147*l*.; granted, 32 Henry VIII., to Robert Holegate, Bishop of Landaff.

At LITTLE MARCIS. A Benedictine Nunnery, built in the year 1163, by Roger de Clere; rents 26*l*. 6*s*. 8*d*., now worth 526*l*. 13*s*. 4*d*.; granted, 35 Henry VIII, to Robert Holgate, Bishop of Landaff; after him to the Bishop of York.

At MARTON. An Augustine Priory, founded, in the reign of Henry II., by Bertram de Bulmer; rents 183*l.* 12*s.* 4*d.*, now worth 3,672*l.* 6*s.* 8*d.*; granted, 34 Henry VIII., to the Archbishop of York.

At MARYKE. A Benedictine Nunnery, founded, in the reign of HenryII., by Roger de Asac; rents 64*l.* 16*s.* 9*d.*, now worth 1,296*l.* 15*s.*; granted, 37 Henry VIII., to John Uvedale.

At MELSA. A Cistercian Abbey, founded, in the year 1150, by William le Gross, Earl of Albemarle: rents 445*l.* 10*s.* 5*d.*, now worth 8,910*l.* 8*s.* 4*d.*; granted, 3 Edw. VI., to John, Earl of Warwick.

At MIDDLEHAM. A College, founded, in the year 1476, by Richard, Duke of Gloucester, afterwards King Richard III.; rents 16*l.* 9*s.* 4*d.*, now worth 329*l.* 3*s.* 4*d.*

At MIDDLESBURGH. A Benedictine Cell, founded, in the reign of Henry I., by Robert de Bruce; rents 21*l.* 13*s.* 8*d.*, now worth 433*l.* 13*s.* 4*d.*; granted, 6 Elizabeth, to Thomas Reve.

At MOLESLEY. A Benedictine Nunnery, founded by Henry II., in the year 1167; rents 32*l.* 6*s.* 2*d.*, now worth 646*l.* 3*s.* 4*d.*; granted to the Archbishop of York.

At Nun Monketon. A Benedictine Nunnery, built in the reign of Stephen, by William de Arches; rents 85*l.* 14*s.* 8*d.*, now worth 1,714*l.* 13*s.* 4*d* ; granted, 29 Henry VIII., to John, Lord Latimer.

At Mountgrace. A Carthusian Priory, founded in the year 1396, by Thomas de Holland, Duke of Surrey; rents 323*l.* 2*s.* 10½*d.*, now worth 6,462*l.* 17*s.* 6*d.*; granted, 32 Henry VIII., to Robert Strangeways

At Mount St. John. A House of Hospitalers, founded in the reign of Henry I., by William Percy ; rents 102*l.* 13*s.* 10*d.* now worth 2,053*l.* 16*s.* 8*d.* ; granted, 34 Henry VIII., to the Archbishop of York.

At Newburgh. An Augustine Priory, built in the year 1145, by Roger de Mowbray; rents 457*l.* 13*s.* 4*d.*, now worth 9,153*l.* 8*s.* 5*d.* ; granted, 38 Henry VIII., to Margaret Simson and Anthony Bellasis.

At Newland. A House of Hospitalers, founded, by King John ; rents 202*l.* 3*s.* 8*d.* now worth 4,043*l.* 13*s.* 4*d.* ; granted, 36 Henry VIII., to Francis Jobson and Andrew Dudley.

At Newton. An Hospital, built in the year 1179, by William Gross, Earl of Albemarle ; rents 21*l.* 0*s.* 2*d.*, now worth 420*l.* 3*s.* 4*d.* ; granted, 16 Elizabeth, to John Stanhope.

At NOSTELL. An Augustine Priory, built in the reign of Henry II.; by Robert de Lacy; rents 606*l*. 9*s*. 3*d*., now worth 12,129*l*. 5*s*.; granted, 31 Henry VIII., to Thomas Leith.

At OVETON. A Gilbertine Priory, founded, 5 John, by Alan de Wilton; rents 11*l*. 2*s*. 8*d*., now worth 222*l*. 13*s*. 4*d*.

At PONTEFRACT. A Cluniac Priory, built in the time of William Rufus, by Robert de Lacy; rents 472*l*. 16*s*. 1½*d*., now worth 9,456*l*. 2*s*. 6*d*.; granted, 7 Edward VI., to William, Lord Talbot

St. Clement's College, founded, in the reign of William Rufus, by Ilbert de Lacy.

Knolles' College, and Almshouse. Sir Robert Knolles founded, in the year 1385, a College for a Master and six Fellows; and adjoining it an Almshouse for a Master, two Chaplains, and 13 poor men and women; revenues 200*l*. 5*s*. 10½*d*., now worth 4,005*l*. 0*s*. 10*d*.

St. Nicholas's Hospital, founded, in the reign of Henry I., by Robert de Lacy; rents 97*l*. 13*s*. 4*d*., now worth 1,953*l*. 6*s*. 8*d*.; it maintained until the dissolution one Chaplain and 13 poor persons.

Dominican Friary, built before the year 1266, by Simon Pyper; granted, 36 Henry

VIII., to William Clifford, and Michael Wildbore.

Franciscan Friary.

At RERECROSS HOSPITAL. An Hospital, built in the year 1171, by Ralph de Multon ; granted, 7 Edward VI., to William Bucton, and Roger Marshall.

At RIBSTANE. An Hospital of Templars, founded in the reign of Richard I., by Robert, Lord Ross ; rents 265*l*. 9*s*. 6½*d*., now worth 5,359*l*. 10*s*. 10*d*. ; granted, 33 Henry VIII., to Charles, Duke of Suffolk.

At RICHMOND. A Benedictine Cell, founded, in the year 1100, by Wymar, Steward to the Earl of Richmond ; rents 43*l*. 16*s*. 8*d*., now worth 876*l*. 13*s*. 4*d*. ; granted, 4 Edward VI., to Edward, Lord Clinton.

A Premonstratensian Abbey, founded, in the year 1151, by Roald, the Constable of Richmond ; rents 188*l*. 16*s*. 2*d*., now worth 3,776*l*. 3*s*. 4*d*. ; granted, 14 Elizabeth, to John Stanhope.

St. Nicholas's Hospital, founded by King Henry II. ; rents 10*l*. yearly now worth 200*l*.

A Franciscan Friary, founded, in the year 1258, by Ralph Fitz Randal, Earl of Middleham ; granted, 36 Henry VIII., to John Banaster, and William Metcalf.

At RIPPON. A College, built and and endowed in the reign of William the Conqueror, by Archbishop Alfred, on the ruins of a Monastery that had been founded before the year 661 by Alchfrid, king of Northumbers, but afterwards burnt down in the civil wars ; seven Prebends made here at the dissolution 361*l*. 19*s*. 6*d*., six Vicars Choral 36*l*., other revenues 47*l*. 16*s*. 3*d*. total 445*l*. 15*s*. 3*d*. ; now worth 8,915*l*. 5*s*.

St John's Hospital, founded, before 4 John, by the Archbishops of York ; rents 12*l*. 0*s*. 4*d*., now worth 240*l*. 6*s*. 8*d*.

Magdalen Hospital, founded, by the Archbishops of York for lepers ; rents 24*l*. 0*s*. 7*d*., now worth 480*l*. 11*s*. 8*d*.

At RIVER. A Cistercian Abbey, founded, in the year 1131, by Walter Espec ; rents 351*l*. 14*s*. 6*d*., now worth 7,134*l*. 10*s*. ; granted, 30 Henry VIII., to Thomas, Earl of Rutland, in exchange for other lands.

At ROCH. A Cistercian Abbey, built in the year 1147, by Richard Fitz Turgis ; rents 271*l*. 19*s*. 4*d*., now worth 5,439*l*. 6*s*. 8*d*. ; granted, 38 Henry VIII. to William Ramesden, and Thomas Vavasor.

At ROSEDALE. A Benedictine Nunnery, founded, in the reign of Richard 1., by Robert de Stuteville; rents 41*l*. 13*s*. 8*d*., now worth 833*l*.

13s 4d.; granted, 30 Henry VIII., to Ralph, Earl of Westmoreland.

At SALLAY. A Cistercian Abbey, founded, in the year 1146, by William de Percy; rents 221l. 15s. 8d., now worth 4,435l. 13s. 4d.

At SELBY. A Benedictine Abbey, founded, in the year 1069, by William the Conqueror; rents 819l. 2s. 6d., now worth 16,382l. 10s.; granted, 32 Henry VIII., to Sir Ralph Sadler.

At SINNINGTHWAITE. A Cistercian Nunnery, founded, in the year 1160, by Bertram Haget; rents 62l. 6s., now worth 1,246l.; granted, 30 Henry VIII., to Robert Tempest.

At SNAITH. A Benedictine Cell, founded in the year 1106, by Girard, Archbishop of York; granted, 4 Edward VI., to John, Earl of Warwick.

At SPORTBURGH. An Hospital, founded, in the year 1363, by Mr. Fitz Williams; rents 9l. 13s. 11d., now worth 193l. 16s. 8d.

At SUTTON. A College; valued at 13l. 18s. 8d. yearly, now worth 278l. 13s. 4d.

An Hospital; valued at 7l. 18s. 4d., now worth 158l. 6s. 8d.

At SWINHEY. A Cistercian Nunnery, founded, in the reign of Stephen, by Roberd de Verli ; rents 134*l.* 6*s.* 9*d.*, now worth 2,686*l.* 15*s.* ; gran'ed, 32 Henry VIII., to Sir Richard Gresham.

At THICKHED. A Benedictine Nunnery, founded, in the reign of Richard I., by Roger Fitz Roger ; rents 23*l,* 12*l.* 2*d.*, now worth 472*l.* 3*s.* 4*d.* ; granted, 33 Henry VIII., to John Aske.

At TICKHILL. A College founded, by Eleanor, Queen of Henry II. ; granted, 4 Edward VI., to Francis, Earl of Shrewsbury.

At TOCKWITH. An Augustine Cell, founded, in the year 1114. by Jeffery Fitz Pain ; rents 8*l.* now worth 160*l.* ; granted, 31 Henry VIII., to Thomas Leigh.

At WARTER. An Austin Priory, built in the year 1132, by Jeffrey Fitz Pain ; rents 221*l.* 3*s.* 10*d.*, now worth 4,423*l.* 16*s* 8*d.* ; granted, 32 Henry VII., to Thomas, Earl of Rutland.

At WATTON. A Gilbertine Priory, succeeded in the year 1150 a Nunnery that was built 686 ; income 453*l.* 7*s.* 8*d.*, now worth 9,067*l.* 13*s.* 4*d.* ; granted, 3 Edward VI., to John, Earl of Warwick.

At WELLE. An Hospital, founded, in the year 1342, by Sir Ralph de Neville ; income 65*l.* 5*s.* 7*d.*, now worth 1,305*l.* 11*s.* 8*d.*

YORK.

At WHITBEY. A Benedictine Abbey grew up in the time of Henry I., instead of an ancient one built by St. Hilda in the year 657 ; income 505*l*. 9*s*. 1*d*., now worth 10,109*l*. 1*s*. 8*d*., granted, 4 Edward VI., to John, Earl of Warwick.

At WIDKIRK. An Augustine Cell, built in the reign of Henry I., by William, Earl of Warren and others ; income 47*l*. 0*s*. 4*d*., now worth 940*l*. 6*s*. 8*d*.; granted, 7 Edward VI., to George Talbot and Robert Saville.

At WILBURFOSSE. A Benedictine Nunnery founded in the year 1153, by Alan de Cotton income 28*l*. 8*s*. 8*d*., now worth 568*l*. 13*s*. 4*d*. ; granted, 7 Edward VI., to George Gale.

At WYKHAM. A Cistercian Nunnery, founded, in the year 1153, by Pain Fitz Osbert de Wykham ; rents 25*l*. 17*s*. 6*d*., now worth 517*l*. 10*s*.; granted, 32 Henry VIII., to Francis Poole.

At YARUM. An Hospital, founded, before the year 1185, by the Brus family ; income 5*l*., now worth 100*l*.

Dominican Friary, founded, in the year 1271, by Peter de Brus ; surrendered by Miles Wilcock, Prior, five Friars and Novices, 1539.

At YORK. A Cathedral, built in the year 1137,

by the care of Archbishops, Roger, Romane, Milton, and Thoresby, in the place of a Church originally founded, 627, by King Edwin, on his conversion to Christianity, but was burnt down in 741 ; yearly revenues of the Archbishop 2,035*l.* 3*s.*7*d.*, Canons 439*l.* 2*s.* 6*d.*, Dean 308*l.* 10*s.* 7*d.* ; total 2,772*l.* 16*s.* 8*d.* ; now worth 55,456*l.* 13*s.* 4*d.*

St. Mary's, a Benedictine Abbey, founded and endowed by William Rufus, in the year 1088 ; income 2085*l.* 1*s.* 5½*d.*, now worth 41,701*l.* 9*s.* 2*d.*

St. Clement's, a Benedictine, Convent, or Nunnery, founded in the year 1130, westward of the town, by Archbishop Thurston ; revenues 55*l.* 11*s.* 11*d.*, now worth 1,111*l.* 18*s.* 4*d.* ; granted, 33 Henry VIII., to Edward Shipwith.

St. Andrew's, a Gilbertine Priory, founded, in the year 1200, by Hugh Murduc ; income 57*l.* 5*s.* 9*d.*, now worth 1,145*l.* 15*s.* ; granted, 37 Henry VIII., to John Bellew and John Broxholm.

Trinity, or Christ Church. An Alien Priory, founded, in the year 1089, by Ralph Painell ; yearly income 196*l.* 17*s.* 2*d.*, now worth 3,937*l.* 13*s.* 4*d.* ; granted, 34 Henry VIII., to Leonard Beckwith.

All Saints, a Benedictine Cell, built by the bounty of William Rufus ; completely demolished at the Reformation, so that it could not be ascertained where it stood.

Beddern, or Vicar's College founded, in the year 1252, by Walter Gray, Archbishop, for the Choristers and other officers of the Cathedral ; revenues 255*l.* 7*s.* 8*d.*, now worth 5,107*l.* 13*s.*

St. Sepulchre's College, founded, in the year 1161, by Roger, Archbishop of York ; income 138*l.* 19*s.* 2½*d.*, now worth 2,779*l.* 4*s.* 2*d.*

St. William's College, founded, in the year 1460, by Richard Neville, Earl of Northumberland, and his brother George Neville, Bishop of Exeter ; yearly income 22*l.* 12*s.* 8*d.*, now worth 452*l.* 13*s.* 4*d.* ; granted 4 Edward VI., to Michael Stanhope and John Bellew.

Boutham Hospital, founded, in the year 1314, by Robert Pykering, Dean of York ; income 11*l.* 6*s.* 8*d.*, now worth 226*l.* 13*s.* 4*d.*

Boutham Hospital, Minor, built in the year 1481 by John Gyseburgh ; rents 9*l.* 6*s.* 8*d.*, now worth 186*l.* 13*s.* 4*d.*

Fossgate Hospital, founded, 45 Edward III., by John de Rucliff, for the poor ; income 6*l.* 13*s.* 4*d.* now worth 133*l.* 6*s.* 8*d.* ; still in being.

St. Nicholas' Hospital, said to have been founded, by the Empress Maud, for leprous persons ; income 29*l.* 1*s* 4*d.*, now worth 581*l.* 6*s.* 8*d.*

St. Peter's or Leonard's Hospital, founded, by King Stephen, for a Master, 13 Brethren, four secular Priests, eight Sisters, 30 Choristers, two Schoolmasters, 206 Beadmen, and six Servitors ; with revenues of 362*l.* 11*s.* 1½*d.*, now worth 7,251*l.* 2*s.* 6*d.* ; granted, 6 Elizabeth, to Robert, Lord Dudley ; it is now called the *Mint Yard.*

St. Thomas's Hospital, founded, before the year 1391, yet stands.

An Augustine Friary, founded, in the year 1278, by Lord Scroop ; granted, to Thomas Rawson.

A Franciscan Friary, founded, by King Henry II., and the City of York ; granted, 34 Henry VIII., to Leonard Beckwith.

A Carmelite Friary, founded, in the year 1255, by Lord Vesey and Lord Percy ; granted, 35 Henry VIII., to Ambrose Beckwith

WALES.

ANGLESEY (County).

At GLANNAGH. A Benedictine Priory, founded in an island in the east part of Anglesey in the year 1221, by Lleweline, Prince of North Wales; income 40*l.* 17*s.* 9½*d.*, now worth 817*l.* 15*s.* 10*d.* ; granted, .6 Elizabeth, to John Moore.

At HOLY HEAD. A College rose instead of a Monastery built in the year 380, by St. Kebius; income 24*l.*, now worth 480*l.* ; granted, 7 James I., to Francis Morrice and Francis Filips.

BRECKNOCK (County).

At BRECKNOCK. A Benedictine Priory, built in the reign of Henry I,, by Bernard de Newmarch ; yearly income 134*l.* 11*s.* 4*d.*, now worth

CAERMARTHEN.

2,691*l.* 6*s.* 8*d.* ; granted, by Henry VIII., to John ap Rice.

A College, made of a Dominican Friary, is standing to this day.

CAERMARTHEN (County).

At ABERGWILLY. A College, founded, in the year 1287, by Thomas Beck, Bishop of St. David's ; rents 42*l.*, now worth 840*l.*

At ABELANDA. A Cistercian Abbey, founded, in the year 1143, by Bernard, Bishop of St. David's ; yearly value 153*l.* 17*s.* 2*d.*, now worth 3,077*l.* 3*s.* 4*d.* ; granted, 36 Henry VIII., to Henry Audley and John Cordel.

At CADWELL. A Benedictine Priory, founded, in the year 1130, by Roger, Bishop of Salisbury ; rents 29*l.* 10*s.*, now worth 590*l.*

At CAERMARTHEN. An Austin Priory, founded before the year 1148 ; rents 164*l.* 0*s.* 4*d.*, now worth 3,280*l.* 6*s.* 8*d.* ; granted, 35 Henry VIII., to Richard Andrews and Nicholas Temple.

A Franciscan Friary ; granted, 5 Edward VI., to Sir Thomas Gresham.

At TALLAGH. A Premonstratensian Abbey, founded in the year 1197, by Rhese Griffith Price, of South Wales; income 153*l*. 1*s*. 4*d*., now worth 3,061*l*. 6*s*. 8*d*.

CAERNARVON (County).

At BANGOR. A Cathedral Church, founded at some early time; the revenues of the Bishoprick were valued at 131*l*. 16*s*. 4*d*., now worth 2,636*l*. 6*s*. 8*d*.

A Dominican Friary, founded in the year 1276, and granted, 7 Edward VI., to Thomas Brown, and converted into a Free School, 1557.

At BARDSLEY, Isle of Birds. An Abbey, founded, before the year 516; it produced great numbers of holy men; yearly income 56*l*. 6*s*. 2*d*., now worth 1,126*l*. 3*s*. 4*d*.; granted, 3 Edward VI., to John, Earl of Warwick.

At BETHKELERT. An Augustine Priory, founded very anciently; yearly value 69*l*. 3*s*. 8*d*., now worth 1,383*l*. 13*s*. 4*d*.; granted, by Henry VIII., to Lord Radnor.

CARDIGAN (County).

At CARDIGAN. A Benedictine Cell, with revenues of 13*l.* 4*s.* 9*d.*, now worth 264*l.* 15*s.* ; granted, 31 Henry VIII., to William Cavendish.

At LLANDEWI-BREVI. A College, founded, in the year 1187, by Thomas Beck, Bishop of St. David's, in honour of St. David, who preached at a Council held in 519, and thereby extinguished the Pelagian heresy; rents 38*l.* 11*s.*, now worth 771*l.*

At LLANLEIR. A Cistercian Nunnery, of yearly income 57*l.* 5*s.* 4*d.*, now worth 1,145*l.* 6*s.* 8*d.* ; granted, 7 Edward VI., to William Sackville and John Dudley.

At STRATA FLORIDA. A Cistercian Abbey, founded, in the year 1164, by Rhesus, son of Griffith of South Wales ; income 122*l.* 6*s.* 8*d.*, now worth 2,446*l.* 13*s.* 4*d.*

DENBIGH (County).

At MAYNAN. A Cistercian Abbey, founded, in the year 1283, by King Richard I. ; revenues

162*l*. 15*s*., now worth 3,255*l*..; granted, 5 Elizabeth, to Elezeus Wynne, in whose family it continues still.

At RUTHIN. A College, founded, in the year 1310, by John de Grey, Lord of Dyffryn, Clywd; granted, 4 Edward VI., to William Winlove and John Stevens.

At DE VALLE CRUCIS LLANEGWAST. A Cistercian Abbey, founded, in the year 1200, by Madoc ap Griffith Maylor, Prince of Powis; income 213*l*. 5*s*. 5*d*., now worth 4,283*l*. 8*s*. 4*d*.; granted, 9 James, to Edward Wotton.

FLINT (COUNTY).

At ST. ASAPH. A Bishoprick, founded, in the sixth century, by a holy and good man, St. Asaph, or Aassaph. This See, and a Monastery that had been also there, were frequently destroyed and rebuilt during the wars between the English and Welsh; revenues 187*l*. 11*s*. 6*d*., now worth 3,751*l*. 10*s*.

At BASINGWERK. A Cistercian Abbey, founded, in the year 1131, by Ranulph, Earl of Chester; rents 157*l*. 15*s*. 2*d*., now worth 3,155*l*.

3*s.* 4*d.* ; granted, 32 Henry VIII., to Henry ap Harry.

At RHUDLAND. A Dominican Friary, founded in the year 1268 ; granted, 32 Henry VIII., to Henry ap Harry.

GLAMORGAN (COUNTY).

At LLANDAFFE. A Bishoprick, founded, about the year 522, by St. Dubritius ; suffered much in the wars ; revenues 242*l.* 7*s.* 1*d.*, now worth 4,847*l.* 1*s.* 8*d.*

At MORGAN. A Cistercian Abbey; founded, in the year 1147, by Robert, Earl of Gloucester ; rents 188*l.* 14*s.*, now worth 3,774*l.* ; granted, 32 Henry VIII., to Sir Richard Moxell, and is now the property of Thomas, Lord Marsel.

At NETH. A Cistercian Abbey, founded, in the reign of Henry I., by Richard de Grainville ; rents 150*l.* 4*s.* 9*d.*, now worth 3,004*l.* 15*s.* ; granted, 33 Henry VIII., to Sir Richard Williams, alias Cromwell.

At SWANSEY. An Hospital, founded, in the year 1332, by Henry, Bishop of St. David's ; rents 20*l.*, now worth 400*l.*

At WENNY. A Benedictine Cell, founded, in the year 1141, by Maurice of London; rents 59*l.* 4*s.*, now worth 1184*l.*; granted, 37 Henry VIII., to Edward Carn.

MERIONETH (County).

At KINNER. A Cistercian Abbey, founded, in the year 1200, by Lleweline, the son of Gervase; rents 58*l.* 15*s.* 4*d.*, now worth 1,175*l.* 6*s.* 8*d.*

MONTGOMERY (County).

At LLANLUGAN. A Cistercian Nunnery, founded in the year 1239; rents 22*l.* 13*s.* 8*d.*, now worth 453*l.* 13*s.* 4*d.*; granted, 37 Henry VIII., to Sir Arthur Darcy.

At YSTRAT MARCHEL, or PAOL. A Cistercian Abbey, founded, in the year 1170, by Owen Keveliog rents 73*l.* 7*s.* 3*d.*, now worth 1,467*l.* 5*s.*; granted, 8 Elizabeth, to Rowland Howard and Thomas Dixton.

PEMBROKE (County).

At Caldey. A Tyrone Cell, the gift of Robert Fitz Martin's mother; rents 5*l*., now worth 100*l*.

At St. David's. A Bishoprick, founded by St. Patrick about 470; underwent several convulsions afterwards; revenues at the dissolution 193*l*. 14*s*. 10*d*., now worth 3,874*l*. 16*s*. 8*d*.

A College, founded, in the year 1365, by John, Duke of Lancaster; revenues 106*l*. 3*s*. 6*d*., now worth 2,123*l*. 10*s*.; dissolved by Edward VI.

At St. Dogmael. A Tyrone Abbey, founded, in the reign of Henry I., by Robert Fitz Martin; rents 87*l*. 8*s*. 6*d*., now worth 1,748*l*. 10*s*.; granted, 35 Henry VIII., to John Bradshaw.

At Haverford. An Austin Priory, founded, in the year 1200, by Robert of Haverford, Lord of the place; rents 135*l*. 6*s*. 1*d*., now worth 2,706*l*. 1*s*. 8*d*.; granted, 38 Henry VIII., to Roger and Thomas Barlow.

At Pembroke. A Benedictine Cell, founded, in the year 1098, by the Earl of Pembroke; yearly value 113*l*. 2*s*. 6*d*., now worth 2,262*l*.

10*s.* ; granted, 37 Henry VIII., to John Vaughan.

At PILLA, or PILLE. A Benedictine Priory, founded, in the year 1200, by Adam de Rupe ; yearly income 52*l.* 2*s.* 5*d.*, now worth 1,042*l.* 8*s.* 4*d.* ; granted, 38 Henry VIII., to Roger and Thomas Barlow.

At SLEBAGH. A House of Hospitalers, founded, in the year 1301, by Wizo, and Walter his son ; rents 184*l.* 10*s.* 11½*d.* ; now worth 3,690*l.* 19*s.* 2*d.* ; granted, together with several things in these parts, to Roger and Thomas Barlow.

RADNOR (COUNTY).

At CUMHIRE. A Cistercian Abbey, founded, in the year 1143, by Cadwathelan, though it seems that the fabric was finished ; the revenues, at the dissolution, made 24*l.* 19*s.* 4*d.*, yearly, now worth 499*l.* 6*s.* 8*d,* ; granted, 37 Henry VIII., to Walter Henley and John Williams.

THE ISLE OF MAN.

DUFFGLASS. Near this place was a Nunnery, which is now a dwelling house.

At **RUSSIN.** A Cistercian Abbey, founded, in the year 1098, by Mac Manis, Governor of the island. This foundation continued for some time after the general suppression of such houses in England. The Isle of man was converted to Christanity by St. Patrick, about the year 447.

IRELAND.

ANTRIM (COUNTY).

At **BALLYCASTLE.** An Abbey, when founded, is not known, but it seems, from an inscription on a chapel that had been built in the year 1612, by Randal Mac Donnell, Earl of Antrim, that the Abbey stood until the Reformation.

At BONAMARGY. A Monastery, founded, during the fifteenth century by Mac Donnell, granted, to his Apostate descendants.

At CARRICKFERGUS. A Franciscan Abbey, founded, in the year 1232, by Hugh Lacy, Earl of Ulster; granted to Sir Arther Chichester; is now the Mansion of the Earls of Donegal.

CLUAIN. An Abbey built in the early ages by St. Olcar; now the Protestant place of worship.

At GLENARM. A Franciscan Abbey, built in the year 1465, by Robert Bisset, a Scotchman; granted, to Alexander Mac Donnell, ancestor to the Earl of Antrim.

At GOODBORN. A Premonstratensian Priory, founded, about the year 1242; surrendered in the year 1542 to the Commissioners of Henry VIII.

At KELLS, or DISERT. A Priory, founded, in the year 1200; surrendered, in the year 1542 to the Commissioners of Henry VIII.

At KILITRAGH. A Church built by St. Patrick; now the Protestant place of worship.

ANTRIM.

At LAMBEG. A Franciscan Monastery, founded by Mac Donnell about the year 1500.

At LHANNAVACH. The Church of the Dwarf, founded, by St. Patrick; now the Protestant place of worship.

At MASSAREENE. A Franciscan Abbey, founded about the year 1500, by O'Neil; granted, in the year 1621, to Sir Arthur Chichester, Baron of Belfast.

At MUCKAMORE. A Monastery, founded, in the year 550, by St. Colman; surrendered, after having been for many ages the light of the world, the nursery of saints and of learning, to Henry VII.; granted, in the year 1639, to the Longford family.

At RACHLIN ISLAND. A Church, founded, in the year 546, by St. Columba. This house, celebrated for learning and sanctity, stood in the year 1558, when the Earl of Essex, Lord Deputy, gained possession of the island.

At RATHMOANE. A Church, founded, by St. Patrick, for his disciple St. Ereclasius; now the Protestant place of worship.

RATHMUIGHE (on the sea-shore, eight miles from Dunliffsia, or Dunluce). A Monastery, founded by St. Patrick.

At Tulach. A Church built by St. Patrick, for St. Nehemias, in the diocese of Connor; now the Protestant place of worship.

[Besides these, there are upwards of thirty religious houses on record, which were principally founded by St. Patrick in this county, but they are omitted because there is no proof that they subsisted until the Reformation.]

ARMAGH (County).

At Armagh. An Augustine Abbey, built in the year 457, by St. Patrick.

A Priory of the Culdei, or Choristers of the Cathedral, had for revenues seven bally-boes, or town-lands, worth 46*l*., now worth 920*l*. Sir Toby Caulfield, Lord Charlemount, received, in the year 1620, the rents for Henry VIII.

Temple Fortagh founded by St. Patrick for St. Lupita, his eldest sister, who was buried here; granted, in the year 1618, by King James, to Francis Annesley, Esq.

A Franciscan Friary, founded, in the year 1261, by Archbishop Scanlon. Solomon M'Conny was superior in 1583, when the Reformation was completed.

CLONFEAKLE, that is, the Church of the Tooth, so named from a tooth of St. Patrick, which was preserved here ; is now the Protestant place of worship ; five miles from Armagh.

At KILMORE. A Church founded, by St. Mochtee ; now the Protestant place of worship ; three miles from Armagh.

At KILSLERE. A Franciscan Monastery. Thomas Ornay was superior in the year 1457.

At KILLEVY. A Nunnery, built about the year 517, by St. Donerca, otherwise called Monenna, sister to St. Patrick, at the foot of Sliev Gullen ; now a Protestant place of worship.

At STRADHAILLOYSE. A Franciscan Monastery, founded, in the year 1282.

[There are five religious foundations of St. Patrick and his disciples omitted in this county as in the preceding.]

CARLOW (COUNTY).

At ATHADDY. An Augustine Nunnery, founded, in the year 1151, by Dermot, son of Murchard, King of Leinster.

At BALLY M'WILLIAM-ROE, near Clonegall. A Preceptory of Templars, founded about the year 1300.

At KILLARGE. A Preceptory of Templars, (which was afterwards granted to the Knights of St. John of Jerusalem,) founded, in the reign of King John, by Gilbert de Borard ; granted, 1590, by Queen Elizabeth, to the wife of Gerard Aylmer.

At LEIGHLIN, a town formerly of considerable note. The Great Abbey, founded, by St. Gobban, celebrated for the Synod held there in the year 630, regarding the celebration of Easter. St. Laserian, Abbot in 632, had at one time 1500 Monks under him ; he was consecrated Bishop by Pope Honorius, and was Legate from the Holy See.

LEIGHLIN BRIDGE. A Carmelite Mona tery, founded, in the reign of Henry III., by one of the Carew family ; had many endowments and privileges from Kings Henry III., Richard II., and Henry IV. ; was finally converted, at the suppression, into a fort.

At St. MULLIN's. An Abbey of Augustines, founded, in the year 632, by St. Moling ; plundered and burnt before the year 1138.

At TULLAGH. An Augustine Abbey, built in the reign of Edward II., on a grant of land made by Simon Lumbard and Hugh Tallon ; granted, 1557, by Queen Elizabeth, to Thomas, Earl of Ormond.

CAVAN (County).

At BALLYLINCH. An Hospital, when founded, by whom and with what endowments, is unknown; granted by King James, 1605, to Sir Edward Moore, ancestor to the Earl of Drogheda, for three pence yearly rent.

At CAVAN. A Dominican Monastery, founded, in the year 1300, by Giolla O'Reilly, of the dynasty of Breffiny; stood until the general dissolution, but there is not now the least remains of it.

At DROMLOMMAN. An Hospital, leased by King James to Sir Edward Moore, for 2s. 6d. yearly rent.

At DRUMLANE or DRUMLAHAN. A Monastery, founded, before the year 550, as some suppose, by St. Maidoc, because he was born in that year; granted, 13 Elizabeth, to Hugh O'Reilly, head of the Brenie sept, for the term of 21 years, at the rent of 8l. 14s. 8d., now worth 174l. 13s. 4d.

At KILLACHAD. An Abbey, founded, before the year 800, by St. Tigernach, who was buried there in the year 805, plundered by the English in the reign of Henry II.

At KILMORE. An Abbey, founded, in the sixth century, by St. Columb ; now the Protestant Bishop's See.

At LOUGH OUGHTER. An Abbey, founded, in the year 1237, by Clarus M. Moylin, Archdeacon of Elphin ; granted, 1570, by Queen Elizabeth, to Hugh O'Reilly of the Brenie, head of his sept; for 21 years, at the rent of 2*l.* 15*s.* 8*d.*, now worth 55*l.* 13*s.* 4*d.* Perhaps he was ejected for non-payment of rent ; for, by an inquisition taken, 27 Elizabeth, he was found in arrears for 11½ years rent, for this and the Monastery of Drumlan, above said.

At MOUNTERCONAGHT. An Endowed Hospital, granted by King James to Sir Edward Moore, at 1*s.* 3*d.* yearly rent, now worth 1*l.* 5*s.* See Ballylinch.

CLARE (COUNTY).

At CLARE. An Augustine Abbey, founded, in the year 1195, by Donald O'Brien, King of Limerick ; granted, 1661, to Henry, Earl of Thomond.

At CORCUMROE. A Cistercian Abbey, founded, in the year 1194, and largely endowed by

Donald O'Brien, King of Limerick; granted to Richard Harding.

At ENNIS. A Monastery of Franciscans, built in the year 1240, by Donagh Carbrac O'Brien; it is the place of interment of the family of the O'Briens; granted, 1621, to William Dongan, Esq.; is now the Protestant place of worship.

At GLAN CHOLUIMCHILLE. An Abbey, founded by St. Columb; is now a Protestant place of worship in the diocese of Kilfenora.

At INCHYCRONANE, an Island on the river Shannon. A Monastery, founded in the year 1190, by Donald O'Brien, King of Limerick; granted, 1661, to Henry, Earl of Thomond.

At INCHMORE, an Island in the Shannon. An Abbey, founded by St. Senan, who placed over it his disciple St. Liberius.

At INISANLAOI. A magnificent Abbey, built in the year 1305, by Turlogh, King of Thomond, where he is buried.

At INISKELTAIR, an Island in Loughderg. An Abbey, founded, in the year 653, by St. Camin, who is interred there. This Island is one of the stations for pilgrimage in the Loughderg.

At INISNEGANANAGH, or the Island of Canons,

in the Shannon. A priory of Augustines, founded, in the 12th century, by Donald O'Brien, King of Limerick; granted, 1661, to Henry, Earl of Thomond.

At INISSCATTERY, a rich and beautiful Island in the mouth of the Shannon. An Abbey, founded by St. Senan, or, as some suppose, by St. Patrick himself, who appointed over it St. Senan; he had eleven churches for Friars, and allowed no women to come into the island. Granted, 20 Elizabeth, to the Mayor and Corporation of Limerick, at 3l. 12s. 8d. rent, now worth 72l. 13s. 4d. This island is a great resort of pilgrims, on certain festivals.

At KILCARRAGH. A Monastery, granted to John King.

At KILLOEN, in the Barony of Islands. A Nunnery, built in the year 1190, by Donald O'Brien, of Limerick. Slaney, daughter of Donogh, King of Thomond, was Abbess, and died in 1260. She excelled all the women then in Munster for piety, alms-deeds, and hospitality.

At KILSHANNY, in the Barony of Corcumroe. A monastery, granted to Robert Hickman.

At QUIN, or QUINCHY, five miles east of Ennis. A Franciscan Monastery, built in the year 1402, by M'Namara; the building is entirely of black marble; granted, 1583, to Sir Tirlagh O'Brien, of Irishdyman. The Roman Catholics repaired this Monastery in 1604.

At SHRADUFFE, an Abbey, granted, in 1611, to Sir Edward Fisher, together with its site and possessions.

At TOMGRANY, four miles east of Loughderg. An Abbey. St. Manchin, Abbot, died in the year 735. It is now the church.

Fifteen religious foundations of the early ages in this county are omitted.

CORK (COUNTY).

At ABBEY MAHON, near Timoleague, by Count M'Sherry-bay. A Cistercian Monastery, built by the Friars, and endowed by Lord Barry with eighteen plowlands, that is, the whole parish of Abbey Mahon, which were seized by the crown.

At BALLYBEG, near Buttavant. An Augustine Priory, founded, in the year 1229, by Philip de

Barry ; the steeple, the arcade over the dome, remaining yet, together with the traces of many external buildings, show that it had been a magnificent structure ; yearly value 260*l*., now worth 5,200*l*., granted, 16 Elizabeth, for 21 years, to George Boucher, Esq. who forfeited it for non-payment of rent ; then granted to the wife of Sir Thomas Norris, Governor of Munster.

At BALLYMACADANE, four miles south of Cork, on the Bandon Road. An Augustine Nunnery, founded, in the year 1450, by Cormac M'Carthy.

At BALLVOURNEY, or the town of the Beloved. An Abbey or Nunnery, built in the year 650, by St. Abban, for St. Gobnata, descendant of O'Connor the Great, Monarch of Ireland ; her festival is on the 14th February.

At BANTRY, a pretty Town on the Bay of that name. A Franciscan Monastery, built in the year 1466, by Dermot O'Sullivan Beare ; is now demolished.

At BRIDGE TOWN, on the Black Water, above Fermoy. A Priory, pleasantly situated in a deep valley at the confluence of the rivers Aubeg and Black Water.

At BRIGOWNE, near Mitchelstown. A Church, founded by St. Finchu.

CORK.

At BUTTEVANT, formerly a corporate town, governed by a Mayor and Aldermen. A Franciscan Monastery founded in the year 1290, by David Oge Barry, Lord Buttevant; the walls of the choir and nave are yet entire; the steeple, a high square tower, standing on a fine gothic arch, fell in 1822. There is a beautiful window in the east end.

At CAPE CLEAR. An island on the south-west coast of Ireland, containing 12 plowlands, 300 houses, and about 1,200 inhabitants.

At CARIGILIKY, in the parish of Myros, West Carberry. A Monastery, built in the year 1172, by Dermot M'Carthy, King of Desmond; granted, with all the possessions, 30 Elizabeth, to Nicholas Walshe for ever, at the yearly rent 28*l.* 6*s.* 6*d.*, now worth 566*l.* 10*s.*

At CASTLE LYONS. A Dominican Monastery, founded in the year 1307, by John de Barry. The Earl of Cork obtained the possessions and bestowed them on the Countess of Barrymore, his daughter.

A Carmelite Abbey, founded in the Barry family.

At CLONMENE, in Duhallow. An Augustine Monastery; founded, by Mr. O'Callagan.

At CLOYNE, a town near Youghal. A Cathedral Monastery, and Nunnery destroyed ; the revenues preserved for parsons.

At CORK. A Monastery founded, in the year 600, by St. Finbar ; it is recorded, that in the eighth century 700 Monks and 17 Bishops were living there a contemplative life ; the possessions were granted, 33 Elizabeth, to Cormac M'Carthy and to Sir Richard Grenville ; a Protestant place of worship was erected on the site.

A Franciscan Friary, founded, in the year 1214, by Dermot M'Carthy Reagh ; granted, 8 Elizabeth, to Andrew Skydy, at 2*l*. 18*s*. 8*d*., now worth 58*l*. 13*s*. 4*d*. This building stood on the north side of the city.

A Dominican Friary, founded, in the year 1229, by Philip de Barry ; it stood on an island in the south of the city ; granted, 35 Henry VIII., to William Boureman, for 9*s*. 6*d*. yearly rent, now worth 9*l*. 10*s*.

An Augustine Monastery, founded, in the reign of Henry IV., by Lord Kinsale, granted, 19 Elizabeth, to Cormac M'Carthy, at 13*l*. 16*s*. 8*d*. yearly rent, now worth 276*l*. 13*s*. 4*d*. ; it is converted into a sugar-house now called the red Abbey.

A Nunnery, founded, by William de

Barry, about the year 1327; it is thought it stood where the market-house now is.

A Preceptory of Templars ; built in the year 1292.

Priory of St. Stephen, founded, for lepers, before the year 1295 ; converted into the Blue-coat Hospital in 1674.

At DONAGHMORE, eight miles north-west of Cork. A Monastery, founded, by St. Fingene, disciple of St. Finbar ; it is now the Church.

At FERMOY, a large town. A Cistercian Abbey, to which Maurice Flemming was a benefactor ; granted, 33 Elizabeth, to Sir Richard Grenville, at 15l. 18s. 4d. yearly rent, now worth 318l. 6s. 8d.

At GLANWORTH. A Dominican Monastery founded, in the year 1227, by the Roche's family.

At INISCARA, on the river Lee, five miles above Cork. An Abbey, built by St. Senan of Iniscattery ; dissolved.

At INISHIRCAN. near Cape Clear. A Franciscan Monastery, founded, in the year 1460, by Florence Moar O'Driscoll; the walls and steeple are still in good order.

At KILBEACAN, in Muscryciure. A large

Monastery, founded, in the year 650, by St. Abban ; St. Beacan presided there.

At KILCREA. A Nunnery, where St. Chera was Abbess.

A Franciscian Monastery, founded, in the year 1465, by Cormac M'Carthy Moor, King of Desmond ; great part of the building still remains ; granted, by Oliver Cromwell 1641, to Lord Broghill.

At KINSALE. A Priory of regular Canons dedicated to St. Gobban.

A Carmelite Friary ; when founded, is not known, it flourished in 1350.

At LEGAN. A Monastery, stood in the year 1301 ; at the suppression of religious houses, the Prior of St. John in Waterford was seised of this house.

At LUEIM, near the city of Cork. A Monastery, of which David de Cogan was patron in the year 1318.

At MIDDLETON. An Abbey, founded, in the year 1180, by the Fitzgeralds, or, as some think, by the Barrys ; Gerald, Bishop of Cloyne, endowed it with several vicarages in 1476.

At MONANIMY, on the Black Water, three

miles below Mallow. A Commandery, for the support of which the parishes of Clenor, Carrigdownen, Carig, and Templebodane, were charged in the King's books with 3*l.* 10*s.* crown rent, now worth 70*l.*

At MOURNE, or BALLYNAMONA, three miles south of Mallow, on the Cork road. A Preceptory, first of Templars, and afterwards of Hospitalers, founded, in the reign of John, by Alexander de Sancta Helena.

At ROSS CARBERRY. An Abbey, founded in the year 590 by St. Fachnan Mougah, or the *hairy*, because he was covered with hair at his birth; he was Abbot of Molona, in the county of Waterford also; a city with a large seminary grown up here.

It was also an Episcopal See. This diocese is now joined to the diocese of Cloyne.

At TIMOLEAGUE, in the Barony of Barryroe, eight miles west of Kinsale. An Abbey of Franciscans, founded at Cregan, and translated hither in the year 1279, by William Barry, Lord of Ibaun. At the suppression, the possessions fell to Lord Inchiquin. The walls, arcades, and tower are still in good order.

At TRACTON, two miles south of Carigline. A Cistercian Abbey, built in the year 1224, by

M'Carthy ; great numbers of pilgrims resorted hither on Holy Thursday to venerate the Holy Cross ; granted, by Queen Elizabeth, 1568, to Sir James Craig and Henry Guilford ; the former assigned it to the Earl of Cork.

At WEEME, near Cork. An Augustine Priory, stood at the fourteenth century, and, without doubt, until the general dissolution.

At YOUGHAL, a large sea port town. A Franciscan Monastery, built in the year 1224, by Maurice Fitzgerald, Lord Chief Justice of Ireland, who died and was buried in 1257, after having spent many years here under the habit of a Monk. This house stood to the South of the town ; there are no traces of it now.

A Dominican Friary, built to the north, in the year 1268, by Maurice, descendant of Lord Offaly ; granted, 23 Elizabeth, to William Walsh, at 1s. 10d. yearly rent, now worth 1l. 16s. 8d.

DERRY (COUNTY).

At ARRAGELL, in the Barony of Coleraine. A Monastery, founded, by St. Columb, to which the Protestant place of worship has succeeded.

DONEGALL.

At BADONEY, in Glaun Aicle, two miles from Derry. A Church, founded, by St. Patrick.

At COLERAINE. A Priory of regular Canons, founded, it is thought, by St. Carbreus, a disciple of St. Finian of Clonard.

A Dominican Friary, founded, in the year 1244, by the O'Cahanes; Shane O'Boyle, the last prior, surrendered it to the King's Commissioners, 1 Jan. 1542.

At DERRY. An Augustine Abbey, founded, about the year 521, by St. Columb.

A Nunnery founded, in the year 1218, by Turlogh O'Neil, of Strabane.

A Dominican Friary, built in the year 1274, by O'Donnel, Prince of Tyrconnell; the house supported generally 150 Monks.

At DEZERTOGHILL. An Abbey, built by St. Columb, is now converted into a Protestant place of worship.

At DONAGHMORE. A Church, built in the time of St. Patrick, is now converted into the Protestant place of worship.

At DUNGIVEN. An Augustine Priory, founded, in the year 1100, by Prince O'Cahane; it stood to the fourteenth, and, without doubt, to the sixteenth, century.

At MAGILLAGAN, near Loughfoyle. A Monastery, founded, by St. Columb.

At MOYCOSQUIN, near Coleraine. An Abbey, founded, in the year 1172; it stood until the fifteenth century.

DONEGALL (COUNTY).

At ASTRATH, on the river Erne, near Ballyshannon. A Cistercian Abbey, built in the year 1178, by Roderick O'Cananan, Prince of Tyrconnell; by a valuation of Queen Elizabeth, the revenues made 19*l*. 11*s*. 8*d*. yearly, now worth 39*l*. 13*s*. 4*d*.

At BOTHCHONAIS, in Inis-eoguin. A monastery, in which St. Coemgall was Abbot in the eighth, and St. Maelisa (whose writings are still extant) in the eleventh century.

At CLONLEIGH, on the river Foyle. A Church built by St. Columb, where his disciple, St. Lugad, is honoured; St. Carnech was Abbot and Bishop here about the year 530. It is now the Protestant place of worship in the diocese of Derry.

At CLONMANY, near the sea. A Monastery, built by St. Columb ; now the Church.

At CONWALL, near the river Sevilly. An Abbey, founded about the year 587 ; now a Church of worship, in the diocese of Raphoe.

At CNODAIN, on the river Erne. A Monastery, in which St. Conan was Abbot.

At DOMNACHGLINNE TOCHUIR, in Inisoen. A Church, founded by St. Patrick, in which he appointed Maccarthen, brother to the Saint of Clogher, Bishop ; there are still preserved the Saint's penitential bed, and other sacred relics ; a great resort of pilgrims on St. Patrick's day, 17th March.

At DONEGALL. A Franciscan Monastery, founded, in the year 1474, by Odo Roe O'Donnell, Prince of Tyrconnell. The place of interment of great men and scholars.

At DRUMHOME, on the Bay of Donegall. A Monastery, in which St. Ernan lived in the year 640 ; continued to the general dissolution ; now the Protestant place of worship.

DONEGALL.

At FAHAN, six miles north-west of Derry, on Loughswilly. A noble Monastery, founded by St. Columb. This grand edifice was held in the greatest veneration, from the reverence paid to the patron saint, from the many monuments of antiquity preserved there, and from its being the interment of many illustrious saints and great men. The only relics still remaining are some fragments of the acts of St. Columb, written in Irish verse by St. Muran, a large chronicle, and the crosier of St. Muran, richly ornamented with jewels, which is preserved by the O'Neils.

At FANEGARAGH. A Franciscan Friary, built by M'Ruinifaig.

At GARTON, two miles west of Kilmacrenan. A Monastery, founded by St. Columb ; now the Protestant place of worship.

At HILFOTHUIR. A Cistercian abbey, built in the year 1194, by O'Dogharty.

At INVER, five miles east of Killybegs. A Franciscan Friary, founded, about the year 1500, on the ruins of an ancient Monastery, that was built, 563, by St. Natalis.

At INIS KEEL, an island off the coast, an Abbey.

An INES SAMER. Some Religious House ; in

which Flaherty, King of Tyrconnell, died in re-
tirement in the year 1197, after having laid off
his crown and wordly cares.

At KILBARON, on the Bay of Donegall. A
Church, founded by St. Columb; now the Protestant Church.

At KILCARTAICH. A Church in which St.
Carthach was Bishop about the year 540; it is
supposed to be Killcarr, which is a Protestant
house in the diocese of Raphoe.

At KILLYBEGS. A Franciscan Friary, built
by M'Sweeny-bannig.

At KILMACRENAN, on the river Gannon. An
Abbey, richly endowed by St. Columb; and a
Franciscan Friary, built by O'Donnel, which is
now the Protestant Church.

At KIL O'DONNEL. A Franciscan Monastery, founded, before the year 1600, by O'Donnell; by an inquisition ordered by James I., the
revenues made 3s. annually, now worth 3l.

At LOUGHDEARG, in the parish of Templeca-
ran; there are several islands, and in the largest
called St. Dabeoc, was an Augustine Priory,
founded, by St. Dabeoc, about the year 492. St.
Patrick's purgatory, celebrated all over Europe,
and visited by all nations, particulary in the four-

teenth century, is situated in one of these islands ;
the lough continues still to be the resort of great
numbers of pilgrims.

At MOVILL on Loughfoyle. A Monastery,
founded by St. Patrick ; now the Protestant
place of worship.

At RAPHOE. A Monastery, founded by St.
Columb.

At RATHMULLIN on Loughswilly. A Carmelite Friary, founded by M'Sweeny Fannagh.
The revenues valued, 43 Elizabeth, at 6s. 8d.,
now worth 6l. 13s. 4d.

At SEINGLEAN, in the diocese of Raphoe. A
Monastery, founded by St. Columb.

At TAUGHBOYNE. A Monastery, founded by
St Baithen, disciple and kinsman of St. Columb,
in the year 584.

At TORRE ISLAND. A Monastery, founded before the year 650, in which St. Ernan was
abbot.

At TULLY, near Loughswilly. An Abbey,
founded by St. Columb.

DOWN (County).

At Achadhcaoil, near the Bay of Dundrum. An Abbey, in which St. Killen was Abbot in the fifth, and St. Senan in the sixth century.

At Bangor, or the White Choir, formerly the Vale of Angels. An Abbey, founded, in the year 555, by St.Corngall, of noble parentage in Ulster, and disciple of St. Fintan in Clonagh. This house continued until the Reformation a celebrated school for great men ; and an asylum for Kings and Princes from the busy stage of the world; by an inquisition held 5 James I. the revenues were worth 3*l*., now worth 60*l*.

At Black Abbey, in the Great Ardes. A Benedictine Abbey, founded by St. John de Courcey; granted by James I. to the Protestant Bishop of Armagh.

At Bretain, near the town of Down. An Abbey, in which St. Loarne was Abbot, in the year 540 ; is now a Nobleman's seat.

At Castle Buy, near the Lough of Stranford. A Commandery, built in the year 1200, by Hugh de Lacie ; now in ruins. The Echlin family possess the property.

DOWN.

At CUMBER, on the Lough of Strangford. An Abbey, founded, about the year 1201, by the O'Neils of Clandeboy. By an inquisition held, 1 James I., John O'Mulligan was Abbot; the revenues made then 23*l*. 19*s*. 4*d*., now worth 479*l*. 6*s*. 8*d*.

At DOWNPATRICK, a town on the Lough of Strangford. An Abbey, founded, by St. Patrick, in which he was interred in the year 493.

A Priory of Regular Canons, founded in the year 1138, by Malachi O'Morgair; granted to Gerald, Earl of Kildare.

A Priory of Crossbearers, founded by Sir John de Courcey; granted to the above Nobleman.

A Cistercian Abbey, founded, about the year 1200, by a Mr. Bagnal.

A Cistercian Nunnery, founded there also.

A Franciscan Friary, built in the year 1240, by Hugh de Lacey, Earl of Ulster; granted to Gerald, Earl of Kildare.

An Hospital of Lepers, granted to the same Earl.

At DROMORE, a town originated by St.

Coleman, a disciple of M'Nissy, Bishop of Connor. A Franciscan Priory, built by him about the year 513.

At DRUMBOE. An Abbey, founded by St. Patrick, in which St. Mochumma was Abbot in the 7th century; now the Protestant place of worship.

At DUNDRUM, in the Barony of Lecale. A Castle, built by Sir John de Courcey, for the Templars, before the year 1313; yearly revenues 6*l*. 13*s*. 4*d*., now worth 133*l*. 6*s*. 8*d*.; granted to Gerald, Earl of Kildare.

At EYNES. A Priory, founded, in the year 1411, by Thomas Chelene; it became the dwelling of Charles Ecklin, Esq.

At GLANGRAGH, VALE OF CHARITY. An Abbey, founded in the year 1200.

GRAY ABBEY, on the Lough of Stranford, founded, in the year 1192, by Africa, daughter of Godfrey, King of Man, and wife of Sir John de Courcey; by an inquisition held in the first year of James I., the revenues made 2*l*., now worth 40*l*.; granted to Gerald, Earl of Kildare; now the Protestant place of worship.

At HOLLYWOOD, on the Bay of Carrickfergus. A Monastery of Franciscans; rents valued, in 5 James I., 1*l*. 3*s*. 4*d*., now worth 23*l*. 6*s*. 8*d*.

At INISCOURCEY, in the Lough of Strangford. A Cistercian Abbey, built by Sir John de Courcey, in the year 1180 ; granted to Gerald, Earl of Kildare.

At KILCLIFF, on the Lough of Strangford. An Abbey, in which St. Eugene and St. Niell were Abbots ; now the Protestant place of worship.

An Hospital for Lepers, under the patronage of St. Peter.

At KILMBIAN. An Abbey built by St. Fergus, Bishop of Down, about the year 583. St. Neman lived here too.

At MAGHERELIN, on the river Lagan, near Dromore. A Monastery, built by St. Colman, who died in the year 699 ; now a Protestant place of worship.

At MOVILLE. An Abbey of Augustines, flourished from the year 559 until 1542, when it had been suppressed after having produced many illustrious saints and great literary characters.

At NEWREY. A Cistercian Abbey, built by Maurice M'Lochlain, Monarch of all Ireland ; made into a Protestant place of worship in 1543. College also destroyed.

At NEWTOWN. A Monastery, founded, in the year 1244, by Walter de Burgo, Earl of Ulster; surrendered 32 Henry VIII.; revenues worth 13*l*. 3*s*., now worth 263*l*.

At SAUL, in the Barony of Lecale. An Abbey, founded, by St. Patrick, where he died, March 17, 493, and in the 120th year of his age, and was buried with great solemnity at Downpatrick; granted to Gerald, Earl of Kildare.

At SLIEVE DONARD, a high mountain. A Monastery, founded, by St. Domangart, a disciple of St. Patrick.

At TOBERGLORY, a well near Downpatrick. An Abbey, founded, by Sir John de Courcey, and richly endowed.

DUBLIN (COUNTY).

At BALDONGAN, in the Barony of Balruddery. A Castle of Templars, that was converted into a Friary and Nunnery alternately.

At BALLYMADUN, in the same Barony. A Cell and a Church ; on the ruins of which Robert Preston, Esq. had his seat in the year 1542.

At CASTLE KNOCK. An Augustine Abbey founded by Richard Tirrel ; now the Protestant place of worship.

At CLONDALKIN. An Abbey, in which St. Cronan Mochua was the first Abbot before the year 776 ; after having produced many Saints, it is made the Protestant place of worship.

At CLONTARF. A Monastery, built in the year 550 ; now a Protestant place of worship.

Commandery of Templars, founded in the reign of King John.

At DUBLIN. Abbey of the Virgin Mary, founded, it is supposed, by the Danes after their conversion to christianity, about the year 948. It was at first a Benedictine monastery, but it was granted to the Cistercians in the year 1139. The house was considerably enriched by the bounty of Bishops, Abbots, and Princes, and always held in the greatest veneration for the numerous saints and learned men it produced, as well as for the sacred relics which it contained. In the year 1180, Fitz Andelm, and Miles Cogane, and Fitz Stephen, brought from Armagh, and bestowed upon this church a stone altar, and the most holy staff of Jesus, which St. Patrick used to carry in his hand ; this staff was covered with gold and overlaid with pearls, being held so sacred that the possessor of it, if a Bishop, was always deemed the canonical owner of the See of Armagh. The history of the staff is thus given by Joceline : " St. Patrick, moved either by divine instinct or angelical revelation, on his tour in the south of Europe, visited one *Justus*, an ascetic in the island of the Tuscan Sea, who was spending a solitary life of the most edifying sanctity. After mutual salutations and discourse on heavenly matters, he presented the Irish Apostle with a staff, which he averred he had received from the hands of Jesus Christ himself. In this island there were some men in the bloom of youth, and others who appeared aged and decrepid. St. Patrick, upon conversing with them, found that those persons seemingly old were sons of those who appeared young. He was astonished at this miraculous appearance, until he was told that from their infancy they had served God; that they were constantly employed in works of charity, and their doors ever open to the traveller and the distressed ; and that one night a stranger, with a staff in his hand, came to them whom they accommodated to the best of their power ; and that in the morning he blessed them, and said, I am Jesus Christ whom you have always faithfully served, but last night you received me in my proper person. He then gave this staff to their spiritual father, with directions to deliver it to a stranger named Patrick, who would shortly visit them. On saying this he ascended into heaven, and left us in that state of juvenility in which you behold us, and our sons, then young, are the old decrepid persons you now see." Joceline goes on then to relate that with this staff our Apostle collected every venemous serpent and snake in the island of Erin to the top of the mountain of Crough Phadruig, or Patrick's Hill, in the county of Mayo, and from thence precipitated them into the ocean. This story was handed down by general tradition in that country since the earliest ages, being related by many authors who flourished prior to the days of Joceline, in the year 1185, This house and possessions were granted 31 Elizabeth, to Edmund Fitz Alexander ; rent 4*l*. 17*s*. 8*d*., now worth 97*l*. 13*s*. 4*d*.

Nunnery of St. Mary de Hogges; founded, in the year 1146, by Dermot son of the King of Leinster ; granted, 6 Edward VI., to James Sedgrave ; rent 11*s*. 8*d*., now worth 11*l*. 13*s*. 8*d*.

Nunnery of St. Mary les Dames ; without the gate.

Abbey of St. Olave.

Priory of All Saints, in Hoggin Green, now called College Green, was founded, about the year 1166, by Dermot, son of Muchard, King of Leinster; granted, 30 Henry VIII., to the Mayor, &c. of the city of Dublin, for the yearly rent of $4l.$ $3s.$ $0\frac{1}{2}d.$, now worth $83l.$ $0s.$ $10d.$

Abbey of St. Thomas, founded, by Henry II., in that part which is now called Thomas Court; the possessions were granted to divers persons in 33 Elizabeth; yearly value $24l.$ $2s.$ $4d.$, now worth $482l.$ $6s.$ $8d.$

Priory of St. John Baptist, founded, in the 12th century, by Ailred le Palmer. In this house was an infirmary, which contained fifty beds for the sick; the house, site and possessions were granted to James Sedgrave of Dublin, for $1,078l.$ $15s.$ $8d.$, now worth $21,575l.$; and the yearly rent of $2s.$ $6d.$, now worth $2l.$ $10s.$

Friary of St. Saviour, near the old bridge, on the north bank, founded, about the year 1202, by William Mareschall, Earl of Pembroke. The King's Inns, containing courts of law, rolls, &c., are built on the site of this sacred edifice.

Monastery of St. Francis, built where Francis-street now runs, by Ralph le Porter, in the year 1235; granted, 24 Henry VIII., to Thomas Stephens, at $2s.$ yearly rent, now worth $2l.$

Monastery of the Holy Trinity, founded, in the year 1259, by the Talbot family; granted, 34 Henry VIII., to Walter Terrell, at the yearly rent of 6s. 1d., now worth 6l. 1s. 8d.

A Carmelite Monastery, in the parish of St. Peter, built in the year 1278; granted, 34 Henry VIII., to Nicholas Stonyhurst, at the yearly rent of 2s. 6d., now worth 2l. 10s.

Hospital of St. Stephen, founded, in the year 1344.

Steyne Hospital, built and endowed in the year 1220, by Henry Loundres, Archbishop of Dublin.

Allen's Hospital, founded, for the poor about the year 1500, by Walter, Archbishop of Dublin.

At FINGLA, two miles from Dublin. An Abbey, founded, as people think, by St. Patrick. St. Kenicus was Abbot and its patron Saint. Here is a well, dedicated to St. Patrick, and remarkable for many miracles, and its sanative effects; now the house is made a Protestant place of worship.

At GLASSMORE. A Nunnery, founded, in the year 1190, by John Comin, Archbishop of Dublin, in this place, which is three miles north of

Swords ; at an inquisition of 33 Henry VIII., the revenues made yearly 112*l*. 1*s*., now worth 2,241*l*.

At HOLM PATRICK. A Priory, founded, by Sitrie, son of Muachard on Inis Patrick. The holy Moel Finian, Prince of the Bregii, resigning his throne, became a Monk here, was afterwards Abbot, and died in the year 898 ; granted, 20 Elizabeth, to Thomas Fitz Williams.

At INIS-PATRICK, IRELAND'S EYE, a small rocky island, north of Howth Hill, where St. Nessau founded, in the year 570, an Abbey, in which he spent the evening of a holy life in praying and fasting.

KILMAINHAM PRIORY, founded, in the year 1174, by Richard Strongbow, Earl of Pembroke, for the Knights Templars, but on the suppression of that order by the Pope, in 1312, the Priory was given to the Hospitalers. By an inquisition taken, 32 Henry VIII., the revenues made 64*l*. 14*s*. 1*d*., now worth 1,294*l*. 1*s*. 8*d*. ; granted, 20 Elizabeth, to William Browne, part of the revenues for 57*l*. 10*s*., now worth 1150*l*. yearly.

At KILSAGHLAN, in the Barony of Castle Knock. A Monastery, valued 28 Henry VIII.; that is all we know of it.

DUBLIN.

At LUSK. An Abbey, founded very early.

At MOORTOWN. A Monastery, in which St. Cronan was the first Abbot, before the year 571.

At PALMERSTOWN, on the Liffey, three miles from Dublin. A Priory of St. Laurence.

At SAGGARD. A Priory, founded about the year 650, by St. Mosacre; now the Protestant place of worship.

At ST. CATHERINE'S. A Priory, amply endowed by Warrisius de Peche, for the salvation of his soul and of the souls of his ancestors, about the year 1220.

At SWORDS. A Monastery, founded, in the year 512, by St. Columb, to which he bestowed a small Missal, written by himself, and appointed St. Finan Lobhair, Leper, as Abbot. This is the church at present.

A Nunnery, founded before the reign of King Edward IV.

At TALLAGHT, five miles from Dublin. A Monastery, founded early by St. Maelwan, they suppose, because he was the first Bishop; now a Protestant place of worship.

FERMANAGH (County).

At CLINISH, an Island in Lough Earn. St. Synell was Abbot of Clain Inis, about the year 550; now a Protestant place of worship.

At DEROUGH. A Collegiate Church, vested in the crown on the general suppression.

At DEVENISH, an Island in Lough Earn, near Enniskillen. An Abbey, built in Daimb-inis, about the year 563, by St. Laserian; it stood until the general plunder.

At GOLA, near Lough Earn. A Monastery, founded, by M'Manus, Lord of the place; granted to Sir John Davis, Knight.

At INIS-MAC-SAINT, an Island in Lough-Earn, an Abbey, founded in 523, by St. Nenn. Remained as a Parish Church till the time of Queen Anne.

At LISGOOL, an Abbey founded very early. Granted to Sir John Davis, Knt.

At ROSS ORRY, on Lough Earn. A Nunnery, founded about the year 480, by St. Fanchea; now a Protestant place of worship, in the diocese of Clogher.

GALWAY (County).

ABBEY GORMOGAN, nine miles east of Lough-rea; granted, 34 Henry VIII., to Ulick, first Earl of Clanricarde.

At ABBEY KNOCKMOY, near Tuam. An Abbey, founded, for the Cistercians, in the year 1190, by Cathol O'Connor, King of Connaught, who took there the religious habit, and died in 1224, and is interred there; valued, 27 Elizabeth, yearly 209*l*. 4*s*., now worth 4,184*l*.; granted to Valentine Blake, Esq.

At AGHRIM, near Ballinasloe. An Augustine Priory, founded, in the year 1200, by Theobald Butler; granted, with several other Houses, to Richard, Earl of Clanricarde, for the yearly rent of 68*l*. 9*s*. 6*d*.

At AHASKERAGH, in the Barony of Kilconnell. An Abbey, in which St. Cuan died in the year 788; now a Protestant place of worship, in the diocese of Elphin.

At ARRAN NAOMH, that is, Arran of the Saints. Many churches were erected in these islands, (three in number,) on the coast of Galway; the bodies of many saints repose in them; the King of Cashell, at the request of St. Albeus, granted the largest of these islands to St. Enna, who built ten churches in it about the year 490.

At the MIDDLE ISLAND. Two Churches.

At ARDOILEN, the third of the Islands of Arran. Three Churches, and a Monastery, which was founded by St. Fechin; the pious Abbot, St. Gormgal, died here in 1017. A Franciscan Friary was founded in these islands about the year 1485.

At ATHENRY. A Dominican Friary, founded, in the year 1241, by Meyler de Bermingham.

A Franciscan Friary, founded in the year 1464, by Thomas, Earl of Kildare, the Earl of Desmond, and by O'Tully.

At BALLYNEHINCH. A Carmelite Monastery, founded in the year 1356, by O'Flaherty.

At BEAGH. A Franciscan Monastery, founded about the year 1441; valued, in the 28 Elizabeth, 618*l.*, now worth 6*l.* 13*s.* 4*d.* yearly.

At BOILEAN CLAIR, in the diocese of Tuam. A rich Franciscan Monastery, founded, in the year 1291.

At CLARE GALWAY. A Franciscan Monastery, built about the year 1290, by John de Cogan;

now a Roman Catholic Chapel is built in its stead.

At CLONFERT. An Abbey, founded, by St. Brendan, about the year 553; he founded several other Abbeys, and had at one time presided over three thousand monks, each of whom did industriously earn a sufficiency for his own support; we find that many saints lived and died here; dissolved at the Reformation.

At CLONKEEN. A Franciscan Monastery, founded, about the year 1435, by Thomas O'Kelly, Archbishop of Clonfert.

At CLONTHUSKERT. A Monastery of Canons, founded, about the year 809, by Boadan; granted to Richard, Earl of Clanricarde

At CLOONEYVORNOGE. An Augustine CELL, founded about the year 1441; worth, according to an inquisition held 28 Elizabeth, 6s. 8d., now worth 6l. 13s. 4d.

At CREVAGHBANE. A Carmelite Friary, founded, in or about the year 1400, by the Earl of Clanricarde; granted to the Burgesses and Citizens of Athenry.

At DUNDRYNAN. A Monastery, in which Thomas was Abbot in the year 1374.

GALWAY.

At DUNMORE. An Agustine Friary, built in the year 1425, on the site of the Monastery founded by St. Patrick; the Market-place and the Protestant place of worship stand in its stead.

At ENAGH DUNE, in the Barony of Clare. An Abbey, founded in the seventh century, of which St. Meldan was Abbot.

A Nunnery, founded by St. Brendan, of Clonfert, for his sister Briga; granted to the Earl of Clanricarde.

St. Mary's Abbey.

A Franciscan Abbey, to which were subordinate all the Connaught and Ulster Monasteries; revenues made yearly 3*l*. 6*s*., now worth 66*l*.

At FALLIG. A Monastery, founded by a Mr. Fallig, an Irishman, for Grey Friars, in the year 1390. The Parson resides there at present.

At FIDHARD. An Abbey, founded by St. Patrick for St. Justus; it is now a Protestant place of worship, in the diocese of Elphin.

At GALWAY. A Franciscan Friary, founded in the year 1296, by Sir William de Burgh, Leigh, or Grey, in the island of St. Stephen, by the north gate.

A Dominican Friary, built first for Nuns, which, when they forsook it, was possessed a long time by the secular Clergy; but finally granted, by Innocent III., to the Dominicans, in the year 1488. Demolished, in 1652, by the orders of Oliver Cromwell.

An Augustine Friary, founded on a hill near the town, in the year 1508, by Stephen Lynch, son to the Mayor of Galway.

A Nunnery, built in the Island of Lough Corrib, west of the town.

At IMMAGH. An Abbey, founded in the year 664, in this island, on the coast of Galway, by St. Fechin, who is the patron saint of the island. Now a Protestant place of worship.

At INISQUIN, an island of Lough Corrib. St. Brendon erected an Abbey, and made St. Meldon Abbot, who died in the year 626.

At KILBOUGHT. A Monastery, built by the Waley family; suppressed by the orders of Queen Elizabeth.

At KILBRENAN. A Monastery, and its appurtenances, granted to the Mayor, &c. of Athenry.

At KILCORBAN. A Dominican Friary; granted, by Thomas Burgh, Bishop of Clonfert, to the

Dominicans, in the year 1446. Pope Eugene IV. confirmed the grant.

At KILCOLGAN. An Abbey, built in the year 580, by St. Colgan, the patron saint; it is now the Protestant place of worship.

At KILCOLGAN, A Monastery, in the diocese of Clonfert, founded by St. Columbkill.

At KILCONNELL. A Franciscan Monastery, founded, in the year 1400, by William O'Kelly, a nobleman, on the ruins of an Abbey, built in the days of St. Patrick, as it is supposed, by the Abbot St. Conall; granted to Charles Calthorpe.

At KILCOONAGH. An Abbey, founded, by Tipraid, a Prince of that country, for St. Columb, who placed over it St. Cuonnan, maternal brother to St. Carthag. This is now a Protestant place of worship.

At KILCREUNATA. A Nunnery, founded, in the year 1200, by Cathald O'Connor Crovderg, for Benedictine Nuns, Lady Fynola, daughter of Felym O'Connor, was Abbess in 1300; granted to Richard, Earl of Clanricarde.

At KILLINE BONAINA. A Franciscan Friary, built about the year 1428.

At KILLOEBHAIN. A religious house of some sort. St. Maccectus of this house was smith to

St. Patrick, and made the famous relic called Finnfaidheach. Now the Protestant place of worship.

At KILMACDUACH. An Abbey, founded, in the year 620, by St. Colman, son of Duack; it became an Augustine Monastery in 1283; here are many venerable and noble ruins that bespeak the former greatness and piety of the Irish. The round tower projects seventeen feet from its perpendicular line. The celebrated leaning tower of Pisa in Italy projects only thirteen feet; granted to the Earl of Clanricarde.

At KILRICKILL. A Nunnery, built by St. Patrick for his sister St. Richella; now a Protestant place of worship, in the diocese of Clonfert.

At KILTULLAGH. A Franciscan Cell, built prior to the year 1441.

At KINALEKIN. A Commandery of Hospitallers, founded, about the 1250, by O'Flaherty.

A Franciscan Friary, founded before the year 1325.

At LOUGHREAGH. A Carmelite Friary, founded, in the year 1300, by Richard de Burgo, Earl of Ulster; granted to Richard, Earl of Clanricarde.

A Leper Hospital was there too.

GALWAY.

At MAGHCE, MAGHELE, or MAGHELLE. Three Monasteries, founded by St. Alban, who died in the year 650.

At MILICK, on the Shannon. A Franciscan Friary, founded by O'Madden, Dynast of that country. Granted to the Earl of Clanricarde.

At MUCINIS. An Abbey, wherein Regulus was Abbot in the time of St. Columb; this place is in Loughdearg, in the county Galway.

At PALLICE. A Carmelite Friary, built in the fourteenth century, by Bermingham, Baron of Athenry; granted, 31 Elizabeth, to John Rawson, at the yearly rent of 8*l.* 12*s.* 7*d.* Irish, now worth 172*l.* 11*s.* 8*d.*

At PORTUMNA. A Cistercian Abbey, which became in the course of time a Dominican Friary; the still existing walls show that it had been a noble structure. The ancient choir is now the Protestant place of worship.

At RATHMATH, on Lough-Corrib. An Abbey, built by St. Fursey, son of Fintan, of the royal race of South Munster, who died about the year 653, being called now Kilfursa; it is the Protestant place of worship.

At ROSS, in the diocese of Tuam. A Franciscan Friary, built in the year 1431.

GALWAY.

At ROSSERELLY. A Franciscan Monastery, founded, in the year 1498, by Lord Gannard; granted to the Earl of Clanricarde.

At SLEUSHANCOGH. A Franciscan Friary; granted to Sir Francis Sammes.

At TEMPLEGAILE, or TEAGH SASSAN. A Franciscan Friary, founded in the reign of Hen. VII., by the Burgo family; granted to the Burgesses and Commonalty of Athenry. Another Franciscan Friary was granted here to Edmond Barret.

At TOMBEOLA, at the head of Roundstowne Bay. A Dominican Friary, founded, in the year 1427, by O'Flaherty, Dynast of that country; demolished in the reign of Elizabeth, and the stones carried away to build a castle in the neighbourhood.

At TUAM. An Abbey, built in the year 487, was converted in the sixth century into a Cathedral by the good St. Jarlath.

A Priory of St John the Baptist, built in the year 1140, by Tirdelvac O'Connor, King of Ireland; granted to Richard, Earl of Clanricarde.

A Premonstratensian Abbey, founded in the reign of King John, by the Burgh family ; granted, 20 Elizabeth, to the Burgesses and Commonalty of Athenry.

KERRY (County).

At AGHADOE. An Abbey, where Aodh, grandson of Auliff Mor. O'Donoghue, King of Aoganacht Lochalein, was buried in the year 1231.

At AGHAMORE. An Abbey, founded, in the seventh century, by the Friars of St. Finbar, of Cork ; it is situated on a small island near the mouth of the Kenmare river.

At ARDFERT. A sumptuous Monastery, built in the sixth century, by St. Brendan ; destroyed repeatedly by fire and wars. Thomas, Lord of Kerry, built, in the year 1253, a Monastery there, which became the burial ground of several illustrious families ; this house was high in estimation for the numerous miracles wrought there. The ruins of this noble edifice stand a little east of the town ; the walls of the steeple, choir, cloisters, dormitory, and chapel for morning are entire. In the church is a figure of St. Brendan in relievo ; the round tower, the finest in Ire-

land, 120 feet high, unfortunately fell in the year
1771.

At BALLYNASKELIGS, or St. MICHAEL'S
MOUNT, in Toragha. An Augustine Abbey,
removed thither from the Island of Great
Skelig; the ruins on the sea shore, that is continually wearing it away, represent the ancient
Abbey as a noble edifice. There is a holy well
consecrated to St. Michael, which is annually
visited on the 29th of September; granted, 28
Elizabeth, to John Blake; rent 6*l.* 13*s.* 4*d.*,
yearly, now worth 133*l.* 6*s.* 8*d.*

At CROEBHEAGH. An Abbey, founded, by
St. Patrick, for his disciple St. Daluan; St.
Trian was Abbot and Bishop here about the
year 450.

At DINGLE. A Monastery, which was a cell
to the Abbey of Killagh, Castlemain.

At INNISFALLEN, an island on the Lake of
Killarney. An Abbey, founded by St. Finian
Lobhar, or the Leper, disciple of St. Brendan,
and son of the King of Munster, in the sixth
century. In 1180 this house was held sacred as
paradise, and the clergy were deemed so holy
and trustworthy, that the treasures and valuable
effects of the whole country were deposited in
their hands, notwithstanding the Abbey was in
this year destroyed by Maolduim, son of Daniel

O'Donaghoe, and many of the clergy were slain, even in their cells, by the M'Carthys. Granted, 37 Elizabeth, to Robert Collan; rent 72*l.* 3*s.*, now worth 1443*l.*

At IRELAGH, near Loughlean. A Franciscan Friary, founded, in the year 1440, by Thady M'Carthy. Granted to Robert Collan at 16*s.* yearly rent, now worth 16*l.*

At KILLACHAD-CONCHEAN. A Nunnery, founded, in the sixth century, by St. Abban, for St. Conchenna.

At KILLAGH. A Priory of Regular Canons, founded, in the reign of John, by Geoffry de Mariscis; granted to Thomas Clinton; rent 17*l.* yearly, now worth 240*l.*

At LISLAGHTIN. A Franciscan Monastery, founded, in the year 1464, by O'Connor, Prince of Kerry; granted to Sir Edward Denny, rent 3*l.* 11*s.* 1½*d.*, now worth 71*l.* 2*s.* 6*d.*

MONASTER NI ORIEL, in the Barony of Glanerought.

At ODORNEY. A Cistercian Abbey, founded in the year 1154; was demolished 39 Elizabeth, and the possessions granted to the Provost and Fellows of Trinity College, Dublin. It is now a shapeless ruin.

At RATTOO, or RATHOY, in the Barony of Clanmaurice. A Monastery of Regular Canons, founded, in the 13th century, in the place of a Commandery of Hospitallers; granted, 23 Elizabeth, to John Zouche, at the rent of 6s. 7d., now worth 6l. 11s. 8d.

At SKELIG, an Island on the Coast of Iveragha. An Abbey, founded, by St. Finian in the year 812. The Danes plundered and destroyed the Abbey, and kept the Monks in close confinement until, through hunger, they perished.

At TRALEE. A Dominican Friary, founded, in the year 1213, by Lord John Fitz Thomas. The general burial place of the Earls of Desmond.

Commandery of the Knights of St. John.

KILDARE (COUNTY).

At ATHY. A Monastery of Crossed Friars, founded, in the reign of King John, by Richard de St. Michael; granted, 17 Charles II., to Dame Mary Meredith.

A Dominican Friary, founded, in the year 1253, by the families of Boiseles and

Hogans ; granted, with all its possessions, 35 Henry VIII., to Martin Pelles : rent 2*s.* 8*d.* Irish, now worth 2*l.* 13*s.* 4*d.*

At CASTLE DERMOT. A Priory of Regular Canons, founded, in the year 500, by St. Dermot, whose festival falls on 21st June.

A Friary of Crouched or Crossed Friars, founded, in the reign of King John, by Walter de Riddlesford ; granted, 23 Elizabeth, to Henry Harrington.

A Franciscan Friary, founded in the year 1302, by Thomas, Lord Offaley.

At CLANE. A Priory, founded about the year 548, by St. Ailbe.

A Franciscan Friary, founded about the year 1266, by Gerald Fitz Maurice, Lord Offaley, as people suppose ; granted, 24 Henry VIII., to Robert Eustace, John Trevor, and others, *in capite*, at the yearly rent of 2*s.* 4*d.* Irish, now worth 2*l.* 6*s.* 8*d.*

At CLONAGH. A Chapel, dedicated to St. Fynan, demolished by John Lye of Rathbridge, according to an inquisition that was held 6 James I.

At CLONCURRY. A Carmelite Friary, built in

the year 1347, by John Roche ; granted, 35 Henry VIII., to William Dickson, at 8*d*. yearly rent ; granted, 8 Elizabeth, to Richard Slayne, for 21 years ; rent 16*s*., now worth 16*l*.

At GRANY, near CASTLE DERMOT. A Nunnery, built in the year 1200, by Walter de Riddlesford ; richly endowed by the benefactions of several ladies and noblemen ; granted, 34 Henry VIII., to Sir Anthony St. Leger.

At GREAT CONALL. A Priory, founded, in the year 1202, by Mayler Fitz Henry, grandson of Henry I. It became the cradle and tomb of great and learned men. Granted, 3 Elizabeth, for sixty-one years, to Sir Nicholas White ; rent 26*l*. 19*s*. 5*d*., now worth 539*l*. 8*s*. 4*d*.

At KILBEGS. A Commandery of Hospitalers.

At KILCOCK. A Monastery, dedicated to the Virgin St. Cocho.

At KILCULLEN. A Monastery, founded by St. Patrick, who appointed St. Isernin superior. He was succeeded by St. Mactalius, who died of the plague in the year 548.

At KILDARE. A Nunnery and Monastery, founded, in the year 453, by St. Brigid, the first Nun in Ireland. The houses and revenues granted by Elizabeth to Anthony Deeringe ; rent 3*l*. 10*s*. 8*d*. Irish, now worth 70*l*. 13*s*. 4*d*.

A Franciscan Abbey, built in the year 1260, by Lord William de Vesey ; granted, 34 Henry VIII., to Daniel Sutton ; rent 2*s*. 3*d*. Irish, now worth 2*l*. 5*s*.

A Carmelite Friary, built in the year 1290, by William de Vesey.

At KILHILL. A Commandery of Hospitalers, built in the 13th century, by Maurice Fitzgerald ; granted to John Allen.

At KILLOSSEY, near KILDARE. An Abbey, founded by St. Patrick for his nephew St. Auxil, who died 27 August 454 ; hence the place was called Kil-usaille, and afterwards Kill-ussi. It is now the Protestant place of worship.

At KILRUSHE. An Augustine Abbey, founded, in the 13th century by William Mareschal, Earl of Pembroke ; granted to the Earl of Ormond.

At LEIXLIP. A Monastery stood in the year 1463 near this village.

At MAYNOOTH. A College, founded about the year 1518, by Gerald, Earl of Kildare, for a Provost, Vice Provost, five Priests, two Clerks and three boys, to pray for his own soul and for the soul of his wife.

KILDARE.

At MONASTEREVAN. A sumptuous Abbey, built by St. Alban, in the 7th century. St. Emin, or Evin, of the Eogonacht's family in South Munster, brought a number of Monks from thence to this house ; his festival is held on 22d December. At the suppression it fell into the hands of the Earl of Drogheda, and is now the mansion of that family, under the name of Moore Abbey.

At MOONE. A large old Church, of which the cross, and several Irish inscriptions, still remain.

At NAAS. An Augustine Priory, founded, in the year 1200, by the Baron of the town ; granted, 1553, to Richard Mannering, at the rent of 35*l*. 18*s*. 2*d*., now worth 718*l*. 3*s*. 4*d*.

A Dominican Friary, founded about the year 1355, by the Eustace family ; granted, 34 Henry VIII., to Sir Thomas Luttrell, at 9*s*. 4*d*. rent, now worth 9*l*. 6*s*. 8*d*.

An Augustine Friary, founded in the year 1484. The possessions were valued, in the reign of Elizabeth, at 6*l*. 12*s*. 8*d*., now worth 132*l*. 13*s*. 4*d*. ; granted to Nicholas Aylmer.

At NEW ABBEY. A Franciscan Monastery, founded, in the year 1460, by Sir Rowland Eustace, Lord Treasurer of Ireland : granted,

1582, to Edmond Spenser; yearly rent 3*l*. Irish, now worth 60*l*.

At St. Wolstan's. A Priory, built in the year 1202, by Adam de Hereford, in honour of St. Wolstan, Bishop of Worcester, lately canonized; granted, 28 Henry VIII., to Allen of Norfolk, at the rent of two knights' fees.

At Timolin. A Priory of Regular Canons, founded here very early; stood in the year 927, and, of course, continued until the general suppression.

A Nunnery, founded, in the reign of John, by Robert, son of Lord Noragh, in which his grand-daughter Lecelina was Nun. This house was richly endowed by the bounty of several Catholic Bishops. Granted, 23 Elizabeth, to Henry Harrington and his heirs, at the yearly rent of 21*l*. 19*s*. Irish money, now worth 439*l*.

At Tully, near Kildare. A Commandery of Hospitalers, founded before the year 1308. This Commandery, with all its possessions, were granted to Sir Henry Harrington, at the rent of 21*l*. 6*s*. 8*d*., now worth 426*l*. 13*s*. 4*d*. It is now held in commendam with the Protestant See of Kildare.

KILKENNY (County).

At CALLAN. An Augustine Friary, founded, as some persons say, by Hugh de Mapilton, Bishop of Ossory, in the year 1251 ; or, as others think, by the Ormonds ; granted, together with the Abbey of Athassel, to Thomas, Earl of Ormond, in the year 1557.

Chantry, of which the nave and aisles are still in good preservation ; the choir being the Protestant place of worship.

At FERTAGH. A Priory, dedicated to St. Kieran, by the Blanchfield family, in the thirteenth century ; granted, 9 Elizabeth, to James Butler, jun. ; rent 12*l.* 13*s.* 3*d.*, now worth 253*l.* 5*s.*

At FIDDOWN. An Abbey, by St. Maidoc, in the year 590. Now a Protestant parochial place of worship.

At FRESHFORD. An Abbey, founded by St. Lactan, Bishop and Abbot ; he died in the year 622. There is a celebrated fountain near Cashell dedicated to him. This is now a Protestant place of worship, and called a Prebend of Aghour.

At GRAIGNEMANAGH. A Monastery, founded, in the year 1212, by William Mareschal, Earl of

Pembroke; this was enriched by the bounty of several Bishops and Nobles. The house, with all its possessions, were granted, 8 Elizabeth, to the Butlers.

At JERPOINT, near THOMASTOWN. A Cistercian Abbey, founded, by Donogh O'Donoghoe, (in the year 1180,) King of Ossory; and richly endowed by him. The house with all the possessions were granted to James, Earl of Ormond, at the annual rent of 49*l*. 3*s*. 9*d*.; now worth 983*l*. 15*s*.

At INISTIOGE on the NOIRE. An Augustine Priory, built in the year 1210, by Thomas Seneschal, of Leinster; granted, with all the possessions, to James Butler and his heirs at the rent of 28*l*. 12*s*.; now worth 572*l*. A rectory granted in Whitchurch to the Earl of Ormond, 31 Elizabeth.

At KELLS. An Augustine Priory, founded, in the year 1193, by Jeffrey, for the salvation of Earl Richard, Governor of the country, Granted, by Henry VIII., to James, Earl of Ormond.

At KILLAGHY. An Abbey, in which St. Sinchell was Abbot, and died of the plague, 26th of March 548, in the 130th year of his age; he was interred in this place.

At KILLAMARY, five miles south of Callan. St. Gobban presided here over a thousand monks; the place is now a Protestant place of worship.

At KILCLEEHEEN, opposite the City of Waterford. A Nunnery, built in the year 2151, by Dermot, son of Murchad, King of Leinster. It was sumptuously endowed by himself and other Noblemen. Catherine Motyng, the last Abbess, surrendered the Abbey, 2d April, 31 Henry VIII.; granted, 26 Elizabeth, to the Mayor, Sheriffs, and Corporation of Waterford; rent, yearly, 59*l.* 1*s.* 8*d.*; now worth 1181*l.* 13*s.* 4*d.*

At KILFANE. An Abbey, erected by St. Phian; it is now a Protestant place of worship, seven miles from Kilkenny.

At KILKENNY, a large handsome town on the river Noire, and capital of the County; it can justly boast of three singular properties —fire without smoke, water without mud, and streets paved with marble.

The Cathedral of St. Kenny, though long since made the Protestant place of worship, still remains the ancient Catholic Cross, and many statues of Saints and Catholic Bishops, with several other reliques of Catholicity.

KILKENNY.

St. John's Abbey, founded, in the year 1211, for the relief of the indigent poor, by William Mareschal, Earl of Pembroke ; and richly endowed by him with several lands. Richard Cantwell, the last Prior, surrendered this house with all the possessions, 31 Henry VIII. ; granted to the mayor and citizens of Kilkenny, with 100 acres of land, 40 gardens, a water-mill in Magdalen-street, a wood called Channonsgrove in the liberties of the town, with 200 acres of land adjoining, ten messuages and 200 acres in Drakeland, in the county, and another messuage in the town.

The Black Abbey, in the Irishtown. A Dominican Priory, founded, in the year 1225, by William Mareschal, jun., Earl of Pembroke ; he was interred in the choir in the year 1231. The house was endowed by King Henry VI., and the Bishops of Ossory. Peter Cantwell, the last Prior, surrendered it ; and, 35 Henry VIII., it was granted to Walter Archer, the sovereign, and to the burgesses of Kilkenny for ever, at the yearly rent of 12s. 4d. Irish money ; now worth 12l. 6s. 8d.

A Franciscan Friary, founded, on the bank of the Noire, by Richard Mareschal, Earl of Pembroke, 15th October 1244. King Henry III. granted 20l. to be paid annually for buying tunicks for the Franciscans of Kilkenny, Dublin, Cork, Waterford, and Athlone. 17th Nov. 1338, a great flood destroyed all the bridges, mills, and buildings in and about Kilkenny, but did not approach the great altar of this Monastery. The noble and venerable ruins of this edifice stand yet, reaching from the city wall to the river. Yearly value of the possessions was then 9*l.* 7*s.* 1*d.*; or in money of the present day, 187*l.* 1*s.* 8*d.*

At KILMANAGH. An Abbey, founded, in the year 563, by St. Natalis.

At KNOCKTOPHER. A Carmelite Friary, founded, in the year 1356, by James, the second Earl of Ormond ; granted, with all the appurtenances, to Patrick Barnwall, 34 Henry VIII., for ever, at the yearly rent of 4*s.* Irish ; now worth 4*l.*

At ROSSIBERCAN. A Monastery, founded, 1267, by the Walsh family ; granted, 31 Henry VIII., to Luke Blake, of New Ross, County Wexford.

At THOMASTOWN. A Dominican Friary.

At TIBRACH, on the Suir below Carrick. An Abbey, where St. Dominic lived in the sixth century ; now a Protestant place of worship

THE KING'S (County).

At BIRR, now PARSONSTOWN, a beautiful town, fifty-seven miles west of Dublin. An Abbey, founded by St. Brendan, son of Neim.

At CLONEMGRE. An Abbey, founded, by St. Pulcherius.

At CLONEFERTMULLOE. An Abbey, founded, in the sixth century, by St. Molua, or St. Luan, the son of Carthar, of Munster. Clonefert-mulloe is now a Protestant place of worship. [Clone, with which these names are compounded, is an Irish word and signifies enclosure ; and *ferta*, another Irish word, signifying miracles, so that this name signifies the miracle-retreat of St. Mulloa.]

At CLONMACNOISE. on the Shannon, in the Barony of Garycastle. St. Kieran having received this place, and the Island of Saints, together with one hundred Churches in Meath, from Dermid, son of Cervail, monarch of Ireland, and having bestowed the church of Clonard upon his master, St. Finian, and the island upon St. Domnan, he founded, in the year 548, an Abbey for himself at Clonmacnoise, which became a celebrated Monastery. Besides a Cathedral Church, there were ten small churches built by different provincial Kings, and a Nunnery with a Church, which was accidentally burnt in 1180, and rebuilt by the Queen of Meath.

At DURROW. A Monastery of Augustine Canons, founded in the sixth century, which flourished in learning and sanctity for many ages, until it was granted, 4 Elizabeth, to Nicholas Herbert, Esq., for the term of twenty-one years, at 10*l.* yearly rent; now worth 200*l.*

At FRANKFORD, formerly called KILCORMUCK, on the Shannon. A Monastery of Carmelites, founded by Odo O'Molly, a chief of that country. In the year 1479, died Charles O'Molly, a brave and holy man. This house with all the possessions were granted to Robert Leicester.

At GALLEN. A Monastery, founded, in the year 492, by St. Canoc; granted, with all the possessions, 4th June 1612, to Sir George Moore, at the yearly rent of 15*l.* 7*s.* 11*d.*; now worth 307*l.* 18*s.* 4*d.*

At GLEANE, or GLIN, on the river Brusna, near Firbance. A Monastery, founded by St. Dermid, whose feast is held on the 8th of July; it stood till the eleventh century, and, of course, until the general dissolution.

At KILCOLGAN. An Abbey, founded, in the

year 580, by St. Colgan, in the Barony of Gary-castle.

At KILCOLMAN. An Abbey, founded, in the year 570, near the parish of Birr, by St. Colgan, Son of Aengus, King of Munster ; now a Protestant place of worship.

At KILCOMIN, near Roscrea. An Abbey, founded, or governed by St. Cumene, surnamed the White, who was educated in the Abbey of Hy.

At KILLEGALLY. An Abbey, in which St. Trena was Abbot in the sixth century ; now a Protestant place of worship in the Barony of Garycastle.

At KILLEIGH. A Priory of regular Canons, in which the Abbot St. Sincheal died of the plague in the year 550. This house, 18 Elizabeth, with three messuages, 124 acres of arable land, 24 of pasture, 3 of meadow, and 4 of wood, and three messuages, six cottages, 24 acres of arable land, and 7 of pasture, in the town of Donfeigh in this county, with the tithes, &c., were granted to Gerald, Earl of Kildare, and his heirs, at the yearly rent of 1l. 13s. 4d., now worth 33l. 6s. 8d., with the condition that he maintain besides one able horseman.

A Nunnery, founded by the Warren

family soon after the arrival of the English. A Domincan Friary, built in the reign of Edward I., by O'Connor ; granted to John Allee.

At KILLIADUIN. A Nunnery, founded, in the 5th century, by St. Keran, for his mother Liadana.

At KINNITTY, near Birr. An Abbey, founded in the year 557, where St. Finian was Abbot that year. In the year 871, died Abbot Colga M'Conagan, who was esteemed the best and most polished poet of those days in the kingdom, and the principal historian.

At LEMANAGHAN. A Monastery, in which St. Mauchan died of the plague in the year 661 ; became afterwards a Protestant place of worship.

At LEITHMORE. A Monastery, founded, in the year 655, by St. Pulcherius, in the Irish language Mochoemoc. Many Saints and holy Abbots flourished here until the dissolution.

At LYNNALLY. A Monastery, founded 516, by St. Colman.

At MONISTERORAS. A Franciscan Friary, built 1325, by Sir John of Bermingham, Earl of Louth ; granted to Nicholas Herbert.

At MUGNA. An Abbey, founded by St. Finian, of Clonard, on a piece of land which was given him by the King of Leinster, Carbreus.

At RATHBEG. An Abbey, founded, south of Birr, by St. Abban, who died in the year 650.

At RATHLIBTHEN, in the Barony of Fercall. An Abbey, founded by St. Illand about 540; his statue is still to be seen in the church, with his mitre and crosier in his hand.

At REYNACH. A Nunnery, founded by St. Regnacia, sister to St. Finian, who died in the year 563; his mother, Tolacia, was Abbess here; now a Protestant place of worship.

At SEIRKERAN, four miles east of Birr. A Monastery, founded 402, by St. Kieran, native of Cape Clear, in the county Cork. It was consigned, with all the possessions, in the year 1568, to Sir William Taafe, who assigned it to James, Earl of Roscommon.

At TUILEIM. A Monastery, in which Abbot Carnech died in the year 556.

LEITRIM (COUNTY).

At ANAGHDUFFE, near Loughboffin. An Abbey, founded in the year 766; now a Protestant place of worship in the diocese of Ardagh.

At BALLEGUARCY. A beautiful Monastery, founded, in the year 1518, by Cornelius O'Brien ; some writers attach this place to the county of Longford.

At CLONE. An Abbey, formerly of great repute, founded, about the year 570, by St. Fraech; now a Protestant place of worship in the diocese of Ardagh.

At CREEVLEA, on the river Boonid. A Franciscan Friary, founded, in the year 1508, by Margaret, daughter of Lord O'Brien, and wife to Lord O'Roirk ; she died in 1512, and was interred here ; dissolved in the reign of James I.

At DOIREMELLE, in Lower Breffiny. A Nunnery, founded by St. Tigenach for his mother St. Mella, who died before the year 787.

At DROMLEAS, on Loughgille. A Monastery, built by St. Patrick for St. Benignus ; now a Protestant place of worship.

At DROMAHAIRE. See CREEVLEA.

At FENAUGH, in the Barony of Leitrim. A Monastery, in which St. Callin was Abbot in the time of St. Columb. This place was formerly celebrated for the School of Divinity, and was the general resort of students from all parts of Europe; half a mile from the edifice is a well, dedicated to St. Callin; now a Protestant place of worship in the diocese of Ardagh.

At JAMESTOWN. A Franciscan Friary.

At KILDAREIS, or Cell of the Two Palms of the Hands; called also Carcuirshineill, or the Reclusory of St. Sinell, is situated in Lough Melvin. St. Sinell, who was bell-founder to St. Patrick, died in the year 548.

At KILNAILE. St. Natalis, or Naal, was Abbot of the Abbey here, and died in the year 563; the festival is on the 27th of January.

At LEITRIM, on the Shannon. An Abbey, in which St. M'Leigus was Abbot.

At MOHILL. An Abbey, founded, in the year 608, by St. Manchan, who was the patron of seven churches. Many glebes, fees, lands, and tithes, were given to this house; they were valued at the dissolution at 2*l*. 6*s*. 8*d*.; now worth 46*l*. 13*s*. 4*d*.

At THACINELING, a house for Grey Friars, founded, in 1414, by William O'Reily.

LIMERICK (County).

At ABBINGTON. A Monastery, founded for the Cistercian Monks in the year 1205, by Theobald Fitzwalter, Lord of Carrick, who richly endowed it, and was interred here in the year 1206. December 6, 5 Elizabeth, this Monastery was granted, with its appurtenances in the counties of Limerick, Kerry, and Carlow, to Peter Walshe, at the yearly rent of 57*l*. 2*s*. 3*d*., Irish money, now worth 1,142*l*. 5*s*. ; he was to maintain one horseman on the premises besides.

At ABBEYFEAL. A Cistercian Abbey, built in the year 1188.

At ADAIRE, formely a respectable place, though now but a miserable village. A Friary of the Order of the Holy Trinity, founded in the reign of Edward I., by John, Earl of Kildare ; granted, 37 Elizabeth, with all the possessions, together with the possessions of the Grey Friars, Preaching Friars, and Augustinian Friars, the Abbey of Monasternenagh, and the Nunnery of St. Katherine, to Sir Henry Wallop, at the rent of 26*l*. 17*s*. 8*d*., now worth 537*l*. 13*s*. 4*d*., he being bound to maintain two horsemen on the premises.

Augustine Friary, founded about 1315, by John, Earl of Kildare ; granted to Sir

Thomas Wallop, together with the possessions. Of this friary remain, still in good
preservation, the steeple, which is supported on an arch, the choir, nave, and aisle ;
there are some beautiful cloisters with Gothic
windows, the sides of which are ornamented
with escutcheons and saltire crosses alternately ; the workmanship is both simple and
elegant.

Grey Friary, founded in the east part of
the town, in the year 1465, by Thomas, Earl
of Kildare, and Joan his wife, daughter to
the Earl of Desmond ; they presented unto
the house two silver chalices and a bell that
cost 10*l.*, now worth 200*l.* The Countess
was interred in the choir in the year 1486.

The Friary, with its possessions, sixteen
acres of land, a church, three parks, a
water-mill and water-course, with a fishing
wier on the river Mage, was granted, 37
Elizabeth, to Sir Henry Wallop, Knt.

At ANY, in the Barony of Small County. Augustine Friary, built in the reign of Henry II.,
by sundry persons ; granted, 31 Elizabeth, to
Edward, John, and Mary Absley, at the yearly
rent of 47*l.* 7*s.* 6½*d.*, now worth 947*l.* 10*s.* 10*d.*

At ASKEATON, on the river Deel. There was
a Castle here in the 16th Century which belonged to the Earls of Desmond, one of whom

founded a Monastery adjoining the Castle for Franciscans.

At BALLYNEBRAHER, barony of Small County. A Friary of Conventual Franciscans, founded, 13th century, by the Clangibbon family. Granted, by Henry VIII., to Robert Browne.

At BALLYNEGALL, a Monastery for Dominican Friars, founded, by the family of Roche in the 14th century; granted, by Queen Elizabeth, to the University of Dublin.

At BALLYNIWILLIN, a house for Dominican Friars. Granted, by Henry VIII., to Robert Browne.

At CASTLE-TOWN MACNAIRY. A large Monastery in ruins.

At CLUNCAGH, near Rathkeale. A Convent, built by St. Maidoc, of Ferns, who died in the year 624; now a Protestant place of worship.

At CROAGH, near Rathkeale, formerly a large town. There is a large church, which was anciently collegiate.

At GALBALLY, in the Barony of Cashlea. A large Monastery, founded by the O'Briens: the ruins thereof, which are yet visible, together with the ruins of several other religious foundations, clearly evince the ancient magnificence of this town. This Monastery, with three gardens, six messuages, and six acres of arable land, were granted, 35 Henry VIII., to John Desmond for ever, at the yearly rent of 4d. Irish, now worth 6s. 8d.

At GREANY, formerly a town of Corporation in the Barony of Coanagh. A Collegiate Church, destroyed when the town fell into insignificance and obscurity.

HOSPITAL. This town took its name from a celebrated Hospital of Hospitalers, which was founded in the reign of King John, by Jeffrey de Mariscis, chief Governor of Ireland in the year 1215. Queen Elizabeth granted this hospital and all the possessions to Sir Valentine Brown, ancestor of the noble family of Kenmare in Killarney : he built a magnificent castle on the venerable ruins.

At KILDIMMA, near Adaire. A Monastery, built by Dimma, a Priest, who was the preceptor of St. Declan. See KILMAMHAMBEG, page 85, hujus.

At KILMALLOCK, formerly a respectable walled town, but now a miserable Priory of regular Canons, founded by St. Mocheallog, who died about 639 ; now the Protestant place of worship.

LIMERICK.

Dominican Friary, founded, in the year 1291, by Gilbert, son of Lord Offalley; granted 36 Elizabeth, with the possessions, to Nicholas Maigh, sovereign, and the Corporation, for ever, at the yearly rent of 2*l*. 13*s*. 8*d*., now worth 53*l*. 13*s*. 4*d*.

At KILSHANE, or KILSHONNA, near the county of Cork. A Franciscan Monastery, founded by Fitzgerald, Lord of Clenlis.

A Cistercian Abbey, founded in the year 1198.

At KILTEEL. An Hospitaler's Commandery, founded in the Barony of Counagh.

At KILTEIDHILL, in the Territory of Ara. An Abbey which was the place of interment of the Saints Mumis and Lomchuo, disciples of St. Patrick, and of seven other holy Bishops.

KYNNETHIN. An Abbey stood there in the year 1300, and we may presume that it stood until the general devastation.

At LIMERICK, as celebrated for its brave defence against King William in the year 1691, as for the infamous treachery on his part in violating the articles of capitulation. A Nunnery, founded, in the year 1374, by Donald O'Brien, King of Limerick.

LIMERICK.

A Priory of Regular Canons, founded, by Simon Minor, before the year 1319; granted, at the suppression, to Edmond Sexton.

A Dominican Friary, founded, in the year 1250, by Donogh C. O'Brien, King of Thomond. In the year 1462 died James, son of the Earl of Desmond; the ancient records of this house represent them bound to celebrate annual masses for the soul of this nobleman, and for the souls of his parents and successors, with their wives.

Henry, the last Prior, was found at the suppression to be seized of the site, church, steeple, dormitory, three chambers, a cemetery, and sundry closes, containing one and a half acre, within the precincts; a garden of four acres without the walls of the monastery, and thirty acres of land, called Cortbrecke, in the liberties; salmon weir, St. Thomas's Island, and land near Parteen, called Monabrahir. This house, with all the possessions, were granted, 35 Henry VIII., to James, Earl of Desmond, *in capite*, at the yearly rent of 5s. 2d., now worth 5l. 3s. 4d. A part of the Friary is converted into a tan-yard, and a large barrack is built on the other part.

A Grey Friary, founded, in the time of Henry III., by O'Brien, of the royal houses of Limerick and Thomond, outside the walls of the city, on the spot where a court-house was built, which is since converted into an hospital; granted to Edmond Sexton, by King Henry VIII., at the yearly rent of 2s. 2d., now worth 2l. 3s. 4d.; though by a valuation then made, it was worth a great deal more.

An Augustine Friary, founded, in the 13th century, by O'Brien, of the kingly race of Limerick and Thomond, near Quay-lane, but not a trace of it is to be seen now. The possessions of this house in lands and houses, through town and country, were valued at 8l. 6s. 1d., now worth 166l. 1s. 8d.

An Hospital of Templars stood near the above house, but not a vestige of this either is to be seen.

At MILTOWN, or BALLYWULLIN. A Carmelites' Friary, founded, by Nellan O'Mulloy.

At MONASTERNENAGH, in the Barony of Poble O'Brien. A Cistercian Abbey, founded by O'Brien, in the year 1151. This house, with all the possessions, consisting of five plough lands, and many other revenues and privileges, were granted to Sir Henry Wallop.

At MONASTERNACALLIAGH, near Lough-Girr. An Augustine Nunnery, to which belonged the rectories of Drishane, Cullon, Nohavel, Kilmeen, and Dromtariff, in the county of Cork; granted to Sir Henry Wallop.

At MUNGRET, three miles south of Limerick. A Monastery, built prior to the coming of St. Patrick to Munster; he placed St. Nessan over it, who died in the year 551. The Psalter of Cashel relates that there were, within the walls of this Abbey, six churches, that contained 1500 religious; 500 of whom were learned preachers, 500 psalmists, and the remaining 500 engaged in spiritual exercises. The ruins are still visible.

At NEWCASTLE. Hospital of Templars founded here, and then a walled town, which, since the destruction of this hospital or castle, fell into its present insignificance.

At RATHKEALE. A Priory of Augustinians, built by a Mr. Harvey.

LONGFORD (County).

ABBEY SHRULE, near the river Inny, founded by O'Farrell, for Cistercian Monks; granted, 11 Elizabeth, to Robert Dillon, with the appurtenances, twenty-four cottages, in the town of Vore; one hundred and eighty acres of land near it; eighty acres of pasture and underwood, near said town also; one messuage, four cottages in Cranaghe; sixty acres near said town; two messuages and four cottages in Ballynamanoghe; sixty-four acres near the same, for the yearly rent of 10l. 14s. 4d., now worth 214l. 6s. 8d.

At ARDAGH, near Longford. A Monastery, founded by St. Patrick.

At BALLYNASAGGARD. A Franciscan Friary, built by the O'Farrells.

At CLONEBRONE, near Granard. A Nunnery, founded by St. Patrick, for the two Emerias of St. Guasact, Abbot of Lerha. This great asylum of virgins stood until the year 1107, and, of course, until the general dissolution of Abbeys.

At DEIRG, or ABBEY DEIRG. A Priory founded in the time of Joan, by Gormgall O'Quin; value at the suppression 2l. yearly, now worth 40l; granted to Nicholas Aylmer.

At INCHYMORY, or GREAT ISLAND. A Monastery, founded by St. Columb, about the year 450, where St. Boadon, of Inismore, died, on the 14th January. In the year 1414 died Edward M'Findbair, Prior.

At INISBOFFIN, an Island in Lough Rie. An Abbey, founded by St. Risch, son of St. Dorerca, sister of St. Patrick.

At INISCLOTHRANN, an Island in the same Lough. An Abbey, founded, in the year 540, by St. Dhearmuid Naoimb or St. Jerome the Just, and brother to Felix, bishop of Kilmore, who wrote a learned and pious work, in the nature of a Psalter. On the 17th December 1160, died Gilla, or Nehemias O'Dunin, professor and celebrated scholar, poet and historian.

At ISLAND, or ALL SAINTS, in Lough Rie. A noble Monastery, built in the year 544, by St. Kieran. In four years afterwards *he procured a very large endowment for the support of its poor;* and having appointed St. Domnan his successor, he quitted this island, and built the Abbey of Clonmacnoise.

At KILGLASS. A Nunnery, where St. Echea, sister of Mell, was abbess.

At KILINMORE. An Abbey, founded by St. Palladius, who lived in the year 450; now the Protestant place of worship.

At LERHA, near Granard. A Monastery, founded by St. Patrick, for St. Guasacht, the son of his old master; another Monastery, founded in the year 1205, by Lord Richard Tuit, who was

killed in Athlone, in the year 1211, by the falling
of a tower, and was buried here. The possessions, at the surrender, valued at 8*l*. 13*s*. 4*d*.
yearly, now worth 173*l*. 6*s*. 8*d*.

At LONGFORD. An Abbey, founded by St.
Idus, a disciple of St. Patrick, whose feast falls
on the 14th July. In 1400 a fine Monastery was
founded by O'Farrell, for the Dominicans; granted, together with possessions, in the year 1615,
by King James I., to Francis, Viscount Valentia.
The church of this Priory is now the Protestant
place of worship in the parish.

At MOYDOE, three miles from Ardagh. St.
Modan, whose feast falls on the 12th February,
was Abbot in 591.

At ST. JOHN'S-TOWN. There was a Grey Friary
near this town, which had, of course, been ingulf-
ed in the general vortex of the Reformation.

LOUTH (COUNTY).

At ARDEE. A Crouched Friary, founded by
Roger, Lord Ardee, for the salvation of his own
soul, and the souls of his wife, Alicia, his father,
William, his mother, Joan, his brethren, Gilbert

and Peter, in the year 1207, for the Augustinians. The founder, for the better support of this house, and to enable the Friars to exercise more liberally their works of mercy and charity, granted them the carucate of land which Osmond Doubleday held; also full liberty to bring water for the use of the house, and a sufficient cart-way. This house was considerably endowed, by grants and donations, from several other pious Catholics. In the year 1612, James I. granted the house and possessions to Sir Garret More at the yearly rent of 115*l.* 5*s.* 8*d.*, now worth 2,305*l.* 13*s.* 4*d.*

A Carmelite Friary, founded in the time of Richard I. In the year 31 Henry VIII., Patrick, the last Prior, surrendered this house and all the possessions, valued yearly at 1*l.* 7*s.* 2*d.*, now worth 27*l.* 3*s.* 4*d.*

ARDPATRICK. Church founded by St. Patrick.

At CARLINGFORD. A Dominican Friary, founded, in the year 1305, by Richard de Burgh, Earl of Ulster; granted, 34 Henry VIII., to Nicholas Bognell, at the yearly rent of 4*l.* 6*s.* 8*d.*, now worth 86*l.* 13*s.* 4*d.*

At DROGHEDA. A Priory of regular Canons, celebrated for the Synod held there by Cardinal Papiro, in the year 1152.

St. Mary's Hospital, founded by Ursis de Swemele, who by the consent of his wife Christiana, bestowed on this house all his lands and rents in Ireland. The house was seized, 31 Henry VIII., of 60 acres of land in Glaspistell, rent 13s. 4d. ; 30 acres in Carlingford, rent 13s. 4d. ; two messuages in Dundalk, rent 6s. ; two acres in Stabanane, rent 2s. ; besides some other rectories, lands, &c. Granted to the Mayor of Drogheda ; rent 1l. 14s. 4d., now worth 34l. 13s. 4d.

St. Laurence's Priory ; granted to the Mayor of Drogheda.

A Dominician Priory, founded, in the year 1224, by Lucas, Archbishop of Armagh. Granted, 35 Henry VIII., with all the possessions, to Walter Dowdel and Edward Becke, at the rent of 2s. 2d., now worth 2l. 3s. 4d.

A Franciscan Friary, in which some murderers took shelter, and abjured the land, in the year 1300 ; granted, 34 Henry VIII., to Gerald Aylmer ; rent 3s. 6d., now worth 3l. 10s.

An Augustine Friary, founded in the time of Richard I. ; granted to the Mayor, &c. of the town.

LOUTH.

A House of St. Bennet; the parliament held at Drogheda, in the year 1467, under John, Earl of Worcester, the Lord Deputy, it was decreed that several lands and rents would be granted to this house.

At DROMCARR. An Abbey, in which Ceallagh, Abbot, died in the year 811; now a Protestant place of worship, in the diocese of Armagh.

At DRUIMFIOINN. An Abbey, where St. Finian was Abbot and Bishop, in the time of St. Columb.

At DRUMSHALLON. A Noble Monastery, founded by St. Patrick. In 969 the Danes plundered and possessed this house; it reformed in 1247.

At DUNDALK. An Hospital, founded for the sick and the aged of both sexes; founded, in the time of Henry II., by Berthram de Verdon, lord of the town; granted, with all the possessions, in town and country, 1 Elizabeth, to Henry Draycot, at the yearly rent of 11*l*., now worth 220*l*.

A Grey Friary, built in the time of Hen. III., by Lord John de Verdon; granted, 35 Henry VIII., to James Brandon, at the

fine of 9*l.* 10*s.*, and rent 6*d.*, now worth
190*l.* 10*s.*

At FAUGHER, the native place of St. Brigid. A
Nunnery, founded, by St. Monenna, in the year
638, where she presided over 150 virgins, but
resigned it to Orbilla or Sirvila, and built another Nunnery for herself at Kilsleive, in the
county of Armagh.

A Priory of Canons, built in the early
ages, and now become the Protestant place
of worship.

At INISKIN. A Monastery, built by St.
Dageus, smith to St. Kieron; is now protestantized.

At KILCLOGHER, on the Boyne. A Monastery,
founded by St. Nectan, nephew to St. Patrick;
now protestantized also.

At KILSARAN. A Commandery of Templars,
founded, in the twelfth century, by Maud de
Lacie; it was given to the hospitalers, in the
reign of Edward II. This house was rich in
lands.

At KNOCK, near Louth. An Augustine Priory,
founded in the year 1148, by Donchad Hua
Kervail, prince of that country, and Eadan,
Bishop of Clogher. This house and all the possessions were granted, 31 Henry VIII., to Sir

John King, at the yearly rent of 16*l.* 5*s.* 4*d.*, now worth 325*l.* 6*s.* 8*d.*

At LOUTH. A noble Monastery and School, founded by St. Patrick, for St. Mocteus or Mochtalugh, a Briton, who died 19th August 534, at the age of three hundred years. The house and immense possessions were granted to Sir Oliver Plunket.

At MELLIFONT, five miles from Drogheda. A Cistercian Abbey, built by Donogh M'Carrol, Prince of Uriel, to which St. Bernard sent the Monks from the monastery of Clairvaux in France, in the year 1142. A great Synod was held there in the year 1157, at which assisted the Archbishop of Armagh, the then Pope's legate, together with many Bishops and Princes; on this occasion many rich presents were made to the Abbey, particularly by Murchertach O'Loughlainn, King of Ireland; he gave 140 oxen, 60 ounces of gold, and a town-land near Drogheda, called Finnabhuir Naninghean; O'Carrol, Prince of Uriel, gave 60 ounces of gold; Dervorgilla, wife to O'Rourke, Prince of Breffiny, gave 60 ounces of gold, a gold chalice for the high altar, and vestments for nine other altars in the same house. This house, and its extensive possessions, were granted, in the year 1641, to Sir Gerald Moore.

At MONASTERBOICE. A Religious house,

founded by St. Bute, who died 7th December, 521. We find that it continued a celebrated school of religion, and both profane and sacred literature, until the twelfth century, and, doubtless, until the fifteenth.

At TERFECKAN. A Monastery, founded, in the year 665. A Nunnery, founded in the year 1195, by M'Mahon. By an inquisition taken, 33 Henry VIII., the last Abbess, Margaret Hobbert, was found to be seized of one hall, two houses in a ruinous state, a haggard, park wood, three gardens within the precincts of the Convent, valued, besides reprises, 3s. 4d. ; two messuages, two gardens, three parks, and five acres of land in Termonfeghan, value, besides reprises, 17s. 4d.; eight messuages, three parks, six acres, and three stangs of land, and one of meadow in Killiligger, value 1l.; thirteen messuages, four parks, one hundred acres of arable land and four of meadow, and twenty of pasture, in Killaghton, annual value, besides reprises, 4l. 8s., and the church or rectory of Killaghton, value 50s. ; making together 8l. 18s. 8d., now worth 178l. 13s. 4d. ; granted, 20 April 1578, to Catharine Bruton.

MAYO (County).

At AGHAGOWER, five miles from Ballintobber. A Monastery, built by St. Patrick, for St. Senach ; now a Protestant place of worship.

At AGHAMORE. A Monastery, built by St. Patrick, for his disciple St. Loarn ; now a Protestant place of worship.

At ANNAGH. A Franciscan Friary; worth 13s. 4d., now worth 13l. 6s. 8d. ; it stood to the year 1440, when Walter, Lord M'William Oughter died there.

At BALLAGH, in the Barony of Clonmorris. An Abbey, built by St. Mochuo, who was the first Abbot of it, and died in the year 637, whose feast falls on the 1st January.

At BALLENTULLY. A Monastery, worth at the suppression, eight quarters of land, valued each 13s. 4d., now 13l. 6s. 8d. each, or 106l. 13s. 4d.

At BALLYHAUNES. An Augustine Friary, which was founded by the Nangle family, and which, according to an inquisition held 12 May 1608, possessed twelve acres of land.

MAYO.

At BALLINA, on the river Moy. An Abbey; suppressed.

At BALLYNASMALL. A Carmelite Friary, founded, in the 13th century, by the Prendergasts; Donogbuy O'Gormealy was the last Prior, and possessed, at the suppression, lands worth yearly 13s. 4d., now worth 13l. 6s. 8d.; granted to Sir John King.

At BALLINROBE. An Augustine Friary; by an inquisition held 27 Elizabeth, the possessions were worth 14s. 10d., now worth 14l. 16s. 8d.

At BALLINTOBBER, or Town of Well. An Augustine Abbey, founded, in the year 1216, by Cathol O'Conogher, King of Connaught. Inquisition, held 36 Elizabeth, found this house possessed of many lands; granted, in the year 1605, to Sir John King.

At BOGHMOYEN. A Franciscan Friary dissolevd.

At BOPHIN ISLAND, in the Ocean, twelve miles from the Barony of Morisk. An Abbey, founded, in the year 667, by St. Colman; in the year 916 died Abbot Fearadagh.

At BORRISCARRA. A Carmelites' Friary, which Pope John XXIII. gave, in the year 1412, to the Augustine Friars ; at the general suppression it possessed one quarter of land, then valued at 13s. 4d., now 13l. 6s. 8d.

At BOWFINAN. A Franciscan Friary, possessed at the suppression in the year 1608, four quarters of land and their appurtenances.

At BURISHOOL. A Dominican Friary, built, as appears from the bull of Pope Innocent VIII., dated 9th February 1486, by Richard de Burke, Lord M'William Oughter, and the head of the Turlogh family ; consigned to Theobald Vincent Castillogalen.

At CLARA, an Island near the Town of Morisk. A Carmelite Friary, founded, in the year 1224.

At CONG, formerly the royal residence of the Kings of Connaught, now but a miserable village, a magnificent Monastery, built by St. Fechan, who died in 664. Æneas M'Donnell, the last Abbot, surrendered it at the general suppression ; granted, 10 December 1605, to Sir John King, ancestor to the Earl of Kingstone, county of Cork. The ruins of several churches are seen there.

At CROSS. A monastery belonging to the Abbey of Ballintober. By an inquisition, held

27 Elizabeth, it possessed lands then valued at 13s. 4d., now 13l. 6s. 8d.

At CROSSMALYNE. An Abbey. In 1306, three men were indicted for assaulting and imprisoning the Abbot, and for taking away his goods and chattels, to the amount of ten marcs. By an inquisition of 27 Elizabeth, this house possessed four quarters of land, each valuing 13s. 4d., now worth 13l. 6s. 8d. each, or 53l. 2s. 8d. the four.

At DOMNACMOR. An Abbey, founded, by St. Patrick, for St. Muckna.

At EREW. A Friary, erected at the extreme end of Erew, which is a peninsula, stretching out in the barony of Tirawley, in which St. Leogar was Abbot; his feast is held on the 30th September. By an inquisition of 27th Elizabeth, it possessed one quarter of land, then worth 13s. 4d., now 13l. 6s. 8d.

At INCHMEAN, an Island, where there was an Abbey, in which Maoliosa, son of Thurlogh O'Connor, was Abbot, in the year 1223.

At INISTORMOR, An Augustine Friary, built by Eugene O'Gorman and Thady M'Firbiss, on a spot of ground which was granted them, in the year 1454, by Thady O'Doud, which grant was confirmed by a bull of Pope Nicholas V.

At KILLECRAW. A Religious House was seized at the inquisition of 30 Elizabeth, of some lands worth 6s. yearly, now worth 6l.

At KILLEDAN. A Franciscan Friary, possessed, at the inquisition of 1608, several lands and tenements.

At KILLETRYNODE, or the Abbey of the Trinity, endowed with a quarter of land.

At KILFINIAN. An Abbey, founded by St. Finian.

At KILMORMOYLE, in the Barony of Tirawley. A Monastery, founded by St. Olcan, disciple of St. Patrick, now a Protestant place of worship in the diocese of Killala.

At KILNEGARVAN. A Church, founded by St. Fechan, who died in the year 664.

At KILVENY. A Franciscan Friary, which, according to an inquisition of 27 Elizabeth, was worth, in lands and tenements, 13s. 4d. yearly, now worth 13l. 6s. 8d.

At KYLLYN. An Abbey was founded, and Endowed, at the same time, of some lands and tithes.

At MAYO. A Priory of Regular Canons, founded, in the year 670, by St. Colman, who came over from Landisfarne, Northumberland. He was followed hither by St. Gerald and his three brothers, *with three thousand disciples from England.* Many illustrious saints and geat men lived and died here ; granted, 20 Elizabeth, to the Burgesses and Corporation of Galway ; rent 26*l.* 12*s.,* now worth 532*l.*

A Nunnery, in which St. Segretia, the Abbess, (sister to St. Gerald,) and one hundred virgin Nuns died of the plague in the year 664.

At MORISK, a town on the Bay of Newport. An Augustine Friary, founded by the O'Maillies, Lords of the country ; at the suppression it possessed lands valued at 13*s.* 4*d.,* now worth 13*l.* 6*s.* 8*d.*

At MOYNE. A Franciscan Friary, founded in the year 1460, by William O'Rourke ; granted, 37 Elizabeth, to Edmund Barrett, with all the possessions, at 5*s.* rent, now worth 5*l.*

At RATHBRAN. A Dominican Friary, founded by the Dexter family ; granted, in the year 1577, to Thomas Dexter ; the venerable ruins of the sacred edifice stand there amidst a few wretched cabins.

At ROSSERICK. A Franciscan Friary, built by a Mr. Joice ; granted to James Garvey. There is here, and also in Moyne, a confessional of hewn stone for two confessors to sit in, and a hole in each side for the penitents to speak through.

At STRADE, on the Moy, near Athlethan. A Franciscan Friary, built by the sept of McJordan, but it was given to the Dominicans in the year 1252, by Jordan, of Exeter, Lord of Athlethan, at the request of Basilia his wife, daughter of Lord Meiler, of Birmingham ; on the 18th of March, 1434, Pope Eugene IV. granted several indulgences to this house ; granted, 30 Elizabeth, to Patrick Barnwell.

At TARMANCARRA. A Nunnery stood in the peninsula of Mullet.

At URLARE, in the Barony of Costello. A Dominican Friary, founded by the Wangle family, who afterwards took the name of Costello, and became Lords of the Barony. The Dominicans settled there in the year 1430. The house underwent two inquisitions, one on the 12th of May,1608, the other 24th of May, 1610 ; granted to Lord Dillon.

MEATH (COUNTY).

At ARDBRACCAN, a village in the Barony of Navan, an Abbey.

At ARDCATH, a village near Duleck. A church or perpetual chantry, a priest was stationed, with the obligation of celebrating mass; the chantry was a body corporate. The inquisition held 14 James found it in possession of some lands against the statute.

At ARDMULCHAN, near Pains-town. There was a parish church; a perpetual chantry of one priest; but the inquisition of 10th James found it in possession of lands against the statute, which of course was sufficient cause for suppressing it; value 17s. annually, now 17l.

At ARDSALLAGH, a village on the Boyne. A Monastery, founded by St. Finian, who died 12th December, 563.

At ATHBOY. A Carmelite Friary, founded on a site which was given by William, of London, in the year 1517. This Friary, with eleven messuages, three cellars, one orchard, and six gardens, in Athboy, with four acres of meadow, called the Friar's meadow in Advenston, were granted, 34 Henry VIII., to Thomas Casey for ever, at the yearly rent of 2s., now worth 2l.

At BALLYBOGAN, or Priory DE LAUDE DEI. An Augustine Friary, founded, in the 12th century, by Jordan Comin. This house was granted, 34 Henry VIII., to Lord Carbray, at the yearly rent of 4l. 3s. 4d., now worth 83l. 6s. 8d.; some of the possessions were granted 4 Elizabeth to Edward Fitzgerald.

At BEAUBEC. A church of St. Mary and St. Laurence, endowed in the reign of King John, by Walter de Lacie, stood, until the 14th century, and, without doubt until the general dissolution.

At BECTIFF, near Trim. A Cistercian Monastery, founded, in the year 1146, by Murchard O'Melaghlin, King of Meath ; surrendered, 34 Henry VIII., with all the possessions.

At CLONARD. An Abbey of Canons, founded by St. Finian. This Abbey, with all the possessions, were granted, 6 Edward VI., to Thomas Cusacke, at the yearly rent of 8l., now worth 160l. ; some of the possessions were granted, 8 Elizabeth, to Richard Hayne ; rent 3l. 8s. 6d., now worth 68l. 10s. : another parcel of the possessions was granted, 36 Elizabeth, to William Browne.

At COLPE, a village on the Boyne. An Abbey of regular Canons, founded, in the year 1182, by Hugh de Lacie. " At the suppression of Monasteries, the Prior was seized of the following tithes in Meath : Colpe, eight couple of corn ; Newtown, one and half ; St. James, one ; Pylleston, one ; Ballangstone, four and half ; Paynstone, two and half."

MEATH.

At DISERTTOLA. An Abbey, founded by St. Tola, who was made Bishop of Clonard, and died in the year 733. This house stood until the 12th century.

At DONNYGARNEY. A Nunnery, granted to Miss Draycot, who married a Mr. Talbot.

At DONOGH PATRICK, an Abbey, founded by Conol O'Neil.

At DROGHEDA. A Priory of Hospitalers, founded, in the time of Joan, or principally endowed by Walter de Lacie. It possessed immense revenues, though they were granted, 6 Edward VI., to James Sedgrave, for 10s. 10d. yearly rent ; now worth 210l.

A Carmelite Friary, built by the inhabitants of Drogheda. There were two grants made, one by the Corporation, in the time of Edward II., of eighty virgates of land, and another by William Messager, of Drogheda, in the time of Edward III., in the year 1346, of four acres of land to the Friars for the purpose of maintaining lights before the image of the Blessed Virgin in this church.

At DULEEK, an Abbey, the extensive possessions of which were granted, 10 James I., to Sir Gerald Moor.

A Priory of the Virgin Mary. Several inquisitions were held on this house ; all the possessions were granted to Sir Gerald Moor ; rent 9*l.* 11*s.* 7*d.*, now worth 191*l.* 11*s.* 8*d.*

An Hospital, founded before the year 1403.

At Dunshaghlin. A Church, founded by St. Seachlan.

At Indenen, near Slane, an Abbey.

At Kells, a celebrated Monastery, founded about the year 550. Henry VIII. granted it, in the 34th year of his reign, to Gerald Fleming and to Sir Gerald Plunket.

A Priory or Hospital, founded in this town, in the time of Richard I., by Walter de Lacie, lord of Meath. This house was surrendered by the last Prior, with the several possessions, 31 Henry VIII., and granted, 8 Elizabeth, to Richard Slayne, at the yearly rent of 14*l.* 10*s.* now worth 290*l.*

A Chantry for three priests.

At Kilberry, near Navan. A Chantry of two priests or chaplains.

At Killeen, a priory of Canons, founded by St. Eudeus, in the year 540.

A Nunnery, built by St. Eudeus previous to the year 580.

At KILMAINHAMBEG, twelve miles north of Navan. A Commandery of Templars, founded, in the time of Richard I., by Walter de Lacie, Lord of Meath. This Commandery was granted, 33 Elizabeth, to Sir Patrick Barnwall, at the yearly rent of 63*l*. 12*s*. 2½*d*., now worth 1,272*l*. 4*s*. 2*d*. ; now the Church.

At KILMAINHAM WOOD. A Commandery of Hospitalers, built in the 13th century, by the Prestons. Granted, 23 Sept. 1587, to Henry Duke, at the yearly rent of 4*l*. 10*s*., now worth 90*l*,

At KILSHIRE. An Abbey, founded in the year 580.

At LISMULLEN, near Tarah. A Nunnery, founded in the year 1240. This house, with its valuable possessions, were granted, 33 Henry VIII., to Gerald, Earl of Kildare and to Mabell his wife, and to Robert Harrison.

At LOUGH SHILLEN, near Cavan. A Friary, built on an island in this lake, which is still a remarkable burying-place.

At NAVAN. A Monastery, built or rebuilt in the 12th century, by Joceline de Angulo or

Nangle ; it stood with a great deal of celebrity until 31 Henry VIII. ; it was granted, with all the possessions ; the horse-barrack is now erected on the site of it.

At NEWTOWN. A Priory of Canons, founded in the year 1206, by Simon de Rochfort ; it flourished for many centuries, and possessed many valuable lands and tenements ; granted by the Parliament, in the year 1536, to King Henry VIII. ; he granted, in 1550, a parcel of them to Henry Draycot, at 4*l.* yearly rent, now worth 80*l.*

A Priory or Hospital of Cross-bearers, or Crouched-friars, founded by the Bishop of Meath, in the 13th century ; granted to Robert Dillon.

At ODDER. A Nunnery, founded by the Barnwall family, before the year 1195. This house, and all the possessions, were granted, 15th Elizabeth, to Richard Power.

At PIERSTOWN. An Abbey, founded in the early ages.

At RATHOSSAIN. A Monastery, founded by St. Ossian, who died 17th February, 686.

At RATOATH, thirteen miles north of Dublin ; an Abbey that possessed, in the reign of Henry

III., forty acres of land, value 6s. 8d., now worth 6l. 13s. 4d.

A Chantry for three priests ; by the inquisition of Henry VIII., they were found to possess some lands contrary to statute, and were suppressed.

At ROSSE, near Tarah. An Abbey, founded by St. Coeman Breae, who died 14th Sept. 614.

At SKRINE, an Abbey of regular Canons; granted, 34 Henry VIII., to Thomas Cusack, at the rent of 5d., now worth 8s. 4d.

A Chantry.

At SLANE, an Abbey of regular Canons; this house, with all the possessions, were granted, 32 Henry VIII., to James Fleming, Knt. ; rent 1d. yearly, now worth 1s. 8d.

At TELTOWN, or KILTALTON. A Church, founded by St. Abbon ; now a Protestant place of worship.

At TREVET, a large Monastery.

At TRIM, a magnificent Monastery, founded by St. Patrick. This house was granted, 34 Henry VIII., with all the lands, &c. to Anthony St. Leger, Knt.

A Gray Friary, founded, by King John, but granted, with all the appurtenances, 34 Henry VIII., to Lodwicke O'Tudor, parson of Roslaye, John Morye, parson of Walterston, and John Wakely; rent 2*l.* 10*s.*, now worth 50*l.* 10*s.* 0*d.*

A Dominican Friary, founded, in the year 1263, by Jeffrey de Geneville, lord of Meath; there was a great Synod held in this church, in the year 1291.

A Priory of Cross-bearers, a magnificent building; the Parliament, in the years 1484, 1487, and 1491, was held in the spacious hall of it; granted, with all the possessions, to Sir Thomas Cusack, 27 Henry VIII., at the rent of 8*s.* 5*d.* yearly, now worth 8*l.* 8*s.* 4*d.*

A Nunnery, founded by some person unknown.

A Church of Grecians, founded very anciently.

A Chantry for three priests.

MONAGHAN (County).

At Clones, a small town. A Priory of regular Canons, Elizabeth granted the house and possessions, in the 19th of her reign, to Sir Henry Duke.

At Monaghan, a Monastery, built by St. Moeldoius, before the 8th century; granted to Edward Withe; Lord Blancy has erected a castle on the site.

At Tehallan, in the barony of Monaghan. A religious house, in which St. Killian was abbot.

QUEEN'S (County).

Abbey Leix, founded, in the year 1183, by Corcherger O'Moore, for Cistercian Monks There were two inquisitions held on this house, one 5 Edward VI., and the other 5 Elizabeth, when the lands were estimated at 820 acres, and were let to the Earl of Ormond for 10l. 5s. yearly rent, now worth 205l.

At AGHABOE, four miles from Montrath, a magnificent Monastery, founded, by St. Canice. The Monastery, with its appurtenances, were granted, 43 Elizabeth, to Florence Fitzpatrick ; rent 5*l.* 18*s.*, now worth 118*l.*

At AGHMACART, four miles west of Durrow, Upper Ossory, an abbey, built about the year 550 ; also a Priory, granted, 43 Elizabeth, together with several other Monasteries and parcels of their possessions, to Florence Fitzpatrick, at the rent of 36*l.* 8*s.* 2*d.*, now worth 728*l.* 3*s.* 4*d.*

At ANNATRIM, in Upper Ossory. An Abbey, founded about the year 550 ; now a Protestant place of worship.

At CLONENAGH, a village in the barony of Maryborough. A magnificent Monastery, founded by St. Fintan. It is now a Protestant place of worship in the diocese of Leighlin.

At CLUAIN CHAOIN an ancient Monastery.

At DESERT ENOS, two miles south east of Maryborough. This is now called Desert, and is a Protestant place of worship, in the diocese of Leighlin.

At DESERT ODRAIN, in the territory of Hyfalgia.

QUEEN'S COUNTY.

At KILLEDELIG, in Upper Ossory, a Monastery, now a Church.

At KILLEBANE, four miles south west of Athy. A sumptuous Abbey, built by St. Abban, about the year 650 ; now a Church.

At KILLERMOGH, in Upper Ossory. An Abbey, built by St. Columb, about the year 558 ; now a place of worship.

At LEAMCHUILL. An Abbey, built by St. Finton-chorach, in the sixth century.

At MUNDREHID, in Upper Ossory. A Monastery, built by St. Lasren, in the year 600.

At ROSSTUIRC. An Abbey near the mountain of Slieve Bloom, governed by St. Brendan.

At SLETTY, near Carlow. An Abbey, by St. Ficah.

At STRADBALLY. A Franciscan Friary, founded, in the twelfth century, by Lord O'Mora ; granted, with all the possessions, in the year 1592, to Francis Cosbey, by Knight's service, or the twentieth part of a Knight's fee, and at the annual rent of 17l. 6s. 3d., now worth 346l. 5s.

At TIMOHOE. A Monastery, built by St. Mochoe, who died in the year 497 ; there is a round tower, with some ruins of the ancient building to be seen yet.

2 B 2

ROSCOMMON (County).

At ARDCARNA, in the Barony of Boyle. An Abbey of Regular Canons; granted, 39 Eliz., to the Provost and Fellows of Trinity College, Dublin, with eighty acres of land in Cloncalliagh; six acres of land in Kilgefin.

A Nunnery of Benedictines, which was a cell to the Abbey of Kilcreunata, in the county of Galway.

At ATHDALARAGH. An Abbey of Canons, where Comgallan was Bishop in the time of St. Patrick. This Abbey existed in the year 1201.

At ATHLOND, a Cistercian Abbey. It was enriched by grants from King John and King Edward I. Granted, with the possessions, 20 Eliz., to Edmond O'Fallon of Athlone.

At BASLICK, three miles south of Castlereagh, an Abbey; now a Protestant place of worship.

At BEALANENY. A Franciscan Friary; granted, together with the possessions, to Edmond O Fallon of Athlone, at the yearly rent of 2*l*. 4*s*. 7*d*., now worth 44*l*. 11*s*. 8*d*.

At BOYLE. A celebrated Cistercian Abbey,

granted with all the property, in the year 1603, to Sir John King.

At CALDRYWOLAGH, in the Barony of Boyle. A Franciscan Friary; granted, 24 Aug. 1582, to Bryan M'Dermot, at the yearly rent of 9s. 4d., now worth 94l.

At CLONRAHAN. A Franciscan Monastery, built by O'Conor Roe, in the reign of HenryVIII.

At CLONSHANVILL. An Abbey, built by St. Patrick; granted to Lord Dillon.

At CLOUNTHUSKERT, seven miles north east of Roscommon. A Priory, founded, in the early ages, by St. Faithlec; granted, 33 Eliz., to Fryal O'Farrell, for 21 years, at the rent of 11l. 9s. 8d., now worth 229l. 13s. 4d.

At CLOONCRAFF. A Monastery, founded by St. Patrick; it existed in the 12th century; now a Protestant place of worship.

At CLUAINEMUIN. An Abbey existed in the 11th century.

At EDARDRUIM. An Abbey, founded by St. Diradius, brother to St. Canoc, who flourished in the year 492; now a Protestant place of worship.

At ELPHIN. A Church founded by St. Patrick, for St. Assicus. The house and possessions were granted to Terence O'Birne.

At FIDHARD, in South Connaught. An Abbey, built by St. Patrick, for St. Justus ; now a Protestant place of worship.

At INCHMACNERIN, an Island in Loughree. A Monastery; granted, with the extensive possessions in lands and tithes, 28 Elizabeth, to William Taaffe, who assigned them to Thomas Spring.

At INCHMORE, an Island in Loughkee. A Priory of Canons, built, as people think, by St. Liberius, whose memory is held in much honour on the island even to this day; granted, 9 Elizabeth, to Lord Delvin, for 21 years, at 6l. 14s. 8d. rent, now worth 134l. 13s. 4d.

At KILCOOLEY. An Abbey, built by St. Olcan; now a Protestant place of worship.

At KILLARAGHT. A Nunnery, built by St. Patrick, for St. Athracta. The inquisition held 10 Aug. 33 Elizabeth, the Abbess of this house was seised of three carucates of land near the water of Lorgbella; two to the north of the waters, and on the west; the whole valued at 5s. besides reprises. Granted to Terence O'Birne, who assigned it to the Earl of Clanrickard.

At KILLUCKIN, four miles north of Elphin. A Nunnery, where St. Lunechaixia is honoured ; she was born before the year 637 ; now a Protestant place of worship.

At KILMORE. An Abbey, built by St. Patrick; now Protestantized.

A Priory, built by Con. O'Flanagan, and consecrated by Donogh O'Conor, Bishop of Elphin, in the year 1232, granted in the year 1580, for 21 years, to Tyren O'Farrel; rent 3*l*. 10*s*., now worth 70*l*.; granted afterwards to Sir Patrick Barnwall.

At KILLOMY. A Monastery, founded before the year 760.

At KILTULLAGH. A Franciscan Friary, founded about the year 1441.

At KNOCKVICAR. A Monastery of Dominicans, founded four miles east of the town; granted, 26 Elizabeth, together with the Abbey of Tocmonia, Clonemeaghan, and Court, in the county of Sligo, to Richard Kendlemarch.

At LOUGHKEE, in this Lake, is Trinity Island, where stood a Monastery dedicated to the Holy Trinity, in the year 700; rebuilt in 1215, by Clarus M'Movlon, Archdeacon of Elphin; granted, 10 August, 36 Elizabeth, with all the possessions, to Robert Harrison, for ever, in free soccage, at 26*l*. 13*s*. 8*d*., now worth 533*l*. 13*s*. 4*d*

At LYSDUFFE. A Priory in O'Conors Country; granted to the Provost and Fellows of Trinity College, Dublin.

At MONASTEREVAN, a Monastery.

ROSCOMMON.

At ORAN, five miles west of Roscommon. A Monastery built by St. Patrick; continues a remarkable place for pilgrimage; now the Protestant place of worship.

At RANDOWN, seven miles north of Athlone. A Priory of Hospitalers or Crossbearers, built in the reign of King John. Phil Nangle was a great benefactor in the reign of Henry III. This town died away, as well as the castle.

A Priory, founded by Clarus Archdeacon of Elphin.

ROSCOMMON, a town that has acquired much respectability from its monastic edifices.

An Abbey of Regular Canons, founded by St. Coemon, disciple of St. Finian. This house was granted, 20 Elizabeth, with the appurtenances, to Sir Nicholas Malleye; rent 30*l*. 5*s*. 10*d*., now worth 605*l*. 18*s*. 4*d*.

A Dominican Friary, founded, in the year 1253; granted, with all the possessions, 29 Jan. 1615, to Francis Viscount Valentia.

At TEAGHNANINGHEAN. A religious house in Connaught, where the seven daughters of Fergus are honoured.

At TIBOHIN. A Church, and formerly a great School; but now a Protestant place of worship.

At TOBERELLY, in the plain of Roscommon. A Franciscan Cell; it possessed some lands of the value of 13s. 4d., now worth 13l. 6s. 8d.

At TOEMONIA. A Franciscan Monastery, founded by O'Connor; granted, with all the lands, 30 Elizabeth, for twenty-one years, to Richard Kyndelinshe, at the yearly rent of 2l. 17s. 2½d., now worth 57l., 4s. 2d.

At TULSK, a Dominician Monastery, built in the 15th century, by M'Duill. It fell under the inquisition which was held 33 Elizabeth.

SLIGO (COUNTY).

At ACHONRY, a small Village and Episcopal See. An Abbey.

At AKERAS, or KILMATIN. A Priory founded, in the year 1280, by the O'Donalds. By the inquisition, this house was found to possess lands to the value of 16l. 8s. 4d., now worth 308l. 6s. 8d.

At ARDNARY. A Monastery for Eremites, following the rule of Augustine, built in the year 1427.

At ATHMOY. A Premonstratensian Monastery, founded, by Clarus M'Maylin, Archdeacon of Elphin, in the year 1251 ; possessions were granted to Robert Harrison, who assigned them to William Crofton.

At BALLINGDOWN, in the barony of Tirerril. The family of M'Donogh founded a Monastery in 1427, for the Nuns of the order of St. Dominick. Elizabeth's inquisition valued the possessions at 6s. 8d. per annum, English money; now worth annually 6l. 13s. 4d., granted to Francis Crofton.

At BALLINLEY, in the barony of Tyreragh, are the ruins of an Abbey of which nothing is known.

At BALLYMOTE, in the barony of Corran. A Monastery founded by one of the M'Donoghs for Franciscan Friars. Granted to Sir Henry Broncard, who assigned it to Sir William Taafe. Knt.

At BALLYSADARE, in the Barony of Tirerril, a Monastery, founded by St. Fechin, and richly endowed. Elizabeth's inquisition found it possessed of lands, tenements, and tithes, to the annual value then of 2l. yearly, value at this day 20l.

At BENNADA, a Barony of Leyney, a Friary of Crenites, founded, in 1423, through the industry of a brother of the order, called Charles. No value stated.

At BILE. An Abbey founded by St. Fechin, and now the parish church.

At CLONYMEAGHAN. A Monastery founded, 1488, for Dominican Friars. Valued at 13s. 4d. worth now 13l. 6s. 8d. yearly, granted to Richard Kyndelinshe.

At COURT, barony of Leyney, a small Monastery built by O'Hara for Franciscan Friars. Valued at 1l. 6s. 8d. annual ; worth now 26l. 13s. 4d. a year, granted to Richard Kyndelinshe.

At DRUMCLIFFE, a celebrated Monastery, founded by Saint Columba in 590. Parish Church built on part of its foundation.

At DRUMCOLLUMB, a church of St. Columb and St. Finbar. Now the parish church.

At DRUMRATT. An Abbey founded by Saint Fechin ; now the parish church.

At ECHENACH, a church built by St. Maveus; now the parish church.

At KILLARAGHT, a Nunnery built by St. Patrick ; now the parish church.

At KILNEMAUAGH, an Abbey founded by St. Fechin. Granted to Richard, Earl of Clanrickard; now the parish church.

At KNOCKMORE, a Friary, erected, in the 14th Century, by O'Gara.

At SLIGO, a Monastery founded, 1252, for Dominican Friars, by Maurice Fitzgerald, granted to Sir William Taafe. This place is described as having been very spacious and beautiful.

TIPPERARY (COUNTY).

At ARDFENNAN, on the river Suire, in the barony of Offa and Iffa, an Abbey and Friary in ruins; built, 1184, by John, Earl of Morton.

An ABBEY OF REGULAR CANONS, founded by St. Finian in 903.

A Friary for Conventual Franciscans.

At ATHASSELL, in the barony of Clanwilliam, William de Burgo founded a priory for the regular Canons of the order of St. Augustine. With its lands and tithes, valued in the reign of Edward VI. at 141l. 14s. 2d., or, of present money 2,834l. 3s. 4d. annually. It was reduced very much ; and, in the reign of Philip and Mary, let to the Earl of Ormond. Elizabeth granted it in fee to the same Nobleman. One of the largest and richest Abbeys in the kingdom.

At CAHIR, in the barony of Offa and Iffa, Geoffry of Camvill founded a priory for Augustine Canons. Leased by Queen Elizabeth to Peter Sherlock, for 24l. 11s. 6d. per annum.

At CARRICK, William de Cantell and Dionisia his wife, founded a Priory for the Canons of St. Augustine. Granted to the Earl of Ormond.

At CASHEL, An Hospital for the poor with fourteen beds and chaplains, was founded by Sir David le Latimer. It was endowed by two succeeding Bishops.

A Dominican Friary, founded, in the year 1243, by David M'Kelly, Archbishop of Cashel ; granted, 35 Henry VIII., with the appurtenances, to Walter Fleming, at the yearly rent of 2s. 6d., now worth 2l. 10s.

Hore Abbey, or St. Mary's Abbey, of the rock of Cashel, founded by the Benedictines, but given, in the course of time, to the Cistercian Monks. This really splendid edifice was richly endowed ; granted to

TIPPERARY.

Thomas Sinclair, 42 Elizabeth, at the yearly rent of 2s., now worth 2l.

Hacket's Abbey, belonging to the Franciscans. The house and its possessions were valued, when surrendered by the last Prior, at 3l. 10s. 2d. ; granted, 30 Henry VIII., for ever, to Edmund Butler, Archbishop of Cashel, at the yearly rent of 2s. 10d., now worth 2l. 16s. 8d.

At CLONAUL. An Hospital of Hospitalers, founded before the thirteenth century.

At CLONMELL. A Dominican Friary, founded in the year 1269.

A Franciscan Friary, built in the year 1269, by Otho de Grandison. There was a miraculous image of St. Francis. This splendid house and all its extensive possessions were granted, 34 Henry VIII., to James, Earl of Ormond and to the Commonalty of Clonmell.

At DONAGHMORE, in the barony of Offa and Iffa. There was an Abbey by St. Farannan; now a Protestant place of worship.

At EMLY, an ancient and celebrated Archiepiscopal city, in the county of Tipperary.

A Monastery, founded by St. Ailbe, who was styled a second St. Patrick ; he died in the year 527, and was interred here.

At FETHERD. An Augustine Monastery. By an inquisition of 31 Henry VIII., this house had possessions to the amount of 7*l.* 13*s.* 4*d.*, now worth 153*l.* 6*s.* 8*d.* Granted to sir Edmund Butler, at the yearly rent of 5*s.* 4*d.*, now worth 5*l.* 6*s.* 8*d.*

At HOLY CROSS. A Cistercian Monastery, built by Donogh O'Brien, King of Limerick. This was a sumptuous house, and was very richly endowed in lands and other tenements. Granted, 5 Elizabeth, with all the appurtenances, to Gerald, Earl of Ormond, at the yearly rent of 15*l.* 10*s.* 4*d.*, now worth 310*l.* 6*s.* 8*d.*

At INISLOUNAGH, in the barony of Offa and Iffa, on the Suir. An Abbey, founded by St. Mochoemse, who died on the 13th March, 655 ; he was succeeded by Congan, about the year 1153, who supplied St. Bernard with materials for writing the Life of St. Malachy. Donald O'Brien, King of Limerick, rebuilt this Monastery in 1187, and endowed it, with the assistance of Malachy O'Foelan, Prince of the Decies ; granted, 33 Elizabeth, to Edward Geogh ; rent 24*l.*, now worth 480*l.* There is a holy well, which is frequented by people from all quarters.

TIPPERARY.

At KILCOMIN. A Benedictine Priory, founded by Philip of Worcester, chief governor of Ireland, in the year 1184. He supplied it with friars from the Abbey of Glastonbury.

At KILCOOLY. A Cistercian Abbey, built by Donogh Carbragh O'Brien, in the year 1200; it had extensive possessions; granted, 31 Henry VIII., to Thomas, Earl of Ormond.

At KILMORE, in Upper Ormond. An Abbey, founded, in the year 540; now a Protestant place of worship.

At KILLINENALLAGH. A Franciscan Friary, built in the time of Henry VI.; granted, 35 Henry VIII., with the possessions, to Dermot Ryan; rent 4d. Irish, now worth 6s. 8d.

At LORRAH, a small village in Lower Ormond, near the Shannon. An Abbey, founded by St. Ruadan, who presided over 150 monks, and died in the year 584. Turgesius and his Norwegians burnt and destroyed this town, with all the religious houses, in the year 845. This is now a Protestant place of worship.

A Dominican Friary, founded, in the year 1269, by Walter de Burgo, King of Ulster.

At MONAINCHA, situated almost in the centre of the great bog of Monela, three miles south east of Roscrea, a Monastery of Culdean Monks.

TIPPERARY.

The house and revenues were granted, 28 Elizabeth, to Sir Lucas Dillon.

At MOYLAGH, two miles west of Carrick. A Nunnery, under the invocation of St. Brigid; granted to Sir Henry Radcliff.

At NENAGH. A Hospital for Augustines, who were to attend constantly the sick and infirm; it was endowed by Theobald Walter. Though the possessions of this house were immense, they were granted, together with the house itself, 5 Elizabeth, to Oliver Grace, for the rent of 39*l*. 0*s*. 10*d*., now worth 780*l*. 16*s*. 8*d*.

A Franciscan Friary, built in the reign of Henry III., by the Butler family; granted, 30 Elizabeth, to Robert Collum, at the yearly rent of 22*l*. 17*s*. 8*d*., now worth 457*l*. 13*s*. 4*d*.

At ROSCREA. A magnificent Monastery, built by Saint Cronan.

A Franciscan Friary, founded in the year 1490, by Mulruany na Feasoige O'Carroll, or by his wife Bibiana. An inquisition was held 27 Dec. 1568; this house and the possessions were granted to the Earl of Ormond, who assigned the same to William Crow.

THURLES. A Carmelite Monastery, founded

in the year 1300, by the family of Butler ; granted, together with the possessions, to the Earl of
Ormond.

TIPPERARY. A Monastery of Augustine Eremites, founded in the reign of Henry III. ; granted, with the possessions, 34 Henry VIII., to
Dermot Ryan ; rent 8*d*. Irish, now worth
13*s*. 4*d*.

TIRDAGLASS, on the Bank of Lough Derg.
A Monastery, founded by St. Columba, a disciple of St. Finian ; he died of the plague in the
year 552. His feast falls on 13 Dec. and the
feast of St. Aidbeus falls on 24 May. Many illustrious saints and scholars flourished in this house
until the twelfth century.

TOOME, six miles south of Tipperary. A
Priory of Canons. St. Donan was honoured here,
and it is supposed that he was the founder.
Queen Elizabeth granted this for twenty-one
years to Miler Magragh, Archbishop of Cashall.

TYRONE (COUNTY).

ARDBOE. A noble and celebrated Monastery,
built by St. Colman.

TYRONE.

BALLINESAGART, in the Barony of Dungannon. A Franciscan Friary, built by Con. O'Neil in the year 1489.

CLOGHER. An episcopal see and borough, three miles and a half south west of Lurgan. A Priory of regular Canons, presided over by St. Patrick, who resigned it to St. Kertern, who founded the celebrated abbey here. King James granted this abbey and revenues to George Montgomery, Bishop of Clogher.

CLUAINDUBHAIN, near Clogher. A large Nunnery founded by St. Patrick.

COROCK. A Franciscan Monastery, built in the fifteenth century; granted to Sir Henry Piers.

DONNAGHMORE, three miles west of Dunganon. An Abbey, built by St. Patrick, in which St. Columb was honoured; it stood until the thirteenth century, and of course until the general dissolution.

DUNGANNON, a borough town. A Franciscan Friary, built by Con. O'Neil, in the reign of Henry VII.; granted to Richard, Earl of Westmeath, who assigned it to Sir Arthur Chichester.

GERVAGHKERIN, A Franciscan Friary, built
2 c 2

in the fifteenth century; granted to Sir Henry Piers, with the friary of Corock.

OMAGH. An Abbey, founded, in the early ages, and in the fifteenth century a Franciscan Friary; granted with the friary of Corock.

PUBLE. A Franciscan Friary, founded, in the fifteenth century; granted to Sir Henry Piers.

WATERFORD (COUNTY).

ACHADDAGAIN. An Abbey, by St. Dogain, who was a strenuous supporter of the ancient mode of celebrating Easter.

ARDMORE, a village four miles east of Youghal. An Abbey, founded by St. Declan, whose feast falls on 24 July. St. Ultan, his successor, was living after the year 550. The splendid round tower, and stately ruins of several churches; the Adam and Eve, with the tree and serpent; the judgment of Solomon, all in alto relievo, strike the traveller's mind with awe, as well as with regret for its fallen degraded state from its ancient wealth and piety.

BALLYVONY, six miles north-east of Dangorvan. A large building in ruins, 150 feet by 90, which is supposed to be a Commandery of Hospitalers.

BEWLEY, two miles south of Lismord. An Hospital of Hospitalers, in ruins.

CAPPAGA, three miles and a half west of Dangorvan. The ruins of a Commandery of Hospitalers.

CARRICKBEG, near Carrick-on-Suir. A Franciscan Friary, built in the year 1336, by the Earl of Ormond; granted, 31 Henry VIII., to Thomas, Earl of Ormond. The steeple still remains, a very curious building, about sixty feet high, rising like a pyramid, which point begins several feet from the ground in the middle of the church.

CLASHMORE, three miles and a half north of Youghal. An Abbey, founded, by Cuanceor, according to the orders of Mochoemoc, who had raised Cuanchear from the dead; that saint died 13th March, 655. Granted to Sir Walter Raleigh.

CROOKE, on the bay, four miles from Waterford. A Commandery, founded, in the thirteenth century, for the Hospitalers, by the Baron of Curraghmore; granted, 27 Elizabeth, to Antony Power, for sixty years; rents 12*l*. 11*s*. 10*d*., now worth 251*l*. 16*s*. 8*d*.

DUNGARVAN. There was a Priory of Canons, founded, in the seventh century, by St. Garbhan, a disciple of St. Finbar.

An Augustine Friary, founded by Thomas, Lord Offaley; the O'Briens were benefactors; granted, with sundry lands, 37 Elizabeth, for twenty-one years, to Roger Dalton; rent 40*l*. 10*s*. now worth 810*l*. There was an hospital also under the invocation of St. Brigid.

KILBARRY, one mile and a half from Waterford. An Hospital of Hospitalers.

KILLUNKART, near Dungarvan. A Commandery of Hospitalers.

KILLURE, two miles east of Waterford. A Commandery of Hospitalers; granted, together with revenues, 25 Elizabeth, to Nicholas Aylmer, for fifty years, at the yearly rent of 13*l*. 6*s*. 8*d*., now worth 266*l*. 16*s*. 8*d*.

Kilmboynan Abbey had a house in Waterford, called the Old Court, which could not escape the all-seeing inquisition of Elizabeth.

LISMORE. An Abbey of regular Canons, founded, by St. Mocheda, in the year 630, together with a celebrated school ; though St. Senan, St. Lugad, St. Neman, and St. Madoc, seem to have been there bishops before him. Corcran Cieirach, anachorite of all Ireland, died at Lismore, in the year 1140. He was a celebrated divine ; and so greatly excelled all the western Europe in religion and learning, that every contest throughout the kingdom was referred to him. In 1127 Cormac M'Carthy, King of Munster, being dethroned, he was compelled to go on a pilgrimage to Lismore, where he erected two churches. In 1135 Daniel O'Brien, King of Dublin, resigned his crown, and died a professed monk in this house.

An Hospital for Lepers, founded, under the invocation of St. Brigid.

A Cell of Anchorites, appertaining to the church of Lismore.

MOLANA, an island in the Bl k Water, two miles and a half above Waterford. There was an Abbey, founded, in the sixth century by St. Molanfide. Queen Elizabeth granted this house and possessions to Sir Walter Raleigh, who assigned them to the Earl of Cork.

MOTHEL, two miles south of Carrick. An

Augustine Monastery, built by St. Brogan, and was succeeded by St. Coan in the sixth century; granted, 33 Henry VIII., with all the possessions, to —— Butler and Power; rent 6*l.* 4*s.*, now worth 128*l.*

RHINCREW, two miles west of Youghal. An Hospital of Hospitalers; granted to Sir Walter Raleigh, who assigned it to the Earl of Cork.

WATERFORD, a large commercial sea-port. An Augustine Priory, founded by the Ostmen; it was richly endowed by different persons in the course of time; granted, with several other possessions, 31 Elizabeth, to Elizabeth Butler, *alias* Sherlock, for twenty-one years; rent 47*l.* 5*s.* 8*d.*, now worth 2,345*l.* 13*s.* 4*d.*

The Hospital of St. Stephen, founded for Lepers, by the Power family.

The Priory of St. John the Evangelist, founded in the year 1185, by John, Earl of Morton, for the Benedictines. This house received several grants of lands and tenements. Granted to William Wyse, Esq., at the annual rent of a knight's fee.

The Monastery of our Saviour, built by the Dominicans, in the reign of Henry III., granted, 34 Henry VIII., to James White; rent 4*s.*, now worth 4*l.* The County Court House is called Black Friars.

A Franciscan Friary, founded in the year 1240, by Lord Hugh Purcell, who was interred here the same year, by the side of the high altar; granted, 33 Henry VIII., to Patrick Walsh and scholars, at the yearly rent of 8s., now worth 8l.; and a fine of 151l. 13s. 4d., now worth 3,033l. 6s. 8d. The Holy Ghost Hospital has been erected on a part of the ruins of this priory.

WESTMEATH (County).

ARDCHARN. An Abbey by St. Beoaid, who died the 8th March, 523.

ATHLONE. This town is built on the river Shannon, partly in the county of Roscommon and partly in the county of Westmeath. A Monastery was built on this side for Franciscans, by Charles, or Cathal Croibh Dearg O'Connor, Prince of Connaught; and by Sir Henry Dillon, who was interred here.

ATHNECARNE. A Dominican Friary, built in the fourteenth century, by Robert Dillon, of Drumrany; granted, with all its possessions in this county, 37 Henry VIII., to Robert Dillon, at the fine of 13l. 13s. 4d., now worth 273l. 6s. 8d.; and a rent of 6d., now worth 10s.

BALLIMORE, on Lough-Seudy, ten miles west of Mullingar. A Monastery, founded before the year 700.

An Abbey, built in the year 1218, by the family of Lacie, for Nuns and Friars: they lived under the same roof, but in different apartments. This house had extensive possessions, and underwent several inquisitions in the reigns of Henry VIII., and Elizabeth.

CLONFAD, five miles and a half east of Mullingar. A Church, founded by St. Ethchen, who died in the year 577. Clonfad is now a Chapel.

CLONRANE, seven miles south of Mullingar. An Abbey, inhabited by several Saints from the sixth to the tenth century; suppressed.

COMRAIRE, near the hill of Usmeach. An Abbey in which St. Colman was honoured; he died in the year 652.

DRUMRANY, or DRUMRATH, six miles northeast of Athlone. An Abbey built in the year 588. In the year 946 this house with 150 persons in it, was burnt to the ground by the Ostmen.

At DYSART, four miles south of Mullingar. An Abbey, built by St. Colman; it became a Franciscan Friary before the year 1331.

At FARRENEMANAGHE. The inquisition of James, in the third year of his reign, finds this Abbey in ruins, though possessed of a cartron of land, tithes, and other tenements, value 12*d*., now worth 1*l*.

FARREN-MAC-HEIGKESE. The inquisition of James III. finds the ruins of a Nunnery that was possessed of some lands.

> There was an abbey here ; and it is recorded that in the year 665, St. Finchin governed three thousand Monks in it.

FORE, once a celebrated town, now an obscure village. This abbey and possessions made, according to the inquisition held, 31 Henry VIII., 161*l*. 12*s*., now worth 3,232*l*. yearly ; granted in the year 1588, for thirty-one years, to Christopher Baron of Delvin.

At CLONCALL, bordering on Kilkenny West. A Monastery, built in the year 486, by St. Munis ; now a chapel.

At HARE ISLAND, in Loughree. A Monastery, by the family of Dillon.

At KENARD, near the county of Longford, north of Inny. A Nunnery, built early.

At KILLARE, in the barony of Raconrath.

Three churches, one dedicated to St. Aid, another called Temple Brigid, and the third the Court of St. Brigid; there were three holy wells St. Cuman was abbot here.

At KILBEGGAN, a borough town. A Monastery, built by St. Becan. Another Monastery, founded on the same, rebuilt in the year 1200, by the family of Dalton. This abbey, and all its extensive possessions, were granted, after having undergone several inquisitions in the reign of Henry VIII. and his son Edward VI., to be held of the King and of the castle of Dublin, in free and common soccage.

At KILBIXY, an ancient town adorned with a castle belonging to the Lacie family; and a Monastery or an Hospital for the lepers, under the invocation of St. Brigid; it stood until the fifteenth century.

KILCONIREGH and CONRY were chapels in the barony of Moycashell; St. Fearfio, son of a smith, was abbot in the year 758.

At KILKENNY WEST. A Friary, built by Thomas, a priest and friar, the grandson of Sir Thomas Dillon, who came into Ireland, in the year 1185; granted, with the possessions, 11 Elizabeth, to Robert Dillon; rent 22l. 10s., now worth 450l. : there was also a holy well here.

At KILLUKEN, five miles east of Mullingar.

WESTMEATH.

An Abbey, built by St. Luican, whose feast falls
on 27th July ; now a Protestant place of worship.

At KILMACAHILL, or KILMICHAEL. A Franciscan Friary built by the family of Petyt ; granted to Robert Nangle.

At KILTOMA, or KILTOAMEN. An Abbey,
built by St. Nennid or Ninn, whose feast falls on
13th November.

At LECKIN, in the barony of Corkerry. An
Abbey, built by St. Crumin, who died in the
year 664 ; now a parish church.

At LYNN, in the barony of Delvin. An Abbey,
founded in the early ages ; now a Protestant
place of worship.

At MULLINGAR, an ancient town. A Priory,
called the House of God of Mullingar ; founded
for Canons in the year 1227, by Ralph Petyt,
Bishop of Meath, who died in the year 1229 ;
this house, with all the possessions, were granted, 34 Elizabeth, to Richard Tuyte ; rent 16*l.*
5*s.* 10*d.*, now worth 325*l.* 16*s.* 8*d.*

A Dominican Friary, founded by the family of Nugent, in the year 1237 ; granted,
8 Elizabeth, to Walter Hope ; rent 10*l.*,
now worth 200*l.*

WESTMEATH.

A Fanciscan Friary, built in the year 1622, by the Friars ; like the lambs building amongst the wolves.

At MULTIFERNAM. A Monastery, built in the year 1235, by William Delamar, for the Franciscans ; granted, with the possessions, 8 Henry VIII., to Edmond Field, Patrick Clynch, and Phil. Petency, for a fine of 80*l.* worth now 1,600*l.* together with the rent of 4*s.*, that is 4*l.* of the present money. It appears that the Friars possessed themselves again of this house until the year 1641.

At RATHUGH. A Monastery by St. Aid ; now a chapel.

At RATHYNE, six miles east of Mullingar. A Monastery built by St. Carthag or Mochuda, where he presided for forty years, over *eight hundred and sixty-seven Monks, who supported themselves and the neighbouring poor by labour.*

At TEAGHBAOITHEN. A Monastery, built by St. Baithen ; stood until the 13th century.

At TEAGHTELLE. A Monastery, built by St. Cera, of Muskerry, but being recommended by St. Munnu to resign the house to St. Tellius, she did, and then returned home to her native country, in the year 576.

At TIPPERT. A Monastery, built by St. Fechin, of Fore; now a chapel.

At TOBER. Pope Innocent VIII. granted licence to Edmond de Lantu Laici to build a Monastery here for Dominicans; granted, 31 Elizabeth, to Henry Matthews.

At TRISTERNAGH, on the banks of Lough Iron. A Priory, founded, by Geoffry de Constantine, an English emigrant, about the year 1200; granted, for twenty-one years, to Captain William Piers, 31 Henry VIII., at the yearly rent of 60l., now worth 120l.

WEXFORD (COUNTY).

At ACHADHABHLA. A Monastery, founded by St. Finian, of Clonard.

At AIRDNE COEMHAIN. A Monastery, by St. Coeman, brother of St. Dagan, who died in the year 639, abbot here.

A BALLYHACK. A Commandery, subordinate to that of Kilcoghan.

At BEGERY, or LITTLE ISLAND, an Island north of Wexford harbour. A celebrated Monastery and a School, founded, by St. Ibor or Ivor, who died in the year 500.

At CAMROS. An Abbey, built by St. Abban, who died in the year 640; and the abbot St. Mosacre died in the year 650.

At CARNSORE. A Monastery, built by St. Domangort, of Ossory, at the foot of a high hill that overhangs the Irish Channel; now a Protestant place of worship.

At CLONMINES. An Augustine Monastery, founded, by the family of Cavanagh, before the year 1385; granted, with the possessions, 35 Henry VIII., to John Parker; rent 2s. 6d., now worth 2l. 10s.

At DARINIS, an island near the town of Wexford. A Monastery, built by St. Nemhan, whose feast falls on 8th March; St. Gobban and St. Caiman were abbots here before the year 540.

At DOWN, six miles from Inniscorthy. A Monastery, built before the arrival of the English, and continued until it was granted, in 1637, to the Lord Baltimore.

At DRUIM CHAOIN. An Abbey, founded by St. Abban, who died in the year 650.

At DUNBRODY, four miles south of Ross. An Abbey, founded, through the bounty of Harvey de Monte Maurisco, Seneschal to the Earl of

Pembroke. The Earl himself and his son Walter were benefactors ; by an inquisition held 37 Henry VIII., the possessions were valued at 25*l.* 4*s.* 8*d.*, now worth 504*l.* 3*s.* 4*d.* ; granted to Osborne Itchingham ; rent 3*l.* 10*s.* 6*d.*, now worth 70*l.* 10*s.*

At INNISCORTHY, a borough town. A Cell to the Abbey of St. Thomas, in Dublin ; founded, and richly endowed for the salvation of his own and the souls of his wife, father and mother, by Gerald de Prendergast, about the year 1225; granted in the year 1581, to Edward Spenser ; rent 13*l.* 5*s.*, now worth 265*l.*

A Franciscan Friary, founded, in the year 1460, by Donald Cavanagh ; granted 37 Elizabeth, to Sir Henry Wallop, for a Knight's service, and rent 10*l.* 16*s.* 4*d.*, now worth 216*l.* 6*s.* 8*d.*

FERNS. Abbey founded, on land given by Brandub, King of Leinster, to St. Moadhog, called also Aidan; it continued a celebrated house until the general suppression. In 1166, Dermot M'Meerchad, King of Leinster, burned the town, and in atonement to God for this sin, he founded an Augustine Abbey here, and richly endowed the same ; granted, with all the possessions, 26 Elizabeth, for 60 years, to Thomas Masternson ; rent 16*l.* 4*d.* ; now worth 320*l.* 1*s.* 6*d.*

GLASSCARIG. On the sea, six miles north of Gorey. Griffin Cordon, Cicilia Barry, his wife, and Roboric Burhe, her father, and three other persons, granted all their lands in Cousinquilos, &c., for building here a Benedictine Priory. Two different inquisitions, one 35 Henry VIII., and the other, 5 Edward VI., found this house in possession of many lands, and other tenements.

HOARTOWN. Carmelite Priory, built in the 14th century by a Mr. Furlong; granted to Sir John Davis and Francis Talbot.

INBHERDAOILE. Monastery, built by Sir Dagain, brother to St. Coemgene, who was also Bishop of Achad Dagain in Leinster, and died 639.

KILCLEGHAN. Near the mouth of the Suir. Commandery built by O'Moore, for the Templars, but on the suppression of this Order, it was given to the Hospitalers; underwent an inquisition 32 Henry VIII.; granted, 30 Elizabeth, to Sir Henry Harrington, for the fourth part of a knight's fee, and rent 35*l*. 16*s*. 8*d*.; now worth 716*l*. 13*s*. 4*d*.

MAGHERE NUIDHE. A noble Monastery, founded by St. Abban, who died in the year 650.

Cross Friary, for the redemption of captives, was built on a rising ground.

Monastery of St. Saviour, erected for the Franciscans, by Sir John Devereux before the year 1300; granted, 30 Elizabeth, to the Earl of Ormond. The east end of the house is now a Protestant place of worship.

Augustine Friary, built in the reign of Edward III.; this house had some valuable possessions, though granted, 35 Henry VIII., to Richard Butler, at the yearly rent of 17d. Irish; now worth 1l. 8s. 4d.

TINTERN. On the Bannowbay, three miles north east of Duncannon Fort. William, Earl of Pembroke, having been in great danger on sea, made a vow to build an Abbey on the first spot where he should land in safety; he put into this bay, and religiously redeemed his vow, by erecting a Cistercian Abbey for Monks, whom he brought from Tintern Abbey, Monmouthshire; he endowed it with many valuable lands; he died in 1219, and King John confirmed his will. Though this house and possessions amounted, according to the inquisition held 31 Henry VIII., to 75l. 7s. 8d., now worth 1517l. 13s. 4d., they were granted to Anthony Colclough, at 26l. 4s. yearly rent; now worth 524l.

WEXFORD. A sea-port town, and a borough. Priory of regular Canons. It was richly endowed by several noblemen. There was an inquisition held on it, 31 Henry VIII., another 1 Edward

VI., when it was granted for ever to John Parker, for the annual rent of 15s. $\frac{1}{2}d$.; now worth 15l. 10s.; but a third inquisition was held, 26 Elizabeth, when the house and possessions were found in the hands of Philip Devereux of Wexford. This Church still remains with a large tower in the middle.

Priory of Hospitalers, founded by William Mareschal, Earl of Pembroke.

Grey Friary, or Franciscan, founded in the reign of Henry III., granted, 35 Henry VIII., to Paul Turner and James Devereux; rent 10d. Irish; now worth 16s. 8d.

Hospital of Lepers, to which Henry IV., in the year 1408, made a grant of lands.

WICKLOW (County).

ARKLOW. Formerly the residence of the Kings of Dublin; a town then of great note, and adorned with a monastery which Theobald Fitz Walter founded for the Dominicans; granted, 35 Henry VIII., to John Travers, rent 2s. 2d.; now worth 2l. 3s. 4d.

BALLYKINE. Six miles and a half west of Arklow Abbey, founded by St. Keivin. On the site of which a Mr. Whaley built a house, called the Whaley Abbey.

BALTINGLASS. A borough town, on the river Slaney. Cistercian Abbey, built in the year 1148, by Dermot M'Murchad O'Cavanagh, King of Leinster; granted, 30 Elizabeth, to Sir Henry Harrington, at 11*l*. 19*s*. yearly rent, now worth 239*l*. ; though it was worth double that sum.

DONARD. A church, built by St. Silvester, who came to Ireland with St. Palladius about the year 430 ; now a Protestant place of worship.

GLENDALOGH. Twenty-two miles from Dublin, and eleven north-west of Wicklow, formerly an episcopal see, and a well inhabited city full of religious edifices. An Abbey founded, and presided over for many years, by St. Keivin, who died 3d June, 618, at the age of 120 years. On the 3d June, immense multitudes of pilgrims visit the seven churches of Glendalogh, to venerate St. Keivin, and his sister, St. Molibba. The seven churches are, the Cathedral Church, St. Keivin's Kitchen, Our Lady's Church, Priory of St. Saviour, the Ivy Church, Teampul na Skellig, the Rhepart.

WICKLOW.

INISBOYNE. Four miles east of Wicklow. An Abbey by St. Baithen.

KILGORMAN. An Abbey, by St. Gorman, nephew to St. Patrick; now a Protestant place of worship.

KILLAIRD. A Nunnery, built in the year 588 by St. Tamthinna.

SRUTHAIR. An Abbey built by St. Mogoroc, brother to St. Canoc; it stood to the 14th century.

WICKLOW. Capital of the county, and a borough. A Franciscan Friary, founded in the reign of Henry III., by the O'Byrnes and the O'Tooles: granted, 7 Elizabeth, to Henry Harrington for 21 years; rent 3*l*. 12*s*. 9*d*.; now worth 72*l*. 15*s*.

THE END.

INDEX.

ENGLAND.

INDEX.

INDEX.

INDEX.

INDEX

INDEX.

INDEX.

INDEX.

INDEX.

INDEX.

INDEX.

Tavistock, Devon
Temple Dynesley, Herts
Temple Bruer, Lincoln
Temple Comb, Somerset
Temple Rockley, Wilts
Temple Hurste, York
Tettenhall, Stafford
Tewkesbury, Gloucester
Thetford, Norfolk
Telesford, Warwick
Thickhed, York
Thobey, Essex
Thomeston, Norfolk
Thornton, Lincoln
Thornholm, Lincoln
Thorney, Cambridge
Thremhall, Essex
Thurgarton, Nottingham
Thurlegh, Kent
Tickhill, York
Tiltey, Essex
Tinmouth, Northumberland
Tintern, Monmouth
Tiptree, Essex
Titchfield, Hants
Tockwith, York
Touge, Salop
Torkesey, Lincoln
Torr, Devon
Tortington, Sussex
Totness, Devon
Towcester, Northampton
Tricengham, Stafford
Truro, Cornwall
Truwardraith, Cornwall
Turbish, Cornwall
Tupholm, Lincoln

Tutbury, Stafford
Twinham, Hants
Tykeford, Buckingham

U

Uphaven, Wilts
Usk, Monmouth

V

Valeroyal, Chester
Vandey, Lincoln

W

Waburn, Norfolk
Waldon, Essex
Wallingford, Berks
Wallingweles, Nottingham
Waltham, Essex
Wangford, Suffolk
Wardon, Bedford ½
Warham, Dorset
Warmington, Warwick
Warrington, Lancaster
Walshingham, Norfolk
Warter, York
Watton, York
Warwick, Warwick
Waverley, Surrey
Welbeck, Nottingham
Welle, York
Wales, Somerset
Welles, Norfolk
Wellow, Lincoln
Wendling, Norfolk
Wencham, Kent

INDEX.

INDEX.

WALES.

INDEX.

IRELAND.

INDEX.

INDEX.

C

INDEX.

INDEX.

INDEX.

INDEX.

INDEX.

INDEX.

INDEX.

B. BENSLEY, PRINTER, ANDOVER.